Political Economy of Post-apartheid South Africa

This book is a product of CODESRIA Textbook Progamme

Political Economy of Post-apartheid South Africa

Vusi Gumede

CODESRIA

Council for the Development of Social Science Research in Africa
DAKAR

ISBN: 978-2-86978-704-9

Typesetting: Alpha Ousmane Dia
Cover Concept: Vusi Gumede
Cover Design: Ibrahima Fofana

Distributed in Africa by CODESRIA
Distributed elsewhere by African Books Collective, Oxford, UK
Website: www.africanbookscollective.com

The Council for the Development of Social Science Research in Africa (CODESRIA) is an independent organisation whose principal objectives are to facilitate research, promote research-based publishing and create multiple forums geared towards the exchange of views and information among African researchers. All these are aimed at reducing the fragmentation of research in the continent through the creation of thematic research networks that cut across linguistic and regional boundaries.

CODESRIA publishes *Africa Development*, the longest standing Africa based social science journal; *Afrika Zamani*, a journal of history; the *African Sociological Review*; the *African Journal of International Affairs*; *Africa Review of Books* and the *Journal of Higher Education in Africa*. The Council also co-publishes the *Africa Media Review*; *Identity, Culture and Politics: An Afro-Asian Dialogue*; *The African Anthropologist* and the *Afro-Arab Selections for Social Sciences*. The results of its research and other activities are also disseminated through its Working Paper Series, Green Book Series, Monograph Series, Book Series, Policy Briefs and the CODESRIA Bulletin. Select CODESRIA publications are also accessible online at www.codesria.org.

CODESRIA would like to express its gratitude to the Swedish International Development Cooperation Agency (SIDA), the International Development Research Centre (IDRC), the Ford Foundation, the Carnegie Corporation of New York (CCNY), the Norwegian Agency for Development Cooperation (NORAD), the Danish Agency for International Development (DANIDA), the Netherlands Ministry of Foreign Affairs, the Rockefeller Foundation, the Open Society Foundations (OSFs), TrustAfrica, UNESCO, UN Women, the African Capacity Building Foundation (ACBF) and the Government of Senegal for supporting its research, training and publication programmes.

Contents

PART I
BACKGROUND

PART II
POLICIES AND PROSPECTS

PART III
TOWARDS A DEVELOPMENTAL STATE

Foreword

This book, *Political Economy of Post-apartheid South Africa*, is an important contribution to the debates about post-apartheid South Africa and the notion of a 'developmental state', particularly as it describes what has transpired since 1994 while giving a historical context for each of the themes it deals with. Unlike experiences in other parts of the world, South Africa has *a priori* declared its ambition to become such a state. This started to filter into policy pronouncements in the mid-2000s, especially in the context of the review of progress in socio-economic transformation after ten years of democracy.

Theorisation around the notion of a developmental state is relatively young; and it has evolved *post facto* in an attempt to generalise experiences of countries that were able to sustain high rates of economic growth for a generation and more. A number of East Asian countries – and few others further afield – are held up as exemplars in this regard. Yet some studies have extended the scope of such theorisation to include, for instance, countries in Europe where social compacts have resulted in sustained growth as evincing a form of developmentalism.

Given his broad canvass of theoretical propositions, Vusi Gumede should be congratulated for discussing the various aspects of the political economy of post-apartheid South Africa. The result is an important addition to the body of literature on developmental experiences. Critically, *Political Economy of Post-apartheid South Africa* contains a systematic analysis of South Africa's post-apartheid development trajectory.

In examining South Africa's post-1994 experience, the author delves into social and economic policies and institutional arrangements for policy-making and implementation. But he doesn't stop there. Contained in this book are ideas on what can further be done towards sustaining and intensifying the transformation project.

This, the author argues, entails building on the progress that has been made since South Africa attained democracy. But it also demands an honest acknowledgement of weaknesses as well as the impact of factors that were, and still are, beyond the control of South Africans. Among the latter are issues such as the global environment within which South Africa set out on its transformation journey, the dependence on and influence of global capital, and the trajectory of the global economy during South Africa's twenty-one years of democracy.

For many years, Vusi Gumede was directly involved in policy development, monitoring and evaluation within South Africa's post-apartheid administrations. That experience and exposure have come handy in crafting a book that can be useful for anyone who wants to know the evolution of the country's numerous political economy issues since 1994. One does not have to agree with his postulates to appreciate that this piece of work has the potential to significantly contribute to sober reflection and introspection.

I recommend the book, not only to academics, researchers and students, but also to policy-makers in both the public and private sectors. I am also certain that members of the public who want to gain new insights on the trajectories of democratic developmental states and know how, as citizens and observers alike, they can exercise agency in influencing South Africa's development trajectory, would gain from this treatise.

South Africa's journey to right a historical injustice is underway. As the country enters the third decade of democracy, it cannot but answer the critical questions about the depth, the speed and the reach of its policies of change. In such a national undertaking, there can be no spectator.

Joel Netshitenzhe

Executive Director
Mapungubwe Institute for Strategic Reflection
Former Head of the Policy Coordination and
Advisory Services in the Presidency

Preface

As I was preparing my departure from government in 2009, I decided that I must write a book. During 2010-2013, I wrote the book I wanted to write and it was scheduled to hit the shelves during 2016 – it was originally hoped that it was going be published in 2015 but it has gone through various iterations as it usually happens with such projects.

While completing the book I am referring to, it occurred to me that another book was necessary, perhaps as a precursor to that book. A straightforward text that explains various aspects of South Africa's contemporary political economy issues can be useful for many reasons: it can be a companion guide to students, policy practitioners, researchers and the like. Most importantly, it can be a good background to the book, *Post-apartheid South Africa: Economic and Social Inclusion*, which I was writing.

South Africa has completed twenty-one years of political independence. There were wide and high expectations in and outside South Africa that the formal end of apartheid in 1994 presented a unique opportunity for the country to pursue a progressive development path in which the rights, wellbeing and dignities of all citizens would be recognised, pursued and preserved in line with the overarching goal of building an inclusive, non-racial, non-sexist and non-discriminatory society. These expectations were based on the recognition of the injustices of the past and the challenges that were looming but also grounded on a firm determination of the political leadership, as it seemed, to confront these seemingly intractable problems through the adoption of an appropriate mix of policies.

Since 1994, various policies have been embarked upon by the successive democratic governments, aimed at achieving the 'dream' of a developmental state which could guarantee an inclusive society. From the Ready to Govern (R2G) document of 1992 which laid the basis for the Reconstruction and Development Programme (RDP) of 1994, the Growth, Employment and Redistribution (GEAR) Policy Framework in 1996, the Accelerated and Shared Growth Initiative for South Africa (AsgiSA) in 2005, the New Growth Path of 2010 and so on, South Africa has been pursuing a democratic developmental state. The overall consensus among scholars that have written on the trajectories of experiences of South Africa in the past 21 years of acceding to the majority democratic rule is that while some progress has been recorded, various challenges in terms of poverty and inequality, unemployment, poor service delivery, and the challenge of nation building and development remain thorny issues that, due to their social implications, deserve urgent attention.

The idea of a developmental state on which the successive post-apartheid governments in South Africa anchored their developmental programmes remains a contested and problematic one, in view of the overriding influence of the skewed global distribution of power on socio-economic policies in the country. While most of the scholarly works on South Africa's development experiences have accepted the daunting challenges of correcting the historical injustices of the past, there is little effort to situate the complexities involved in addressing these challenges within what could be termed 'democratic developmental state debate', especially as it relates to the ability and autonomy of the government to formulate and implement appropriate policies that are in synch with the expressed ideology of reconstruction and development on which the African National Congress (ANC) secured political power in 1994.

This book, *Political Economy of Post-apartheid South Africa*, comes as a background to a more thorough and detailed analysis of what has happened in South Africa in the past 21 years regarding social and economic inclusion. It explains in straightforward terms what has happened in the various selected political economy areas in post-apartheid South Africa.

Vusi Gumede, PhD
Tshwane, South Africa

Acknowledgements

Like most publication projects, many people play roles in ensuring that a manuscript gets published. The first category of people to acknowledge are the research assistants that worked with me on this book: TK Pooe, Tsholofelo Mokone and Babalwa Njezura. The second category is that of former and current colleagues; I need to recognise Joel Netshitenzhe in particular. He was my boss for eight years in the erstwhile Policy Coordination and Advisory Services (PCAS) during the Thabo Mbeki administration. Over and above the inspiration he provided, as I was slowly exiting government he allowed me space to reflect and begin the process of drafting parts that have made it to this book. I also thank him for agreeing to write the Foreword for this book.

I also acknowledge my former colleagues at the University of Johannesburg – and the students that I was teaching – who confirmed that a publication like this is necessary. I acknowledge colleagues at the Graduate School of Public and Development Management (now called the School of Government) at the University of the Witwatersrand. Many of the students I taught during 2009–2014 have shaped this book through the heated debates in and outside class, and so are those who attended sessions I facilitated for the Public Administration Leadership and Management Academy (now renamed the National School of Government).

I have to thank the reviewers. Similarly, I have to thank the publisher, particularly the colleagues directly responsible for publishing this book. Alexander Bangirana, Head of Publications at the Council for the Development of Social Science Research in Africa (CODESRIA) played a critical role in getting this book published. I also thank CODESRIA for the financial support that made this project a reality. A word of gratitude is extended to Tshego Sehlodimela who assisted me with preparing the book for publication through her publishing and editing knowledge.

Parts of some chapters come from previously published materials. I thank the editors and publishers who gave permission that I could re-publish those parts.

I thank my parents for the sacrifices they made to allow a possibility that I can contribute to knowledge production. Thanks also to many people in my life who played different roles that have enabled me to contribute to knowledge production.

Abbreviations

ABET	Adult Basic Education and Training
ACE	Advanced Certificate in Education
ACSA	Airports Company South Africa
AIDS	Acquired Immune Deficiency Syndrome
ANAs	Annual National Assessments
ANC	African National Congress
ANCYL	African National Congress Youth League
ARMSCOR	Armaments Corporation of South Africa
AsgiSA	Accelerated and Shared Growth Initiative of South Africa
AU	African Union
BEE	Black Economic Empowerment
BBBEE	Broad-Based Black Economic Empowerment
BUSA	Business Unity South Africa
CASP	Competitive Agriculture Support Programme
CDE	Centre for Development Enterprise
CES	Centre d' Economie de la Sorbonne
CHE	Council on Higher Education
CLARA	Communal Land Rights Act
Codesa	Convention for Democracy in South Africa
Cosatu	Congress of South African Trade Unions
CPPP	Community Public Private Partnership
CSDP	Competitive Supplier Development Programme
CSIR	Council for Scientific and Industrial Research
CST	Colonialism of a Special Type
CTCP	Clothing and Textile Competitive Programme
CWP	Community Work Programme
DBE	The Department of Basic Education

DED	Department of Economic Development
DoE	Department of Education
DoHE&T	Department of Higher Education and Training
DFI	Development Finance Institution
DPE	Department of Public Enterprise
DPME	Department of Performance Monitoring and Evaluation
DTI	Department of Trade and Industry
DMS	Development Merchant System
EE	Employment Equity
EFF	Economic Freedom Fighters
EIP	Enterprise Investment Programme
EPZ	Export Processing Zone
ESAP	Economic Structural Adjustment Programme
ESKOM	Electricity Supply Commission
ESTA	Extension of the Security of Tenure Act
ETQAs	Education and Training Quality Assurance Authorities
FAO	Food and Agricultural Organisation
FDI	Foreign Direct Investment
FET	Further Education and Training
FGT	Foster-Green-Thorbecke
FOSAD	Forum of South African Directors-General
EPWP	Expanded Public Works Programme
FTLRP	Fast Track Land Reform Programme
GAA	Group Areas Act
GBE	Government Business Enterprise
GDP	Growth Domestic Product
GEAR	Growth, Employment and Redistribution Framework
GHS	General Household Survey
GNU	Government of National Unity
HSRC	Human Sciences Research Council
HIV	Human Immunodeficiency Virus
HDI	Human Development Index
HPI	Human Poverty Index
HPI-1	Human Poverty Index (for developing countries)

HPI-2	Human Poverty Index (for developed countries)
ICT	Information Communication Technology
IDC	Industrial Development Corporation
IDP	Integrated Development Plan
IDZ	Industrial Development Zone
IDTT	Inter-Developmental Task Team
IFI	International Financial Institutions
IFP	Inkatha Freedom Party
IJR	Institute of Justice and Reconciliation
IMF	International Monetary Fund
IPAP	Industrial Policy Action Plan
IPR	Intellectual Property Rights
IRP	Integrated Resource Plan
ISCOR	Iron Steel Corporation
ITAC	International Trade Administration Commission
ITED	International Trade and Economic Development
JIPSA	Joint Initiative for Priority Skills
LRP	Land Reform Programme
LRRP	Zimbabwean Land Reform and Resettlement Programme
MAFISA	Micro Agricultural Finance Institute of South Africa
MDGs	Millennium Development Goals
M&E	Monitoring and Evaluation
MEC	Mineral-Energy-Complex
MERG	Macro-Economic Research Group
MPC	Monetary Policy Committee
MTEF	Medium Term Expenditure Framework
MTSF	Medium Term Strategic Framework
NA	National Assembly
NAMAC	National Small Business Advisory Council
NAP	National Agricultural Policy
NCOP	National Council of Provinces
NDP	National Development Plan
NDR	National Democratic Revolution
NDS	National Democratic Society

Nedlac	National Economic Development and Labour Council
NEET	Not in Education, Employment or Training
NEF	National Economic Empowerment Fund
NECSA	Nuclear Energy Corporation for South Africa
NERSA	National Energy Regulator of South Africa
NFTN	National Foundry Technology Network
NIEP	National Institute of Economic Policy
NIPF	National Industry Policy Framework
Nepad	New Partnership for Africa's Development
NGM	National Gender Machinery
NGOs	Non-Governmental Organisations
NGP	New Growth Path
NHI	National Health Insurance
NIEP	National Institute of Economic Policy
NIPP	National Industrial Participation Programme
NEDP	National Export Development Programme
NLA	Natives Land Act
NLM	National Liberation Movement
NMISA	National Metrology Institute of South Africa
NP	National Party
NPC	National Planning Commission
NPM	New Public Management
NQF	National Qualifications Framework
NSBs	National Standard Bodies
NSF	National Skills Fund
NSDS	National Skills Development Strategy
NSDP	National Spatial Development Perspective
NRCS	National Regulatory for Compulsory Specifications
NYDA	National Youth Development Agency
OBE	Outcomes-Based Education
ODA	Overseas Development Assistance
OECD	Organization for Economic Cooperation and Development
PAC	Pan African Congress
PCAS	Policy Coordination and Advisory Services

PF	Peoples Front
PIC	Public Investment Corporation
PICC	Presidential Infrastructure Coordinating Commission
PFMA	Public Finance Management Act
PPPFA	Preferential Procurement Policy Framework
PRC	Presidential Review Committee
PSRs	Poverty Strategy Papers
QIDS UP	Quality Improvement, Development Support and Upliftment Programme
QLTC	Quality Learning and Teaching Campaign
QCTO	Quality Control for Trade and Occupation
R2G	Ready to Govern
RDLR	Department of Rural Development and Land Reform
RDP	Reconstruction and Development Programme
RNCS	Revised National Curriculum Statement
SABC	South African Broadcasting Corporation
SABS	South African Bureau of Standards
SADC	Southern African Development Community
SANDF	South African National Defense Force
SACP	South African Communist Party
SAIRR	South African Institute of Race Relations
Samaf	South African Micro Finance Apex Fund
Sanac	South African National Aids Council
Sanco	South African National Civic Organisation
SANAS	South African National Accreditation Systems
SAPs	Structural Adjustment Programmes
SAPS	South African Policy Service
Sasol	South African Coal, Oil and Gas Corporation
SAR	South African Railway
SARB	South African Reserve Bank
SAQA	South African Qualifications Authority
SARS	South African Revenue Service
Sawid	South African Women in Dialogue
SDA	Skills Development Act

SETAs	Sector Education and Training Authorities
Seda	Small Enterprise Development Agency
SEZ	Special Economic Zone
SGB	School Governing Body
SHI	Social Health Insurance
SME	Small and Medium Sized Enterprises
SMMEs	Small, Micro and Medium Enterprises
SMTs	School Management Teams
SoC	State Owned Companies
SOEs	State Owned Enterprises
SQAM	Standard Quality Assurance and Metrology
SSA	Sub-Saharan Africa
Stats SA	Statistics South Africa
TB	Tuberculosis
TBVC	Transkei, Bophuthatswana, Venda and Ciskei
TCC	Transnational Capitalist Class
TEO	The Enterprise Organisation
TGRs	Third Generation Reforms
TIA	Technology Innovation Agency
TNPA	Transnet National Ports Authority
TRC	Truth and Reconciliation Commission
TVET	Technical, Vocational Education and Training
UDF	United Democratic Front
UN	United Nations
UNISA	University of South Africa
USAID	United States Agency for International Development
WB	World Bank
WHO	World Health Organization
ZANU	Zimbabwe African National Union

List of Tables and Figures

Tables

Figures

PART I

BACKGROUND

1

Introduction

South Africa became politically independent in 1994, much later than all other African countries – most countries in Africa gained political independence between the late 1950s and the 1970s. This book examines the various political economy issues pertaining to South Africa, with a specific focus on the post-apartheid period (i.e. since 1994). Political economy simply means the interface between the economy and politics. In other words, the study of political economy involves the evolution of societies overtime, taking into account socio-economic and political phenomena. In the context of South Africa, it is important to understand how the post-apartheid dispensation has, among other things, shaped the economy, the politics and social development. It is also important, as part of the study of any political economy, to also assess how the past affects the present and what the future might look like. It is in that context that this book looks at the political history of South Africa (Chapter 2) and examines the extent to which the ideals, such as that of ensuring a developmental state in a democratic South Africa, are being met (Chapter 12).

Background

There are many policy and strategy documents of the liberation movement that shaped what was expected to be a democratic South Africa. By the national liberation movement, the book mainly refers to the African National Congress (ANC) and its Tripartite Alliance made up of the ANC, Congress of South African Trade Unions (Cosatu) and the South African Communist Party (SACP). The liberation movement, broadly, refers to the various organisations that have played a role in the political liberation of South Africa. This would include the United Democratic Front (UDF) and many others. There were also many individuals and institutions that played various roles in ensuring the end of apartheid, including the African Union (formerly Organisation for African Unity).

Among many documents that informed the agenda for what was to be a democratic South Africa is the 1943 Bill of Rights in the Africans' Claims in South Africa, the 1955 Freedom Charter, the 1962 Road to South African Freedom and the 1992 Ready to Govern Discussion Document. The liberation movement also adopted various theories that informed the struggle towards the political independence of South Africa. Some of the main theories include the Colonialism of Special Type thesis and the National Democratic Revolution – these are discussed in detail later.

Post-1994, there are also many policy and strategy documents that shaped policy towards a socio-economically inclusive society. These include the 1994 Reconstruction and Development Programme (RDP), the 1998 Discussion Document on the State, Property Relations and Social Transformation, the 1996 Constitution and many others. The debate on whether these policy and strategy documents, and subsequent policies and programmes, have ensured that South Africa becomes a just and equitable society – given the injustices of over three-hundred years – continues and it is far from being over or settled.

On 24 May 1994, the late president, founding father and first president of a democratic South Africa, Nelson Mandela, in his inaugural address, in accordance with the policy aspirations of the Freedom Charter, opened a Joint Sitting of Parliament with the following words:

> My Government's commitment to create a people-centred society of liberty binds us to the pursuit of the goals of freedom from want, freedom from hunger, freedom from deprivation, freedom from ignorance, freedom from suppression and freedom from fear. These freedoms are fundamental to guarantee human dignity. They will therefore constitute part of the centrepiece of what this Government will seek to achieve, the focal point on which our attention will be continuously focused.[1]

Transition from Apartheid to Democracy

In 1994, the first democratically elected government inherited an economy and a society that were in profound crises. The society was severely divided. The majority of the population was disproportionately bearing the brunt of poverty, marginalisation and underdevelopment. While the South Africa's economy had begun to adjust in the 1990s, the harsh reality of a significantly distorted income distribution and consequent structural distortions in the demand for goods and services eventually resulted in a significant economic crisis. Stephen Gelb, one of leading economists in South Africa, has written extensively about the economic crises that have continuously bedevilled South Africa, both before and after apartheid colonialism. Seraaj Mohamed,[22] from a different perspective, contends that the South African economy, even the post-apartheid one, has been in a crisis. Mohamed attributes the economic crises of the post-apartheid South Africa to neoliberal policies which resulted in internationalisation, financialisation and de-industrialisation.

The apartheid social systems not only prejudiced and disadvantaged Africans, but also failed to meet the socio-economic needs of the country as a whole. High levels of unemployment and poverty, highly unequal income distribution and low levels of investment became deeply entrenched during the economic crisis of the 1990s. Contrary to the experiences of other comparable economies, with similar endowments and/or equivalent initial conditions as economists would put it, from the 1980s South Africa was stagnating with further adverse effects on the economic participation and wellbeing of the majority. From 1994, legislation and policy interventions had to be put in place to redress the ramifications of apartheid colonialism.

The ANC-led government, since 1994, has undertaken extensive policy and institutional reforms in an effort to resolve contradictions brought about by the legacy of centuries of discrimination against the majority of the country and deliberate underdevelopment. The ANC's main overarching goal was, and remains being, the creation of a united, non-racial, non-sexist, prosperous and democratic society. The ANC's strategic preoccupation has always been about uplifting the quality of life of all South Africans, Africans in particular and black people in general, especially the poor.

The ANC is committed to a series of strategic undertakings that intended to combine growth and development, reconstruction and redistribution, popular participation and respect for human rights. It is against this backdrop that the party contested the first democratic elections – on 27 April 1994 – based on a vision of 'A Better Life for All'. The outlines of, and the strategic path towards, the purported 'better life' are elaborated in the 1992 Ready to Govern (R2G) strategy document and particularly in the 1994 Reconstruction and Development Programme – a policy framework underpinned by the vision for reconstruction and development of a new South Africa. South Africa's new Constitution enshrined the right of all South Africans to equality and provided for specific measures to be taken to redress historical imbalances and the monumental historical injustice of apartheid colonialism.

A number of macro-economic policies and/or political economy interventions have been pursued, namely the 1996 Growth, Employment and Redistribution (GEAR) framework, the 2005 Accelerated and Shared Growth Initiative of South Africa (AsgiSA) and the 2010 New Growth Path (NGP). Chapters 4 and 5, as well as 6, to some extent, discuss these economic frameworks and other major policy directives of the successive post-apartheid administrations; and Chapter 13, as the book concludes, discusses similar issues in the context of a developmental state. While post-apartheid South African administrations have made concerted efforts to deal with the historical socio-economic challenges, progress is mixed at best and disappointing at worst. The gains on social development and welfare in post-apartheid South Africa are commendable. Significant progress has been made in expanding access to education, healthcare, housing and providing basic services. But there are many areas, say the economy and the labour market as examples, where progress is disappointing, as discussed later. Even in the areas where progress is registered (i.e. education and healthcare), the quality of service provisioning and services provided remain poor.

Concepts and Ideas

As a study of political economy, this book presents many concepts and ideas in the fields of political studies and economics as well as policy studies. Some of its chapters also have relevance for other fields such as geography, history and broader development studies. The various concepts are explained as and when they are used in the different chapters and a glossary of key terms for each chapter is provided at the end of the chapter, except for the first two chapters which are introductory and therefore have the terms used extensively discussed in the text. Also, Chapter 13 does not contain a glossary of terms because it is a conclusion.

The one concept that needs some explanation, at this very onset, is 'apartheid colonialism'. At a broad level, apartheid colonialism is a shorthand for the totality of the historical experience of colonialism, imperialism, racism, apartheid and other forms of enslavement that black South Africans have endured in over three centuries. In other words, both colonialism and apartheid were formal systems of oppression and racism. South Africa, unlike most other African countries, experienced both colonialism (officially since 1652 until the 1940s) and apartheid (1948–1994). Apartheid colonialism, as a system, also created racial categories of Africans (including Indians and coloureds, over and above blacks) and whites (i.e. Europeans).

The book uses the developmental state framework to discuss the various political economy issues. The Freedom Charter and its understanding of the role of the state – the 'developmental state' – has since served as a philosophical prism through which the understanding of the 'new society' has been articulated. In order to understand the framework of the developmental state, it is important to highlight the emergence of the 'developmental state' in development discourse. The emergence of the notion of 'developmental state' in development discourse follows the rapid rise of the East Asian Tigers (i.e. Taiwan, South Korea, Singapore and Hong Kong) as an economic and consequent political force in the 1990s; Louis Amsden and Chalmers Johnson stand out as the two scholars who have written extensively about this or have significantly influenced the discourse about developmental states. Peter Evans has also written extensively, especially in the context of 'new' developmental states (countries such as Brazil and India). Vivek Chibber, Patrick Heller, Adrian Leftwich, Amiya Bagchi, Ziya Onis and Manuel Castells have also written significantly on the notion of developmental states. Thandika Mkandawire has written extensively about developmental states in Africa while Guy Mhone and Omano Edigeji have written a lot about the notion of developmental states with a specific focus on South Africa. Issa Shivji is also worth mentioning, given his extensive works on matters of development on the African continent, so is Samir Amin – to highlight a few.

Much of what is known to constitute a 'developmental state' is, as a consequence, modelled against the Asian Tigers whose developmental states were, in the main, characterised by state intervention in the economy in the pursuit of socio-economic development. In this regard, as Mhone[3] puts it, the developmental state is a state that steers economic development as well as industrialisation in the interest of the public good. The 'developmental state' concept is said to be an institutional model that adopts a statist approach to account for the high levels of growth of the lately industrialised nations. It affirms the state as central and beneficial in economic development, and in ways that are distinct from Soviet-type communist states. The Keynesian social-democratic states, for instance, have aspects of developmental states because the state is expected to intervene in the market economy in order to accelerate social equality and fairness.[4]

The developmental state emerges in stark contrast to neoclassical (or neoliberal) economics that has long argued that 'state interference' tampers with economic growth as it disrupts market equilibrium with devastating consequences. Institutional economics has since recognised the limitations of orthodox economics, whose failure(s) to explain market 'anomalies' is largely attributable to its failure to recognise the importance of non-market related institutions (i.e. political and cultural institutions) in shaping the very same institutions required to achieve market equilibrium. The developmental state is also in recognition of power relations that shape development.

There is no single and agreed-upon definition of a developmental state – there is, however, a generally wide consensus on the characteristics of a developmental state. A developmental state can be viewed as a state that actively intervenes in the economy with the aim of advancing wellbeing in tandem with a growing economy. The working definition of a developmental state that this book uses supposes that a developmental state 'is a state that is active in pursuing its agenda, working with social partners, and has the capacity and is appropriately organised for its predetermined developmental objectives'.[5] This definition is informed by research on the subject and influenced by Evans'[6] notion of 'embedded autonomy'; Leftwich's[7] model of a developmental state; Cummings and Nørgaard's[8] four dimensions of state capacity; as well as definitions and features of developmental states by South African scholars, such as Luiz,[9] Mhone,[10] Swilling et al,[11] Edigheji.[12] As Dikeni[13] puts it, "developmental state" as a term primarily concerns itself with the ways and means of how a state governs, intervenes in the lives of its citizens, and organises and mobilises resources for itself in order to transform and effect economic and social change in society for development purposes'.

It must be noted, however, that the fact that the idea of a developmental state has currency does not presuppose a consensuses by scholars and policy-makers on the features or even the model South Africa has been following and/or should follow. Alan Hirsch,[14] echoing Ralph Mathekga[15] who says that the 'democratic South Africa is relatively an infant', argues that 'it is too early to say that a democratic developmental state is impossible in South Africa [because] our political system is so young and immature…' Leslie Dikeni[16] makes a related point that, theoretically and conceptually thinking, the term [developmental state] cannot be seen and/or be used as a concept, neither can we attribute the meaning of a 'theoretical model of development to the term… [the term] represents a grouping together of a series of some loosely-related phenomena of "state" and "development" under the rubric of a developmental state'. Thandika Mkandawire[17] could disagree because, in his view, developmental states are 'social constructs' that the states and societies bring about, implying that there is value in the notion of a developmental state, even as a term.

It is suggested that it is not only possible but also necessary to empirically and conceptually gauge the extent to which South Africa can be characterised as a developmental state, especially two decades since the dawn of democracy. For instance, Hein Marias[18] argues that to arrive at a view of whether South Africa is a developmental state or not, one should examine 'features deemed essential' for South Africa to be a developmental state or assess whether South Africa 'is already conducting itself in a manner of a developmental state'. Essentially, therefore, there ought to be attempts, using sound analytical tools, to assess whether a country is progressively becoming a developmental state or not. That would help engage the various views on the notion of a developmental state in South Africa. For instance, Ben Turok[19] concluded that 'South Africa could not presently be characterised as a developmental state but that it has taken several significant steps in this direction'.

It is worth noting that a significant body of the literature on the notion of a developmental state has focused on economic growth and development. Amiya Bagchi,[20] for example, defines a developmental state as a state that prioritises economic development in public policy and a state that is able to design effective instruments to promote such a goal. Critical to this perspective is that industrial policy and structural change in the production system drives economic expansion. In this instance, economic development is largely associated with industrialisation and liberalisation. This perspective seems to feature prominently in definitions of developmental states by leading scholars in the field.

Robinson and White,[21] Leftwich,[22] as well as Cummings and Nørgaard's,[23] on the other hand, have introduced a notion termed the 'state-structure nexus' as a critical attribute of the developmental state. These scholars emphasise the importance of organisational capacity of the state as well as technical capacity in building a developmental state. Important in this regard is the ability to develop industrial elites, ensure relative state autonomy, institutional coherence and economic performance. Institutional reforms, alongside changes in the economic strategy, are seen as critical in the promotion of developmental goals.

As indicated earlier, Mkandawire,[24] on the other hand, argues that developmental states are 'social constructs' by different role-players in a particular society, namely the political elite, the industrial elite and the civil society. This perspective is, in part, shared by Johnson[25] who conceptualised the developmental state in Japan, for instance, as epitomised by a 'plan rational state' where 'the politicians reign and the state bureaucrats rule' – the 'plan rational state' shaped economic development as it intervened in the development processes and established 'substantive social and economic goals'.

Similar to Onis[26] who argues that the East Asian model of a developmental state is the product of political and cultural forces, Castells[27] also identifies three 'cultural' dimensions that reinforce the conceptual makeup of the developmental state in East Asia, namely: the Japanese communitarian approach, the Korean patrimonial logic and the Taiwanese patrilineal logic. Onis[28] highlights the importance of the historical context that sets the stage for the making of the developmental state and argues that East Asian developmental states were, by and large, also shaped by their historical circumstances.

As demonstrated by the different perspectives briefly depicted above, there is no single narrative that accounts for the developmental state. It seems to me, however, that the differences are mainly attributable to differences in emphasis. In other words, one can recognise a developmental state when one sees one. In essence, developmental states are characterised by a number of features or multiple dimensions, namely: ideological (i.e. role of the state versus market), institutional (i.e. state autonomy and capacity), cultural (collectivism versus individualism), and socio-economic attributes (i.e. economic growth, industrialisation, etc).

As indicated above, for the purposes of this book, suitable to South Africa's realities, the developmental state – a contested notion – is defined as a state that is 'active in pursuing its agenda, working with social partners, and has the capacity and is appropriately organised for its predetermined developmental objectives'.[29] This broad definition suggests that a developmental state is essentially made up of a government that has requisite capacities to fulfil a developmental mandate, striking a balance between state and capital as well as working with society as a whole. At the very least, this provides a framework that can guide analysis of whether a particular society would ever have a developmental state or not. The book is guided by this perspective in the discussion of the various political economy phenomena.

Lastly, the other important concept that should be explained at this outset is 'development'. Development – not to be confused with a theoretical notion of developmental state – involves socio-economic progress or improvement in the wellbeing of people. The improvements in wellbeing are normally quantified through the Human Development Index (HDI) which measures human development as a composite indicator made up of life expectancy, literacy and per capita income. In simple terms, human development involves achievements in healthcare, in education and in the standard of living. Another way of thinking about the term 'development' is when countries go through different stages of development, from low to high. It is generally understood that development must involve the people that need development – the people should be able to guide the development needed and also have choices for their livelihoods (as Claude Ake[30] or Amartya Sen[31] would put it).

Scope of the Book

The book is made up of three parts. The first part is on background and a brief discussion on the political history of South Africa. The second part deals with policies and prospects. It covers chapters on policy and law making, economic development, economic empowerment, industrial development, public enterprises, land and agriculture, education and training, poverty and inequality and, lastly, spatial planning. Part three discusses how the South African society has evolved since 1994 and explores South Africa in the pursuit of a developmental state while also proposing policy interventions that can deal with the socio-economic challenges discussed in the second part of the book.

2

Brief Political History of South Africa

Introduction

This chapter discusses the various African communities in the broader southern Africa, their various interactions with one another and the interactions with non-African peoples. The chapter also describes how the various African communities such as the San, Khoi, Nguni, Sotho and Tswana managed their socio-economic and political systems. The role and interactions of non-African communities, such as the Portuguese, the Dutch and the English with African communities are also discussed. In the main, European colonialism negatively impacted the African communities. It is in this context that history is critical in order that the understanding of the post-apartheid political economy is not divorced from the totality of the historical experience that has influenced today's political economy.

The history of southern Africa can be said to be not a single narrative or story but rather a series of contested histories that have been altered and remodelled to shape non-African communities and institutions.[32] That is why this chapter examines the pre-colonial African communities and the key developments which characterised their societies. The chapter also gives a brief background explanation on how South Africa's pre-colonial history was manipulated in order to misrepresent the fact that African peoples/communities did in fact have vibrant and functional pre-colonial interactions and societies.

In describing the history of southern Africa, it is important to first acknowledge the fact that the history did not begin with the Portuguese or British or Dutch (European) arrival, but is rather an interrupted narrative of socio-economic development.[33] There were many African communities that co-existed in southern Africa before the arrival of Europeans – and there were various advanced kingdoms, as epitomised by civilisations pertaining to Mapungubwe and Great Zimbabwe for example. In fact, those originating within the African continent had migrated from different other parts of the continent to the southern parts.[34]

Europeans arrived in southern Africa about two centuries after Africans from other parts of the continent had migrated to the southern tip. It is understood that, in fact, mainly the Khoi and the San – derogatorily called Hottentots – had existed in the southern tip of Africa from time immemorial.[35]

The southern Africa of pre-colonial era was one that did not have clearly identifiable borders, and societies were categorised into kingdoms (i.e. Zulu, Sotho, Venda and others) and smaller hunter (San) or gatherer (Khoi-Khoi) communities.[36] It is important to note that the African communities in that period did have some interactions with non-African communities such as the Portuguese, Dutch and sometimes Arab traders and ship merchants as well as Asians. It is also important to note that Africans are said to have settled at what later became known as South Africa over 2000 years ago and they had occupied the east coast around the sixteenth century[37]. It was during this time that great cities and states like Mapungubwe State, Toutswe State (near Limpopo River), Kilwa and Sofala (along the so-called Indian Ocean coast) were formed and great African leaders like Inkosi Shaka Zulu and Morena Moshoeshoe reigned.[38]

African Communities

As indicated earlier, there is no single history of African communities and kingdoms. Rather, it is a series of histories of different communities who could be divided into different ethnic or language groups. Following is a discussion on (1) San and Khoi-Khoi; (2) Nguni; and (3) Sotho-Tswana and other communities.

San and Khoi-khoi

The San and Khoi-khoi need to be understood as two different and distinct African communities.[39] Each of these two groups was predominantly found in the western hemisphere of southern Africa. They could also be distinguished by their linguistic differences and livelihood strategies (hunters or gatherers). Both these communities were the original inhabitants of the area known today as the Western Cape and had interactions with other African communities, most notably Bantu-speaking Africans.[40]

The Khoi-khoi and San were slightly different from their fellow Africans in the southern African region, in part due to their non-Bantu language, smaller community size and choice of routine – they were nomadic and exhibited hunter-gatherer traits.[41] Despite these obvious and real differences, it is important to note that the San and Khoi-khoi were themselves two different communities who, depending on where they stayed, were expert hunters, trackers, artists and on occasion makers of hunting tools and weapons.[42]

Nguni

The largest African communities in the southern African region were the Nguni communities.[43] The Nguni communities, much like the Sotho-Tswana, were a Bantu-speaking ethnic group.[44] While the Khoi and San communities could be found along the Western Cape area of present-day South Africa, the Nguni communities were to be found along the Eastern Cape and KwaZulu-Natal coastal and inland regions.[45]

Within the Nguni communities, further delineations between communities existed. For instance, the Eastern Cape area had the amaXhosa (this is a generic term that refers to an amalgamation of clans from the broader Eastern Cape) while the KwaZulu area had the amaZulu (who were formed into one nation or kingdom over time). Other Nguni communities, such as the amaSwati and amaNdebele would later come out from the predominantly Zulu kingdom.[46]

The Nguni people of both the Eastern Cape and KwaZulu areas were nation states that came to be formed partly due to the expansionist tendencies of their respective leaders and kings. As mentioned earlier, the Zulu Kingdom came to the fore largely due to the actions of Inkosi Shaka Zulu and the Mfecane process, which had the effect of further delineating the South African and southern African landscape.[47] The Mfecane or Difaqane was a process whereby various ethnic groups were amalgamated to the Zulu Kingdom, while others formed their own kingdoms.

The Eastern Cape amaXhosa was a conglomeration of mini-clans such as the abaThembu, amaMpondo, amaMpondomise, amaXesibe and amaQwathi, to mention but a few.[48] However, these communities did not reach the level or influence of the Zulu Kingdom, partly due to the numerous subsets of chieftaincies and numerous political reasons, such as not having a single leader in the form of Inkosi Shaka Zulu.

Sotho-Tswana

The Sotho-Tswana communities encompassed three small communities, namely the Sotho, Tswana and Pedi (i.e. South Sotho). They were predominantly found in the northern areas of South Africa (present-day Gauteng, Free State, Limpopo, North-West and parts of the Northern Cape provinces of South Africa) and later Botswana in southern African.[49]

Despite sharing the same form of Bantu dialect, both the Sotho and Tswana communities came to occupy different parts of South Africa and southern Africa and later developed into distinct communities.[50] For instance, the Sotho occupied and lived in the central areas of South Africa and eventually became a kingdom

– Morena Moshoeshoe – through the founder of present-day Lesotho.[51] The Batswana would come to be recognised through their royal houses such as the baKwena, baKgatla, baRolong and baHurutshe, which were later integrated into smaller subsets and kingdoms.[52] It was not uncommon for both these communities to be involved in skirmishes, firstly between themselves and also with the San and Khoi-Khoi communities, partly due to the limited resources that characterised non-coastal areas.[53] Despite the differences, the Sotho-Tswana communities, much like the Nguni communities of the coast, did involve themselves in large scale agricultural pursuits and also some form of metal and mining activities in their respective lining areas.[54]

Political and Economic Systems

The political landscape of the early (so-called pre-colonial) southern Africa can be said to have been one that was characterised by the rule of kings or, more precisely, regional kingdoms. It needs to be mentioned that the power dynamics and political system of that time were more complex than has previously been presented, and that the community, especially elders, had significant influence on how respective kings, and on occasion queens, ruled their people.[55] To simply characterise the rule of kings and queens as genetic or divine right-rule would fail to capture the complexity and nuances that characterised how African communities in the most southern tip of the continent functioned and or were organised.

It is important to highlight that one of the biggest political ruptures or events to define early southern Africa had to do with the activities of Inkosi Shaka Zulu. The event referred to came to be known as Mfecane, which was the expansion of the Zulu Kingdom from its coastal areas to the inland areas of the then South Africa.[56] It was during this period that numerous African communities fled to other parts of southern Africa and that resulted in the creation of newer political formations and communities, such as the Shona and Ndebele.[57] The Mfecane greatly reshaped the political landscape of South Africa and southern Africa, as old ruling community structures were either dealt away with or new ones came into existence.

With regards to economic activities during this time, trade between the various African communities did take place.[58] At a basic level, trade of different food stuffs was quite common in the early periods of interaction; however as civilisations came to exploit agricultural and even mining activities, there were shifts in economic activities to relatively advanced trade products. For instance, cattle came to be viewed as an important currency for both practical and even cultural-religious purposes and the more cattle one owned the richer one was thought to be.[59]

Interactions between Africans and non-Africans

The interactions between African communities and non-African communities, especially within the southern African region and South Africa in particular, can be said to have been one based on economic ties and trade.[60] As more and more Europeans, and on occasion Arab travellers, began to manufacture and operate ships for trade purposes, first at a small scale and later at industrial levels, they came to interact with African communities living on the coastal areas of the Western and later the Eastern Cape, and finally KwaZulu region.[61]

The trade that took place between African and non-African communities first began with basic food products and fresh waters and later on advanced to valuable products such as gold and other prized possessions.[62] As this trade advanced, the reach of non-African traders and merchants extended to places as far north as present-day Zimbabwe.

The city state or kingdom of Mapungubwe is an interesting case study for advancing the idea that southern Africa was a developing region, before European colonialism. It thrived as a sophisticated trading centre from around the thirteenth century. As more research work is being done on the area and history of Mapungubwe, what has been revealed thus far shows a fairly advanced African kingdom, with a rich commercial and societal development.

Commercial History

Research and work linked to the study of Mapungubwe show that it was a society at a commercial level which was characterised by small scale mining and metallurgy.[63] While the mining which took place was not the type seen in later centuries, it was able to produce end products like jewellery, potteries and other items which were traded by citizens of this kingdom with non-African merchants, with business extending to not only Europe but also Asia.

It is this commercial activity that clearly illustrates the fact that not only the region of Mapungubwe, but also southern African kingdoms and city states were in the process of economic development. While it is true that more research is needed to uncover how and in what ways other southern African kingdoms and city states were developing, what cannot be denied though is the fact that areas like the Mapungubwe City State illustrates that there exists a long history of southern/South Africa commercial pre-colonial history.[64]

What has also been confirmed by research is that the Mapungubwe City State did have leadership structures and structures of society that were able to first organise commercial activity and then attend to rudimentary governance matters. As Ramsey[65] explains, the findings at Mapungubwe clearly illustrate the fact that development of the city state was led and in some ways governed by ruling elites and royal classes. It has also been explained by Moffat[66] that some of the major governance responsibilities administered by the royalty and ruling class were the issues of trade and commercial activity which even extended to how they interacted with other regional kingdoms and city states.

The ruins of Mapungubwe – just like the ruins of Great Zimbabwe – are not only important for South Africa's early history, but are equally critical to understanding the whole history of southern Africa. It is important to remember that Mapungubwe, though part of modern South Africa, was in the past a stand-alone city state encompassing not only present-day South Africa but also parts of Zimbabwe. Furthermore, the influence of the city state is said to have assisted in the development of the Great Zimbabwe Kingdom that came later. Mapungubwe represents an important argument for the idea that Africa and southern Africa's development was not predicated on European inventions and ideas, but was rather stunted by the colonisation and apartheid regimes.

Conclusion

This chapter sought to highlight, briefly, some important aspects of the history of what is known as South Africa today. Chapter 12 discusses the evolution of post-apartheid South African society. It is critical to understand the early history of any country so as to better understand the present and consider the future, as political economy has to engage with the evolution of societies. For well over three hundred and fifty years of British and Afrikaner rule, according to Thompson,[67] the propaganda was that African peoples in southern Africa neither had the mental capabilities nor the historical hegemony to create kingdoms and governance systems. However, as case studies such as regarding Mapungubwe or even the governance and expansionist history of Inkosi Shaka Zulu show, African people had had a very strong socio-economic development before the advent of European colonialism.

PART II

POLICIES AND PROSPECTS

3

Policy and Law-making

Introduction

This chapter describes how policy is formulated and reformed by the post-apartheid government in South Africa. It also illustrates the processes public policies go through to ultimately become law in South Africa. The main purpose of the chapter is to add to the understanding and knowledge of the public sector by examining policy reforms in the post-apartheid South Africa. The chapter also provides a description of the policy approaches (i.e. models) and other related issues while also discussing the three main levels of the government as prescribed by the Constitution of the Republic of South Africa (Act 108 of 1996), namely, the National, Provincial and Local levels. In addition, some of the important decision-making processes within these spheres are discussed in order to highlight the democratic principles inherent in the South African governmental system.

There are many definitions of public policy. In the main, a policy refers to a plan, principle, programme or an initiative aimed at improving a particular condition or achieving a particular goal. In the context of public policy, policies are intents of what government wants to achieve. For instance, a government would have policies on healthcare, education, the economy, transportation and many other areas. In such cases, there are many role players and processes in the policy formulation and implementation.

Defining Public Policy

According to Gumede,[68] given that public policies usually involve many institutions and various processes, they entail 'all formal and public known decisions of government that come about through predetermined channels in a particular administration'. As this definition suggests, public policies entail decision-making in the administration of government. It is also suggested that public policies have to be publicly known.

Gumede[69] summarises what scholars of 'public policy' have said about this term:

- A label for a field of government activity (such as foreign policy, social policy, etc);
- An expression of general purpose, which would entail many public statements and announcements that members of the cabinet make;
- A set of specific proposals, which could be on how to address – for example – service delivery challenges;
- Formal authorisation for action by ministries or similar set-ups;
- Policy as programme: A series of linked proposals and means of implementation. This might be expressed in a slogan such as the 'war against poverty' (e.g. in the recent case of South Africa's anti-poverty initiatives);
- Policy as output or outcome: Government often attributes a good result in government agency to some policy that may not necessarily be publicly known;
- Policy as process: Policy emerges from the interaction of many people representing many interests. Most policies build on existing activities and institutions which themselves have become an interest, and are modified during implementation as the actions of agency confront the realities on the ground.

In view of the above, public policies can be influenced or shaped by various contexts and are mainly aimed at the welfare of the nation concerned. In other words, they are directed to positively impact a particular group or the population at large. It is also important to note that when policies change or shift, as the environment or context changes, that is referred to as 'policy reform'. In every country, at some point there are policy reforms. A distinction also needs to be made between policy making and policy implementation: policy making involves different processes and decisions in the formulation of public policies while policy implementation is about putting in place programmes and projects that are aimed at ensuring that the goal of a policy is accomplished.

Public Policy Reforms

As indicated above, policy reforms often take place when change or shift occurs either in the context, environment or government. For instance, as leaders in gover-nment change, even within the same political parties at times, policies change or shift. Leaders have different ideals of the country and that influences public policies.

The different policy emphases can be viewed as overarching ideals of the national policies by the national government during the time of the different leaders in the presidency – the emphasis or focus of each leader could also be influenced by the domestic and global context. Given the political history of

South Africa as briefly presented in Chapter 2, Nelson Mandela had to prioritise reconciliation and reconstruction, Thabo Mbeki needed to focus on socio-economic transformation and it makes sense that Jacob Zuma has prioritised rural development and poverty reduction. It should however be noted if the same ruling party leads government for a longer period the various or successive administrations are likely to pursue similar overarching goals. For instance, as indicated in Chapter 1, the African National Congress in South Africa is guided by the National Democratic Revolution theory and shaped by the aspirations expressed in the Freedom Charter. Therefore, even though the different administrations, since 1994, may seem to have prioritised different objectives the main overall goals have not changed.

In formulating national policy, it is of significant importance that the functions and responsibilities of the different role players are clear. In the case of South Africa, the functions and responsibilities are indicated in the 1996 Constitution. Broadly speaking, the national government is responsible for policy formulation, developing standards and norms, as well as rules and regulations. Functional areas for provincial governments include abattoirs, ambulance services, provincial planning, provincial cultural matters, provincial roads and traffic management. Local governments take care of local government matters which include local amenities, municipal abattoirs, municipal roads, pollution and street trading.

In undertaking policy reforms, public management officials require appropriate management tools in both public and private domains. These tools maximise efficiency and the effectiveness of public administration. Public policy development can be described in three ways, namely, the efficient and effective use of all categories of resources for implementing public policies; increase in public policies performances through adaptability to the needs of society; engagement and building of consensus amongst public actors by creating a reflective and action space. This indicates that public management is a commitment to change and maintaining equilibrium of change.

Public administration theory posits two paradigms of influence in many countries, including South Africa. The first theory consists of the bureaucratic system, associated with Marx Weber, namely, the traditional system of public management. The second theory is that of the new public management. Of late, there is also a theoretical proposition called third generation reforms.

Traditional System of Public Administration

According to Stewart and Walsh,[70] the traditional system of public management is based on a set of fundamental characteristics which are: administration, job depersonalisation and functionaries. Stewart and Walsh[71] further suggest that the traditional model of organising and delivering public services is based on the principles of the bureaucratic hierarchy, planning, centralisation and direct control. This implies that the public administrators do not own the technical or financial means of the administration. Therefore, according to Stewart and Walsh, it should be noted that the traditional model was eventually replaced by a management of public services based on the market rules, which was called the new public management.

The New Public Management

Ferlie et al[72] indicate that the methods and techniques specific to the new public management have been used to bring changes into the public services management of the countries that have a relatively unstable economic and social environment. These practices and techniques have been generically named the 'new public management' or the 'new managerialism'.

Bale and Dale[73] describes new public management as 'a move away from input controls, rules and procedures towards outputs measurement and performance targets – the accountability control with improved reporting and monitoring mechanisms, a preference for private ownership, contestable provision and contracting – out of publicly funded services; adoption of private sector management practices in the public sector such as short-term contracts and performance-linked remuneration schemes'.

Although there are still aspects of traditional management and new managerialism in the South African public sector, it would appear that there has been more of a new public management application and the third generation reforms, such as the integrated governance approach.[74] Another important aspect of the government arrangements is that South Africa has put in place what could be characterised as a combination of distributed 'institutional monopoly' and 'institutional pluralism'. This implies a combination of various forms and types of decentralisation, or the devolution of certain decision-making powers to other spheres of government and/or certain agencies of government.[75]

Public Policy Making Approaches

The models or approaches that are generally applied in the formulation of public policies include:

- The rational model,
- The garbage-can model, and
- The incremental and mixed-scan model.

The Rational Model

The rational model, which was influenced by the field of economics, provides a structured and sequenced approach to decision making. The model involves a number of sequential and ordered steps. Additionally, the model suggests that there are interconnections and sequential phases in policy making. The interactions between policy actors and policy makers on the one hand, and affected parties on the other hand, take place during the policy formulation phase. Interactions or consultations could also take place during the issue definition or objective setting stage.

Morse and Stryuk[76] propose six basic steps in policy analysis which have similarities with the rational model of policy making:

Figure 3.1: Policy Process: Sequential Steps and Stages

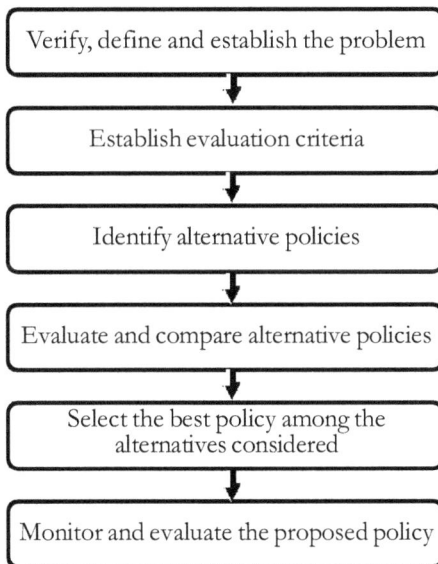

```
┌──────────────────────────────────────────┐
│  Verify, define and establish the problem │
└──────────────────────────────────────────┘
                    ↓
┌──────────────────────────────────────────┐
│       Establish evaluation criteria        │
└──────────────────────────────────────────┘
                    ↓
┌──────────────────────────────────────────┐
│        Identify alternative policies       │
└──────────────────────────────────────────┘
                    ↓
┌──────────────────────────────────────────┐
│   Evaluate and compare alternative policies│
└──────────────────────────────────────────┘
                    ↓
┌──────────────────────────────────────────┐
│       Select the best policy among the     │
│          alternatives considered           │
└──────────────────────────────────────────┘
                    ↓
┌──────────────────────────────────────────┐
│   Monitor and evaluate the proposed policy │
└──────────────────────────────────────────┘
```

Nonetheless, many criticism of the model arise due to claims that the model is impractical and premised on unrealistic assumptions. Although the rational model appears ideal for policy making, it might not apply in reality. For instance, it 'assumes' that there is adequate capacity and time to make a particular policy, do forecasting, undertake a cost-benefit analysis, and so on. The model also 'assumes' that policies are outcomes of an objective of fact and thus ignore the externalities and context that shape public policy making. The model underplays the role and significance of power relations in the policy-making process. It is suggested that, in many times during the policy making process, other factors comes into play. This is so as most policy decisions are effectively political ones and stages such as forecasting are hardly undertaken.

The Garbage-can Model

The garbage-can model can be viewed as a 'messy' policy-making process that does not follow a linear or specific approach and sequence. It is applied in organised 'anarchical' situations where there are no agreed and shared goals or resolution of problems. Furthermore, it does not follow any sequential processes because procedures are non-existent and participants change from time to time.

The garbage-can model involves decision making that is based on three principles:[77]

- That decision making is based on problematic preferences that are generally inconsistent and ill defined;
- That the preferences are broadly a loose coalition of ideals that are often harnessed in a trial-and-error procedure, based on experience and invention of necessity;
- That participation is fluid, as time devoted and effort made differ with actors in the policy sub-system.

The garbage-can model can be compared to an open or upside-down hat into which various problems and solutions are put and from which they are taken out by participants. The mix of 'garbage' in a hat depends partly on the labels attached to the alternatives as well as on what 'garbage' is being produced at that moment, on the mix of cans available, and on the speed with which 'garbage' is collected and removed from the scene (metaphorically speaking). The garbage-can model has been criticised for being ad hoc, haphazard and lacking order. The model is trying to make a point that the goals are often unknown to decision makers. In addition, policy actors simply define goals and choose means as they go along in a policy process that is necessarily contingent and unpredictable.

Organisations are characterised as garbage cans into which problems, people, choice situations and solutions are dumped and selected. A crucial variable in this model is timing. It is assumed that there is a continual stream of people, solutions, choices and problems that flow in an organisation. Every now and then, some clusters of these elements coincide, and a decision is produced. Therefore, Weick[78] argues that the problems may attach themselves first to one choice situation then to another, and the same holds true for people and solutions.

The Incremental and Mixed-scan Models

When the incremental model was developed in the 1960s, it was conceived of as a policy-making process that does not require a thorough review of policy alternatives. The model provides for a broad review of the policy options. This implies that the approach does not require a linear decision-making process and it has most of the attributes of incrementalism and rationality. Such policy making proposes small steps which bring about a change or a shift in an existing policy. Decision makers only consider alternatives for dealing with a problem that differs marginally (incrementally) from existing policies. This posits that incremental policy models do not need to be completely re-created every time a policy decision is made. However, they re-fashion existing policy. For each alternative, only important consequences are considered. Problems confronting the decision maker are continually re-defined.

According to Dye,[79] proponents of the incremental model argue that agreement is often achieved relatively easily when the policy issues contested are only about increases or improvements as compared to when they are about major shifts in a case of 'all or nothing'. Incrementalism is particularly applicable in instances where societal values are contestable.

Alternatively, Mitchell[80] argues that the mixed scanning approach considers both fundamental and incremental decisions. According to Mitchell, the mixed-scan model tries to involve the strengths of the rational planning approach and the incremental model and eliminate the weaknesses. Mixed scanning incorporates a broad-based analysis on occasions and an in-depth analysis at other times. It considers the differing capacities of decision makers.

Public Policy Cycle

A policy cycle refers to the different stages and processes that should be taken into account when formulating public policy. There are five stages in the policy cycle:

Figure 3.2: Public Policy Cycle

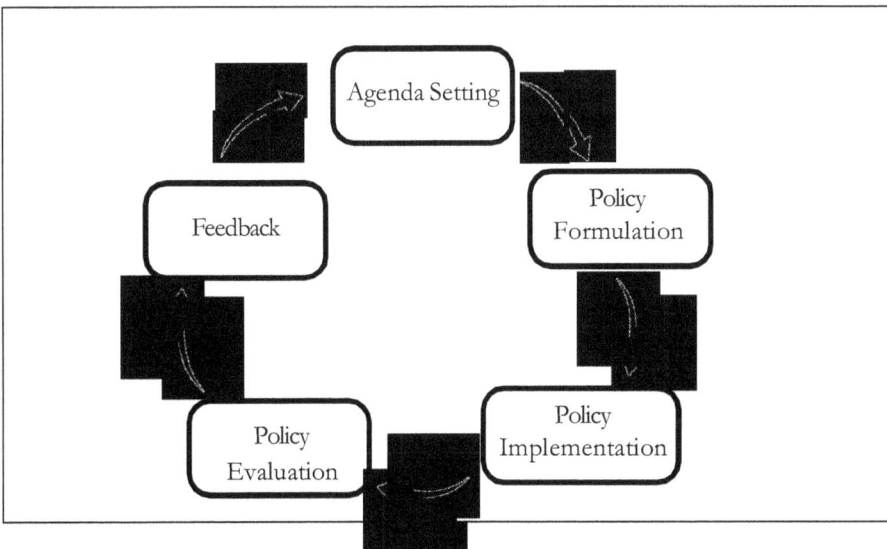

Agenda Setting

The starting point in policy formulation is the acknowledgement of the policy challenge that needs to be addressed. For instance, if all the children that are supposed to be at school are not at school, the policy needs to be formulated to ensure that all children are at school. This recognition and acknowledgement of the policy challenge is called 'agenda setting'. The agenda setting stage is viewed as the most critical stage in the policy cycle because it is the first stage and what happens during this stage shapes the policy making process. According to Howlett and Ramesh,[81] agenda setting refers to a socially constructed process in which actors and institutions, influenced by their ideologies, play a fundamental role in determining the problems or issues requiring action on the part of the government.

Policy Formulation

Policy formulation is the process of deciding on a particular policy option relative to other possible policy alternatives. Once the policy challenge has been identified and discussed, the policy needs to be formulated. There are many factors that come into policy formulation, hence it normally takes a very long to make a policy. There are two types of constraints that affect policy formulation: subjective constraints and procedural constraints. According to Howlett and Ramesh,[82] substantive constraints are related to the nature of the problem itself and entail considerable use of state resources to resolve a policy challenge. Procedural constraints, on the other hand, also affect all aspects of the formulation stage, are characterised either as institutional, based on government procedures, or as tactical, based on relationships between various actors or social groups.

Public servant actors and social groups, as Howlett and Ramesh put it, are component parts of the policy subsystems, and the cohesiveness between the two components with respect to discourse (reflecting values and beliefs) and their social bonds has a fundamental influence on policy formulation. Also, the relationship between the government and social actors is an important factor influencing the formulation of public policies.

Implementation

This is the process of putting public policy into effect. According to Mégie,[83] this is when a decision is carried out through the application of government directives and is confronted with reality. Policy implementation involves carrying out activities and processes towards resolving the policy challenge. Like other stages in the policy cycle, policy implementation is characterised by many challenges. Skills for implementing a policy are among the most important factors for policy implementation. Because of the various challenges, many policies are not properly implemented. Also, policies can have unintended consequences, as another policy challenge might happen while implementing a particular policy.

Policy Evaluation

Once the policy has been formulated, it is important to assess or evaluate its effects: How has the policy worked? How can policy implementation be improved? Answering these questions is essential to providing policy makers with necessary feedback to incorporate into future decision making.

Law-making

The governance arrangements in South Africa are enacted in the supreme law of the country – the Constitution. Public policy, as explained in the proceeding sections, outlines what a government department hopes to achieve and the methods and principles that will be applied to accomplish them. Law, on the other hand, is about ensuring that policies are implemented by holding government legally accountable.

A law refers to set out standards, procedures and principles that must be followed. If a law is not followed, those responsible for not following it can be prosecuted in court (to put it simplistically). This implies that public policy which sets out the goals and planned activities of a department, as an example, may have to be translated into a law to enable government to put in place the necessary institutional and legal frameworks to achieve its objective.

It should be noted that the process of making law in South Africa – and probably in many other countries, if not all – involves a number of structures. By the time the draft legislation reaches parliament (from government departments), where it is tabled as a Bill, it would have gone through a lengthy process. The process generally begins with a discussion document, called a Green Paper, or is followed by it. This is drafted in the ministry or department dealing with the particular issue at hand, with an aim to demonstrate the way that the ministry or department is thinking on a particular policy.

The Green Paper is then published so that anyone who is interested and/or affected can give comments, suggestions and ideas. The Green Paper process is followed by a more refined discussion document called a White Paper, which is a broad statement of government policy. The White Paper is drafted by the relevant department or a task team appointed by the relevant head of that government department. Comments may again be invited from interested parties. The relevant parliamentary committees may propose amendments or make other proposals and then send the policy paper back to the ministry for further discussion and final decisions.

Once approved by the Law Commission and Cabinet, the document is sent to the State Law Advisers who assess the legal and technical implications of the draft law. Before the Bill reaches parliament, it is a requirement that it must have already gone through a public participation process where organs of civil society, other bodies and the general public are given opportunities to make inputs during the drafting of the law. To ensure that public consultation occurs, departments are required to indicate in the explanatory memorandum all those consulted in the process of drawing up the Bill.

Although the law is passed by parliament in sittings of the two houses, that is the National Assembly (NA) and the National Council of Provinces (NCOP), it is only at Cabinet level and its committees and clusters that the details of the draft law are examined. At the provincial level, the power to make laws is vested in the provincial legislature. A provincial legislature is governed only by the Constitution, and if it has passed a constitution for its province, it is also governed by that constitution; and so, must act in accordance with and within the limits of the both the national Constitution and the provincial constitution. In exercising its legislative power, a provincial legislature may consider, pass, amend or reject any bill before the legislature; and initiate or prepare legislation.

A provincial legislature must provide for mechanisms to ensure that all provincial executive organs of state in the province are accountable to it; and monitor the exercise of executive authority in the province, including the implementation of legislation, and any other provincial organ of state. As in the case of the NA and the NCOP, a provincial legislature must ensure involvement of the general public in all legislative processes, whether executed by the legislature itself or by any of its committees, in a regulated manner.

South Africa has what some call 'quasi-federalism' because certain powers and functions are with the provinces. The political discourse remains very robust on this issue because some argue that the current governance arrangements constrain effective service delivery due to limitations imposed on the central government in determining and shaping the affairs of provincial (subnational) governments, although the Constitution does provide some recourse in extreme cases, such as when there is a breakdown in the functioning of a provincial (subnational) government.

Under each provincial government is the local sphere of government. This consists of municipalities which have been established round the whole of the territory of the Republic of South Africa. The executive and legislative authority of a municipality is vested in its Municipal Council. A municipality – either local or district or metro – has the right to govern, on its own initiative, the affairs of its locality, subject to national and provincial legislation, as provided for in the

Constitution. Municipalities have the right to exercise their powers and perform their functions without the control of national or provincial governments. In addition, municipalities are capable of making and administering bylaws for the effective administration of their respective communities. At that level, public participation forms a cornerstone of the administration processes.

Although there is provision for public participation in all spheres of government and its policy making processes, it is mainly the local government sphere that is a product of a conscious policy and institutional design, and this is to ensure accessibility of local governments to communities and citizens at the grassroots. Section 152 (1) of the Constitution of South Africa[84] states the following as some of the objects of local government:

- Providing for a democratic and accountable government for local communities;
- Ensuring the provision of services to communities in a sustainable manner; and
- Encouraging the involvement of communities and community organisations in the matters of local government.

Policy Coordination and Monitoring and Evaluation

Monitoring and Evaluation (M&E), in general, is a practice intended to assist the public sector in evaluating its performance and in identifying the factors that need attention in order to ensure that policies are effectively implemented. M&E provides its users with the ability to draw fundamental connections between the choices of policy priorities, the resourcing of those policy objectives, the programmes designed to implement them, the services actually delivered and their ultimate impact on communities.

It is important to note that monitoring and evaluation has evolved since 1994, or since 2004 in particular when specific institutions and processes were put in place for monitoring and evaluation. From when the Policy Coordination and Advisory Services (popularly known as the Policy Unit) was established in the late 1990s, it undertook policy-making and its various components such as policy analysis, policy coordination and policy advice as well as led medium to long-range planning as well as government-wide monitoring and evaluation. The Policy Unit was disbanded (in 2010) then the National Planning Commission (NPC) and the Ministry for Planning as well as the Department of Performance Monitoring and Evaluation (DPME) were established. However, once the National Development Plan (NDP) was concluded in 2012, DPME was reconfigured to include planning responsibilities hence the name changed to

Department of Planning, Monitoring and Evaluation (DPME). This is meant to briefly illustrate changes that have taken place since 1994 with regard to monitoring and evaluation as well as planning to some extent, at least as far as institutional arrangements are concerned. There are also specific program mes such as *Izimbizo* (where a president visits a particular community to discuss issues that the community is concerned with) and *Siyahlola* (which are surprise visits by the president to front-line offices to examine service delivery).

Similarly, policy coordination has evolved since 1994. As indicated above, one of the key institutions in the policy-making landscape in post-apartheid South Africa – besides Parliament – had been the Policy Coordination and Advisory Services (which used to be normally termed the 'Policy Unit' as indicated above). The Policy Unit was located in the South African state Presidency. Essentially, the Policy Unit was the main clearing-house in the policy-making processes in South Africa. However, with the establishing of the Department of Performance Monitoring and Evaluation in 2010, the government-wide monitoring and evaluation functions were moved to the Department of Performance Monitoring and Evaluation. With the establishment of the National Planning Commission and the Ministry of Planning in the Presidency, also in 2010, planning responsibilities were to be undertaken within the Planning Ministry and the National Planning Commission – a Secretariat dealing with planning was established (also in 2010) to coordinate planning activities. The Planning Ministry and the National Planning Commission appear to have mainly focused on developing the National Development Plan which was unveiled in 2012. It also seems that the Department of Performance Monitoring and Evaluation and its successor (i.e. Department of Planning, Monitoring and Evaluation) have not been dealing with policy coordination. The Jacob Zuma administration established Ministerial Committees on one hand and Implementation Forums made up of Directors-General (i.e. Permanent Secretaries) on the other hand that are supposed to coordinate on the basis of government priorities – this might have been informed by a view that the challenge regarding service delivery relates to implementation and not policies. There is however the Presidential Infrastructure Coordinating Commission (PICC), chaired by the President, whose mandate is to ensure that all infrastructure programmes are planned for and coordinated through one body dedicated to such work. Lastly, with the increase in capacities in the Presidency broadly – as in the numbers of technocrats – and the increase in capacities in the Private Offices of the President and of the Deputy President, it might be that policy coordination would eventually get back, if not better than, the levels observed during the Thabo Mbeki administration.

Conclusion

This chapter has described how policy is formulated and reformed, generally, and by the government of South Africa. It also illustrated the processes public policies go through to ultimately become law in South Africa. It also discussed policy coordination and monitoring and evaluation. The main purpose of this chapter was to add to the understanding and knowledge of the public sector. It discussed the policy formulation and reforms which have taken place in the post-apartheid dispensation. In the main, it would seem that South Africa, since 1994, has put in place rigorous policy and law making processes. However, it appears that there has been weakening of the policy and law making processes since the disbanding of the Policy Unit in 2010. The author has published other aspects pertaining to policy and law making in post-apartheid South Africa,[85] so, those aspects are not covered in detail in the chapter. The next chapters detail the overall performance of the post-apartheid governments so far, by examining the different political economy themes.

Key Terms

Policy: Strategic intent or a plan aimed at achieving a predetermined agenda or outcome

Policy Analysis: Review or evaluation of a policy, including the monitoring and evaluation of a policy implementation.

Policy Coordination: A process that oversees and ensures that all relevant role players are involved in policy-making.

Policy Formulation: Also called policy making or policy development, referring to a process that identifies a policy problem or a challenge that needs to be addressed.

Policy Implementation: Activities and processes carried out towards achieving the objectives of a policy.

Public Policy: Policies pursued by a government in order to achieve the goals of developing a society.

Monitoring and evaluation: the analysis of collected data (i.e. evidence) regarding the effects of policies, programmes and projects.

Wellbeing: The quality of life of an individual and access to opportunities.

4

Economic Development

Introduction

This chapter describes the economic policies designed and implemented in the post-apartheid South Africa. It also discusses the evolution of the country's economic policies as well as the country's economic performance since 1994. In the main, the chapter discusses the main aspects of economic development and economic transformation since 1994[86] and describes the various initiatives aimed at improving economic development and performance during this period.

The performance of South African economy has gone from being an underperforming economy, due in part to international boycotts and sanctions before the 1990s, to one that experienced a relatively good Gross Domestic Product (GDP) growth.[87] Macro-economic stability, accompanied by sound and transparent fiscal and monetary policies, has played a critical role in ensuring the impressive economic performance that South Africa has experienced since the mid-1990s.[88] However, although the growth of the South African economy has been impressive during the first twenty years of political independence, South Africa continues to face mass unemployment, high poverty and rising inequality.

Economic transformation refers to processes aimed at changing economic relations for the better so as to benefit more people. Economic development is understood as economic growth and benefits associated with social development. Social development is about improvements in the wellbeing of people. Economic performance is generally summarised by the rate of growth of GDP, which refers to the total sum of goods and services produced in a country.

Economic Transformation

Political oppression and the apartheid capitalist economic system negatively affected the South African society and economy – many Africans were oppressed and/or exploited. Because of the many centuries of economic exclusion and oppression, many Africans continue to bear the brunt of hardship disproportionately, compared to whites in South Africa.

Economic empowerment is aimed at redressing the economic exclusion that Africans have suffered. Economic transformation, on the other hand, is aimed at structural changes in the economy in order to achieve sustainable economic growth and improve the standards of living of the people. The structure of an economy needs to be changed in order to ensure effective social and economic inclusion. As discussed later, the structure of an economy entails: (a) the sectors and their contribution to economic growth, (b) respective capital and labour intensity of the sectors; and (c) the dominant sectors and their linkages. With regards to sectors and their contribution to economic growth, the discussion centres on the proportions of manufacturing sectors vis-à-vis mining and minerals versus services industries and what they entail. In relation to capital and labour intensity, the discussion involves the extent to which machinery is used more than labour in the various sectors or the proportion of one input relative to the other. The third issue pertains to the main sectors – like the mining and mineral sectors – and linkages to other big sectors – like the energy sector. The other fundamental issue is ownership because ownership determines the structure of an economy.

As indicated in Chapter 1, the National Democratic Revolution (NDR) is one of the perspectives that shape economic transformation in South Africa. The NDR envisages a national democratic society in the context of meeting the objectives of the Freedom Charter. The overall vision of the Freedom Charter is a society in which the people share in the country's wealth.[89] It has been argued that without a fundamental transformation of economic relations, the democracy of South Africa would be in trouble.[90] Since 1994, various initiatives have been pursued towards the economic transformation of the South African economy and society as hoped by the ANC's theory of the National Democratic Revolution.[91] According to Bodibe,[92] the following are the main aspects of the ANC's economic transformation programme:

- An industrial strategy: diversifying the industrial base by building capabilities to export value added manufactured products and modern services;
- De-racialising the economy: broadening capital ownership through affirmative action and broad-based black empowerment;
- Spatial development: changing apartheid geography and settlement patterns;
- Macro-economic policy: ensuring a stable macro-economic environment;
- A campaign to defeat unemployment and poverty: key pillars of the programme include youth community service programmes and apprenticeships, ramping up expanded public works, especially in the social sector; an integrated anti-poverty strategy and a raft of second economy interventions and skills development;

- A developmental state: building the strategic organisational and technical framework necessary to drive and lead development.

Economic Performance

When visiting a doctor, for example, certain diagnoses are performed to assess the wellbeing of an individual. In a similar way, certain checks can be performed on the economy (by analysing economic data) to determine whether the economy is performing optimally or not. These checks are in form of calculations and estimations which produce indicators that provide inference with regards to the performance of the economy. Economic indicators are statistics about an economic activity. They allow an individual to view economic performance at a certain period and then predict future performance of the economy.

Policy makers make use of economic indicators when monitoring or evaluating a policy to assess progress made or not made during the period a policy was implemented. An economic indicator is used not only to formulate economic policies but also to formulate other policies as well. An example of this would be the health policies; the formulation of health policies has to take into account the number of people who are unemployed which affects the tariffs decided on health insurance. As indicated earlier, GDP is the most widely used measure of economic performance.

Calculating GDP

GDP = CONSUMPTION + GOVERNMENT EXPENDITURES +INVESTMENT + EXPORTS – IMPORTS

GDP – Gross Domestic Product

Consumption – This includes items such as durable goods and non-durable goods (food and clothing) and services.

Government Expenditures – This includes spending by government on policy objectives such as defence/military, roads, health and schools.

Investment Spending – This includes spending on non-residential (spending on plants and equipment), residential (single-family and multi-family homes) and business inventories.

Net Export – This is the positive balance after exports have been added to GDP and imports have been deducted from the GDP.

An important aspect in measuring the performance of an economy is the particular periods in which the economy should be monitored or assessed, whether quarterly, monthly or yearly. Furthermore, average economic growth is calculated to assess the growth during a period of specified years.

Calculating Economic Growth Rate

$$\text{Economic Growth Rate} = \frac{GDP_2 - GDP_1}{GDP_1} \times 100$$

Example

Year 1 Revenue: 1000
Year 2 Revenue: 250

$$\text{Economic Growth Rate} = \frac{250 - 1000}{1000} \times 100$$
$$\text{Economic Growth Rate} = -0.75 \times 100$$
$$\text{Economic Growth Rate} = -72 \text{ per cent}$$

Note that a negative indicates loss

Example

Year 1 Revenue: 150
Year 2 Revenue: 500

$$\text{Economic Growth Rate} = \frac{500 - 150}{150} \times 100$$

$$\text{Economic Growth Rate} = 2333 \times 100$$
$$\text{Economic Growth Rate} = 233 \text{ per cent}$$

Note that the growth rate in this example is positive

Unemployment

A person is defined as unemployed if he/she desires employment but cannot find a job. The rate of unemployment is determined by expressing the number of those unemployed as a percentage of the total number of people willing and able to work (those called economically active people/population).

A discouraged job-seeker is a person who was not employed during the reference period, wanted to work and was available to work but did not take active steps to find a job within a period of four weeks, provided that the main reason given for not seeking work was any of the following: no jobs available in the area; unable to find work requiring his/her skills; lost hope of finding any kind of work.

Persons in informal employment comprise all persons in the informal sector. The informal sector has the following two components:

1. Employees working in establishments that employ fewer than five employees, who do not deduct income tax from their salaries/wages; and
2. Employers, own-account workers and persons who are helping, unpaid, in their household business and who are not registered for either income tax or value-added tax.

The labour force comprises all persons who are employed plus all persons who are unemployed. Labour force participation rate is the proportion of the working-age population that is either employed or unemployed.

---

*   Long-term unemployment: Persons in long-term unemployment are those individuals among the unemployed who were without work and had been trying to find a job or start a business for one year or more.
*   Not economically active: Persons aged 15–64 years who are neither employed nor unemployed in the reference week. Underemployed persons (time-related) are employed persons who were willing and available to work additional hours, whose total number of hours actually worked during the reference period were below 35 hours per week.

Underutilised labour comprises three groups which are defined as follows: persons who are underemployed, persons who are unemployed, and persons who are discouraged.

Calculating Unemployment

Unemployment = Number of persons unemployed in the age groupe (15 – 64) years x 100

Total population in the age groupe (15 – 64) years

Number of persons unemployed in the age groupe (15 – 64) years X 100

Total population in the age groupe (15 – 64) years

Economic Development Since 1994

Among the important documents that were meant to shape economic development in the politically independent South Africa is the 1992 *Ready to Govern (R2G)* discussion document. The R2G document framed post-apartheid economic policies around the need for a new path of economic growth and development aimed at building a strong, dynamic and balanced economy.[93] Another important discussion document, discussed in Chapter 1, is the *State, Property Relations and Social Transformation* discussion document published in 1998. This discussion document made an important attempt at clarifying the ANC's approach on the South African economy and society.

The following paragraph captures the essence of what was (to be) pursued in the post-apartheid South Africa:

> [South Africa] is pursuing the kind of state whose character is developmental. Development is about improving the quality of life; it is about equity and justice. As the RDP document asserts, development entails a growing economy in which redistribution is a critical element; it includes modernisation of the productive forces and a redefinition of production relations. It includes the preservation and development of human resources in the form of skills-training, job-creation and the provision of education, health services, infrastructure, adequate social security system, and so on. It is also about democracy and popular participation (*State, Property Relations and Social Transformation*, 1998).

The *State, Property Relations and Social Transformation* discussion document also explains in detail the type of developmental state that politically independent South Africa needed. The discussion document contends that the South African developmental state:[94]

- should use the resources that it commands to ensure redistribution of wealth in the interest of the poor and disadvantaged;
- should put in place regulatory and other mechanisms that not only seek to obviate market failure, but also afford the state the capacity to intervene in a proactive way to facilitate growth and redistribution;
- should also be able to strike the correct balance between state ownership of productive forces and private ownership, guided *inter alia* by the pre-rogatives of strategic interest, efficiency, technology-transfer, affordability of services and narrow cost-benefit considerations; and
- should define and regulate its interaction with private capital in such a way that mutual benefit can be derived. This includes an industrial policy that

helps to direct private capital into critical sectors; and a labour market policy that prevents super-exploitation and encourages skills development and workplace democracy. It includes offering aspirant black capitalists opportunities which in fact encourage the expansion of this class.

Economic Development Initiatives

As the 2014 World Bank Report on South Africa indicates, impressive economic growth since 1994 could not have been realised without the aid of appropriate government policies, strategies and programmes which were focused on economic growth, job creation and wealth distribution among South Africans citizens.[95] This section highlights some of the main economic development policies that have been implemented since the mid-1990s.

Reconstruction and Development Programme

The 1994 Reconstruction and Development Programme (RDP), conceived in the main by the Congress of South African Trade Unions (Cosatu), was essentially about meeting the basic needs of South Africans and building a united nation. In order to achieve this goal, the RDP envisioned removing racial biases from the economic and social structure of South Africa, so as to address poverty and socio-economic inequalities. It is for this reason that certain government structures, most notably the Presidency of the Republic of South Africa, explained that the RDP and its associated projects played an important role in laying the foundation for a framework that would ensure service delivery.[96] According to Hanival and Maia,[97] the RDP was a socio-economic programme as opposed to an integrated macro-economic policy framework. This implied that the implementation of its full vision depended on access to substantial resources, requiring complementary policy initiatives.

The 2011 Census indicated that there has been impressive progress in access to basic services. The Census results indicate that an overall of 91 per cent of households have access to tap water and 85 per cent of household have access to electricity. This is compared to 80 per cent household with access to water and 58 per cent household with access to electricity in 1996. Furthermore, access to a flush toilet increased from 83 per cent in 1996 to 91 per cent in 2011. There has also been steady progress in people's access to schooling, healthcare, electrification, roads, telecommunications and public transport, although much work still needs to be done in the reconstruction and transformation of the South African society.

In 1996, large and unplanned exchange rate depreciation threw macro-economic policy into spotlight.[98] An uncoordinated response caused further crisis, leading to a contraction of the economy and loss of jobs and possible threats to the government's programme of reconstruction and development. In response, government developed the Growth, Employment and Redistribution Strategy (GEAR). It should be mentioned that GEAR was not only responding to economic challenges emanating from the 1996 exchange rate depreciation; rather, it was broadly aimed at stabilising the South African economy, given that prior to 1994 the economy was having many major problems, and was effectively in a recession.

Growth, Employment and Redistribution (GEAR)

GEAR was justified on the grounds that the economy needed macro-economic stabilisation. Before political independence, the economy was in a bad shape, with double-digit inflation, very high interest rate, negative GDP growth rate and other problems such as a very high government debt. GEAR was essentially aimed at:

- Fast-tracking economic growth in order to generate formal employment for work-seekers;
- Redistributing income and generating opportunities for the poor;
- Creating a society in which sound health, education and other services are available to all; and
- Enabling an environment in which homes are secure and places of work are productive.

It has been argued that the objectives of GEAR were adversely impacted by external events associated with the East Asian crisis in 1998. The rand depreciated considerably (about 28 per cent in nominal terms against the US dollar from April to August 1998), prompting a monetary policy response that resulted in short-term rates soaring 700 basis points.[99] Another period of global instability set in early in the new millennium, with the rand depreciating by 21 per cent in nominal terms against the US dollar between September and December 2001. However, the monetary authorities' reaction was more measured, as short-term interest rates increased by 400 basis points while long-term bond yields rose slightly. Both of these external shocks to the South African economy amounted to temporary, albeit serious, set-backs to investment activity and overall growth.

There are other views regarding the performance of GEAR. The debate about GEAR also deals with ideological issues: many argue that GEAR was a neo-liberal economic policy which focused on free market philosophy. There are those who argue that GEAR actually performed well because it met some of its targets and it stabilised the South African economy.

Accelerated and Shared Growth Initiative (AsgiSA)

It is indicated that an analysis of the post-apartheid South African economy revealed that the pace of economic growth and structural change have not been sufficient enough to make a significant dent on unemployment and poverty levels, despite a sustained positive performance.[100] This implied that the objectives of RDP and GEAR were not fully achieved. In response, the Accelerated and Shared Growth Initiative for South Africa (AsgiSA) was launched in 2005 with the aim of accelerating economic growth and ensuring that economic growth is shared widely. Such acceleration in growth was deemed necessary to halve the incidence of poverty and unemployment by 2014.[101] AsgiSA also included infrastructure development, the upgrading and building of the energy infrastructure, railways and ports, and the road network.

Hanival and Maia[102] however argue that although AsgiSA's objective for growth was necessary, there are binding constraints to economic growth that needed attention. These are (a) the volatility and level of the currency; (b) the cost, efficiency and capacity of the national logistics system; (c) shortages of suitably skilled labour, amplified by the impact of apartheid spatial patterns on the cost of labour; (d) barriers to entry, limits to competition and limited new investment opportunities; (e) the regulatory environment and the burden of small and medium businesses; and (f) deficiencies in state organisation, capacity and leadership.

National Development Plan (NDP)

The NDP can be viewed as a consensus-building mechanism towards some envisaged end in which poverty inequality and unemployment would be drastically reduced. The NDP offers a long-term perspective. It defines a desired destination and identifies the role different sectors of society need to play in reaching that goal.

The National Planning Commission indicates that:

> The NDP is a plan for the whole country.... Government will engage with all sectors to understand how they are contributing to implementation, and particularly to identify any obstacles to fulfilling their role effectively.[103]

In addition, the NDP states that South Africa can realise these goals by drawing on the energies of its people, growing an inclusive economy, building capabilities, enhancing the capacity of the state, and promoting leadership and partnerships throughout society.

Perspective Box: National Development Plan

Arguments against the NDP	Arguments for the NDP
The NDP draws from some gover-nment policies and programmes and does not consider other policies and programmes. It is said to be a long- term plan, yet it tries to replace other key policies and strategies, such as NGP and Indus-trial Policy Action Plan. In other words, it does not significantly draw from past and existing policies in making its recom-mendations.	The NDP emphasises growth and prosperity as the best way to fight poverty and unemployment. It pro-motes participatory development. The plan necessitates the state to grant everyone an opportunity and an enabling envi-ronment to better themselves through increased access to education and other essential services.
The plan is not realistic in its ap-proach and understanding of the country's socio-economic chal-lenges. For one, it aims at reducing poverty, unemployment and inequalities that persist in society. It however takes a narrow under-standing of these challenges in society by using the narrow defi-nition of unemployment instead of the broader one. This will lead to socio-economic challenges if not well addressed. Furthermore, the kinds of jobs that the plan aims at creating are of low quality and unsustainable.	The plan aims at creating good conditions to attract investment and create jobs.

Source: Gumede (2015a: 238)

Medium-term Planning

The South African government has a five-year mini-plan for every political calendar – the political calendar refers to the five years between the general and the next election date. The mini-plans are called Medium Term Strategic Framework (MTSF). The MTSF focuses on the priorities of the government for the five years a particular political party leads government.

For instance, the 2009-2014 MTSF priorities were to:

- Halve poverty and unemployment by 2014;
- Ensure a more equitable distribution of the benefits of economic growth and reduce inequality;
- Improve the nation's health profile and skills base, and ensure universal access to basic services;
- Improve the safety of citizens by reducing incidents of crime and corruption;
- Build a nation free of all forms of racism, sexism, tribalism and xenophobia.

New Growth Path (NGP)

The NGP was introduced as a successor to AsgiSA. Its aim of the NGP is to increase economic growth to sustainable rates of between 6 and 7 per cent per year in order to create 5 million jobs by 2020, thereby reducing the unemployment rate to 15 per cent.[104] The NGP further acknowledges the need for government to create decent work, reduce inequality and defeat poverty. The NGP emphasises that this can only occur by restructuring the South African economy to improve its performance in terms of labour absorption as well as the composition of the economy and its rate of growth.[105] It draws from the Industrial Policy Action Plan and identifies various structural and social impediments to accelerated growth and made recommendations towards improving the macro-economic environment.[106]

Other Policies, Strategies and Initiatives

Expanded Public Works Programme (EPWP)

The Expanded Public Works Programme (EPWP) was launched in May 2004 with the purpose of providing an important avenue for labour absorption and income transfers to poor households in the short to medium term.[107] Furthermore, it is a deliberate attempt by the public sector to use the expenditure on goods and services to create work opportunities for the unemployed.[108] This is done through integrated and coordinated labour-intensive methods for public sector delivery of infrastructural projects and service provision.[109]

The programme is focused on the following sectors: infrastructure, non-state, environment and culture, and social. This is achieved through the following programmes:

- An increased labour intensity of government-funded infrastructural projects, under the Infrastructure sector;
- Creating work opportunities through the Non-Profit Organisation Programme (NPO) and Community Work Programme (CWP), under the Non-State sector;
- Creating work opportunities in public environment and culture programmes, under the Environment and Culture sector; and
- Creating work opportunities in public social programmes, under the Social sector.

Looking at the period April 2004–March 2009, EPWP programmes have been reported to produce the following:

- The infrastructure sector created more than 1 million jobs;

- The economic sector programmes created 20,514 work opportunities;
- The environment and culture sector was able to create more than 450,000 work opportunities;
- The Working for Coast programme was able to create more than 8,000 jobs;
- The Working for Water programme was able to create more than 180,000 work opportunities;
- The Land Care South Africa programme created more than 160,000 work opportunities;
- The Social Sector provided 1,840,965 training days and created 175,769 job opportunities.[110]

Joint initiative for priority skills acquisition (JIPSA)

The Joint Initiative for Priority Skills Acquisition (JIPSA) was launched in March 2006 as the skills empowerment arm of AsgiSA.[111] It was to address the shortage of skills across numerous professional categories as this was identified as a constraining factor to economic growth.[112]

The following areas were identified as the areas of focus for skills acquisition:

- City, urban and regional planning and engineering skills for the municipalities;
- High level engineering and planning skills for the transport and telecommunications network industries, as well as for energy sectors;
- Artisan and technical skills for infrastructural development;
- Management and planning skills in education, health and local government;
- Teacher training in mathematics, information and communications technology (ICT), science and language competency in public education;
- Skills needed by municipalities to execute local economic development, especially development economics.

Economic Performance in Post-apartheid South Africa

When comparing the South African economy to that of the entire world (see Figure 3), the economy performed reasonably well for most of the first twenty years of political independence. Apart from the Asian crisis, from 1994 to 2008, the GDP grew by an avarege of 3.6 per cent per year. Growth in sub-Saharan Africa in general has received strong positive support from the strong world demand for commodities fuelled by strong East Asian growth.[113] However, from

2009 the growth of the South African economy declined. Some studies suggest that the South African economy was negatively affected by the international financial crisis and the 2009 global economic recession.

Figure 4.1: South African GDP Compared to World GDP Growth, 1982–2012

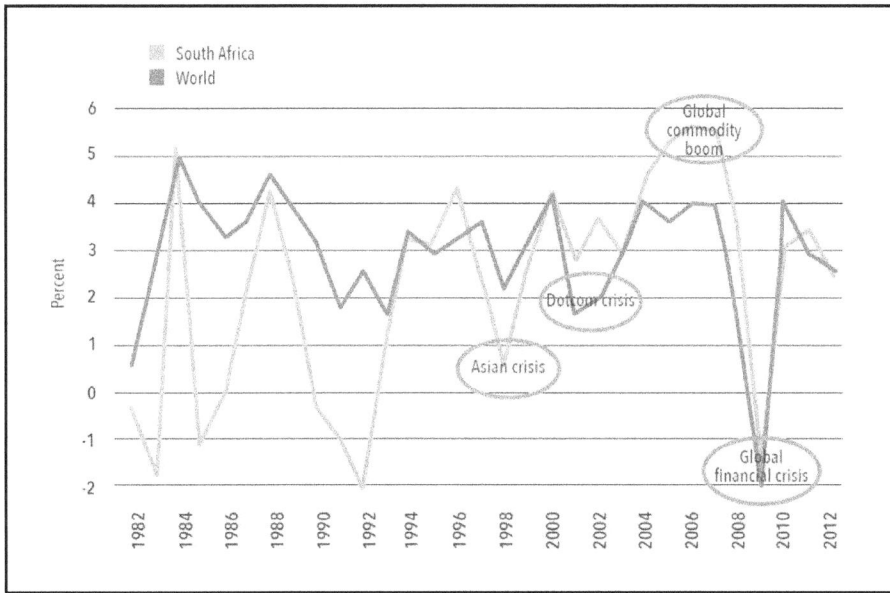

Source: Industrial Development Corporation (2013)[114]

Fedderke suggests that there are three major factors which affect South Africa's economic growth drivers and constraints.[115] These include market distortions, inadequate human capital provision and political economy questions. Others have emphasised political economy constraints. Fedderke,[116] for instance, indicates that the public sector's performance is worsening and the level of perception with regards to corruption is higher in the public sector than in the private sector.

It is useful to discuss the economic performance of one country in relation to other comparable economies. Table 4.1 indicates that, when compared to other countries, South Africa has not performed well enough for the size and potential of its economy.

Table 4.1: Gross Domestic Product, SA and Other Countries (2000-2010)

Country	South Africa	Botswana	Brazil	India	Malaysia
2000	4.2	5.9	4.3	4.0	8.9
2001	2.7	3.5	1.3	5.2	0.5
2002	3.7	9.0	2.7	3.8	5.4
2003	2.9	6.3	1.1	8.4	5.8
2004	4.6	6.1	5.7	8.3	6.8
2005	5.3	1.6	3.2	9.3	5.3
2006	5.6	4.5	4.0	9.3	5.8
2007	5.5	4.8	6.1	9.8	6.5
2008	3.6	2.9	5.2	4.9	4.7
2009	-1.5	-4.9	-0.6	9.1	-1.7
2010	2.9	9.7	7.5	9.7	7.2

Source: Development Indicators (2011)

As indicated earlier, the structure of an economy entails (a) the different sectors and their contribution to economic growth; (b) the capital and labour intensity of the sectors; and (c) the dominant sectors and their linkages. The third issue about the structure of an economy is about the major sectors, like the mining and mineral sectors, and linkages to other big sectors, like the energy sector. As discussed in Chapter 1, the South African economy is characterised as Mineral-Energy Complex, and it is also largely capital intensive (meaning that the economy uses more machinery than labour). Next is a discussion of the structure of the South African economy from the perspective of the share, composition or contribution of the various sectors to it.

Figure 4.2: Sectorial Contribution to the South African Economy

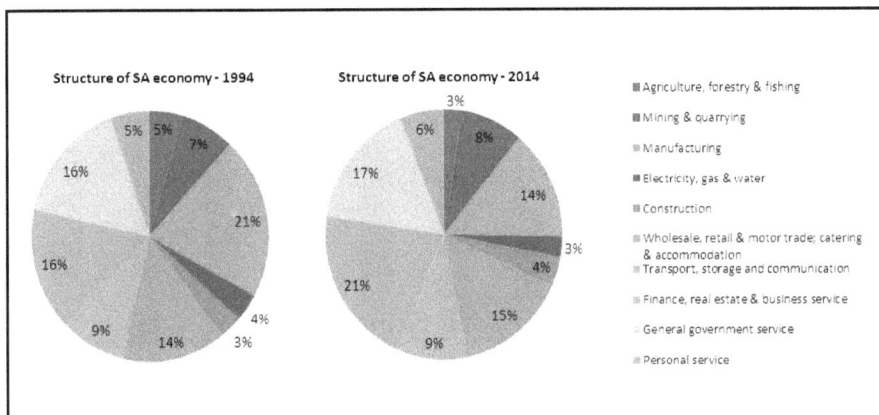

Source: Own Calculations Using Statistics South Africa Data

As indicated in Figure 4.1, the economic structure has not changed much. However, there are some industries whose contributions to the economic activity of South Africa have increased slightly. In particular, the sub-sectors in the services sector have increased their contribution to the economy. For instance, the contribution of the Finance, Real Estate and Business Services sector increased from 16 per cent in 1994 to 21 per cent in 2014. The contribution of the manufacturing sector however decreased from 21 per cent in 1994 to 14 per cent in 2014.

With regard to economic performance in terms of the nine provinces of South Africa, Figure 4.1 shows average real annual economic growth rates per province for the years 2003–2013. In the year 2013, the South African economy recorded an average growth rate of 3.7 per cent. Western Cape and Gauteng were above the national average, both with rates of 4.2 per cent. They were closely followed by KwaZulu Natal with a growth rate of about 4 per cent. All other provinces performed below the average growth rate.

Figure 4.3: Growth Rates by Province in South Africa

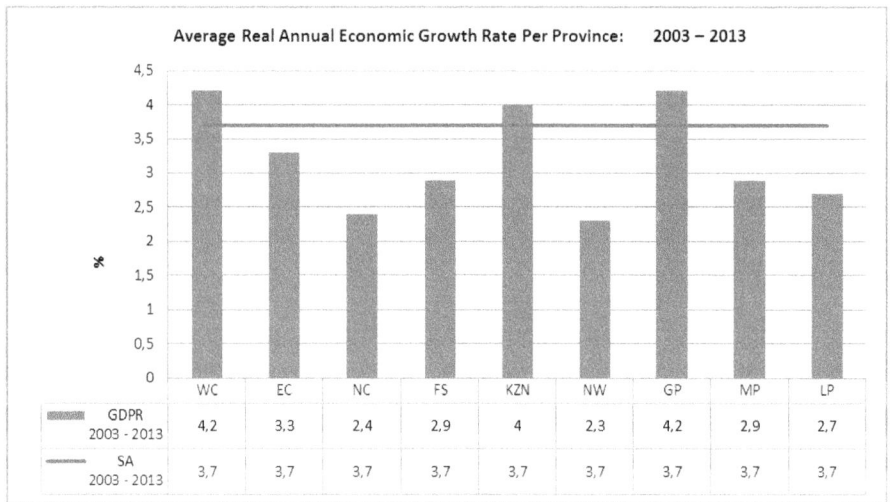

Average Real Annual Economic Growth Rate Per Province: 2003 – 2013

	WC	EC	NC	FS	KZN	NW	GP	MP	LP
GDPR 2003 - 2013	4,2	3,3	2,4	2,9	4	2,3	4,2	2,9	2,7
SA 2003 - 2013	3,7	3,7	3,7	3,7	3,7	3,7	3,7	3,7	3,7

Source: Own Calculations Using Statistics South Africa Data

The relative ranking of the contribution of the nine provinces in the South African economy did not significantly change between 1995 and 2013, as shown in Figure 5. Gauteng remains the largest (33.8 per cent), followed by KwaZulu Natal (16 per cent) and Western Cape (13.7 per cent). These three dominant provinces (collectively contributing nearly two-thirds to the South African economy) have, however, shown a slight decline in their combined contribution over the period.

Employment

One of the most critical challenges facing the post-apartheid government and society broadly is employment creation. Unemployment or employment rates are calculated by looking at the labour market (where labour is demanded and supplied). Studies show that the employment performance of the economy has not adequately met the needs of the society. The number of jobs created has lagged behind in relation to the demand for jobs required. A number of newly created jobs have been precarious and of poor quality and many of those jobs have disappeared as a result of recession and poor economic management.

According to Table 4.2, the unemployment rate was recorded as 25.2 per cent during the first quarter of 2014 as compared to 23.2 in the first quarter of 2008, which indicates an increase in the number of people who are unemployed. As Mayer and Altman[117] have put it, employment response to a given quantum of growth has been bad and very uneven across sectors. This has led some analysts to characterise the nature of unemployment in South Africa as structural

Table 4.2: Labour Force

	Jan-Mar 2008	Jan-Mar 2009	Jan-Mar 2010	Jan-Mar 2011	Jan-Mar 2012	Jan-Mar 2013	Jan-Mar 2014
	'000	'000	'000	'000	'000	'000	'000
Total	**31 544**	**32 135**	**32 732**	**33 335**	**33 945**	**34 558**	**35 177**
Population 15-64 (years)	**18 808**	**18 982**	**18 410**	**18 501**	**19 053**	**19 420**	**20 122**
Labour Force	14 438	14 616	13 797	13 904	14 284	14 558	15 055
Employed	9 934	10 161	9 695	9 785	10 121	10 242	10 780
Formal sector (Non-agricultural)	2 433	2 284	2 148	2 277	2 212	2 334	2 336
Informal sector (Non-agricultural)	838	778	683	627	694	764	709
Agriculture	1 233	1 393	1 271	1 214	1 257	1 219	1 231
Private households	4 371	4 366	4 612	4 597	4 769	4 862	5 067
Unemployed	12 736	13 153	14 323	14 834	14 892	15 138	15 055
Not economically active	1 202	1 233	1 890	2 243	2 380	2 401	2 355
Discouraged work-seekers	11 534	11 921	12 432	12 591	12 512	12 737	12 700
Rates (per cent)	**23.2**	**23.0**	**25.1**	**24.8**	**25.0**	**25.0**	**25.2**
Unemployment rate	45.8	45.5	42.2	41.7	42.1	42.1	42.8
Employed / population ratio (Absorption)	59.6	59.1	56.2	55.5	56.1	56.2	57.2

Source: Based on Statistics South Africa Data

for the most part, with a notable mismatch between skill endowments of the majority of the labour force and the nature of skills demanded by employers (see, for instance, Bhorat et al[118]).

Figure 4.4: Age Groups of those employed by First Quarter of the Periods (2008-2014)

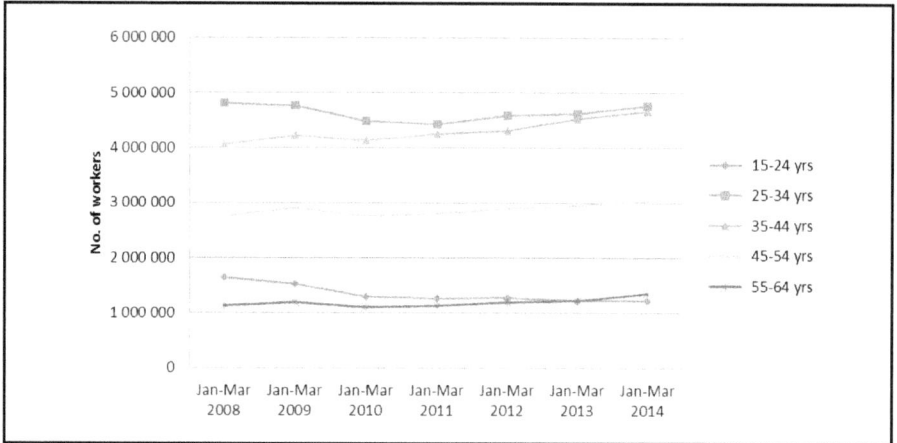

Source: Based on Statistics South Africa Data

Figure 4.2 shows that the large number of workers during 2008-2014 is in the age group 25-34 years of age. These are followed by those in the 35-44 years age group. Although the pattern across the age groups has also remained consistent throughout, there is a slight increase in employment observed of those in the 34-44 years age group.

Figure 4.5: Age Groups of those employed by First Quarter of the Periods (2008-2014)

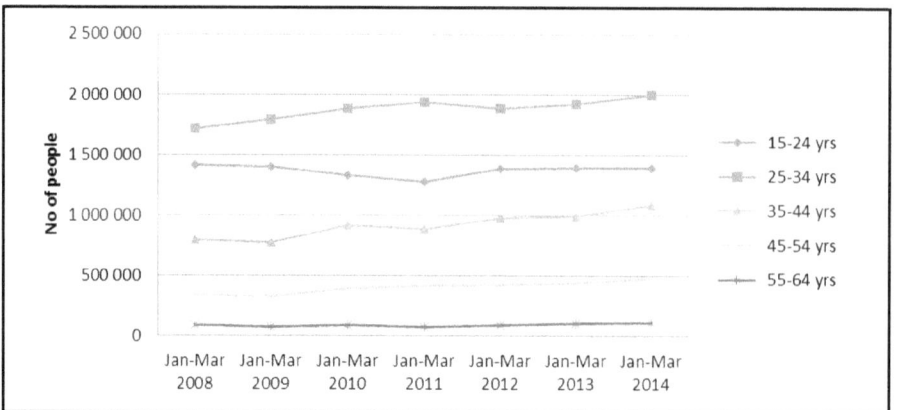

Source: Based on Statistics South Africa Data

Figure 4.5, on the other hand, shows those that are unemployed in the first quarters during 2008-2014. The pattern is slightly different from those that are employed. There is a significant number of people that were recorded as unemployed in the age group 25-34 years. In the year 2011, 42 per cent of those that were unemployed were in the 25–34 age group. Also the numbers of those unemployed in the older age group, that is 35-44 years and 45-54 years, have increased over time during 2008-2014.

Selected Economic Indicators

Figure 4.6 shows foreign debt as a percentage of GDP. A low debt-to-GDP ratio indicates an economy that produces and sells goods and services sufficiently to pay back debts without incurring further debt. However, the figure shows that, in South Africa, foreign debt has been increasing significantly from the year 2011.

Figure 4.6: Foreign Debt as a percentage of GDP

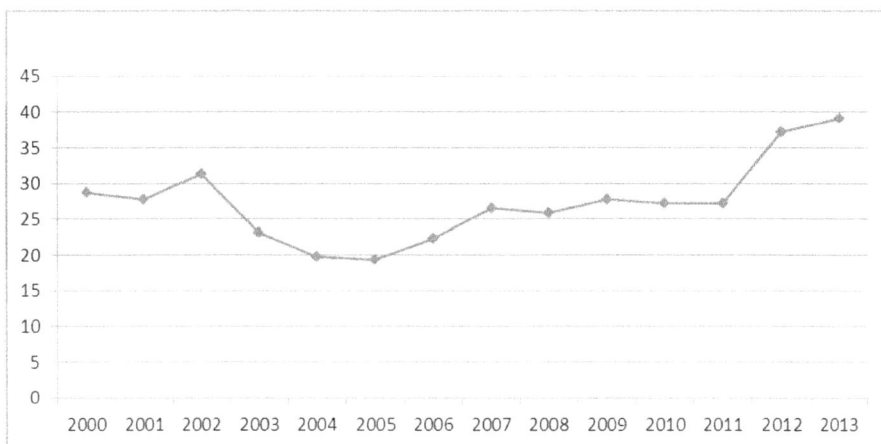

Source: Based on South African Reserve Bank Data

Table 4.3 shows selected economic indicators during the periods 1991 to 2013. In observing inflation from the year 1994, it reached 10.4 per cent in 2007. Household debt ratios are important indicators as they are used by policy makers, analysts, economic researchers and others to evaluate households' financial situation. They can also be used when forecasting consumption expenditure. Table 4.3 also shows that household savings decreased from 2.7 per cent in the year 1994 to zero in the year 2013. Table 4.3 shows that households' consumption expenditure has reached more than 60 per cent of South Africa's GDP.

Table 4.3: Selected Economic Indicators

Period	Gross saving-GDP	House-hold-saving/Income	Share of GDP to emplo-yees	Con-sump-tion-GDP	GDP growth income	Unem-ploy-ment	infla-tion	Inte rest rate
1994	16.8	2.7	55.9	62.3	3.2	31.5	8.4	14
2001	15.3	0.4	52.2	63.1	2.7	31.7	5.73	10.5
2007	14.3	-1.2	50	62.7	5.5	33.2	10.04	11
2008	15.5	-1.2	49.5	61.7	3.6	27.4	7.29	13
2009	15.5	-0.7	50.3	60.7	-1.5	29.7	4.1	8
2010	17.1	-0.6	50.7	59.3	3.1	25.3	5.01	7
2011	16.8	-0.3	51.4	59.4	3.6	25.7	5.75	6.5
2012	14.2	0	52.2	60.8	2.5	24.9	5.8	5
2013	13.5	0	52.9	60.8	0.7	24.7	5.5	5.5

Source: Based on the South African Reserve Bank Data and Statistics South
Africa Data

Overall, table 4.3 also supports the view that the South African economy recently has not been performing very well. Household savings have been zero since 2012, GDP growth has been declining (reaching 0.7 per cent in 2013) and the unemployment rate has remained very high.

Conclusion

This chapter has described the economic policies and programmes designed and implemented in the post-apartheid South Africa. It has also discussed economic performance as well the evolution of the economic policies in the country since 1994. Overall, the South African economy has performed relatively well since the mid-1990s, following the GEAR framework. In the main, although economic growth has performed relatively well, South Africa continues to face mass unemployment, high poverty and rising inequality. In the main, the structure of the South African economy has not changed since 1994.

Key Terms

Economic Development: Economic growth and improvement in wellbeing

Economic Growth: The increase in Gross Domestic Product, from one year to the other or from one quarter to the other

Economic Policy: Interventions or instruments for stabilising and growing an economy

Economic Structure: The composition of an economy by sectors and sub-sectors

Economic Transformation: Processes to change the structure and pattern of economic development

Gross Domestic Product: The total sum of goods and services produced in a particular country

Macro-economic Policy: Economic policy that focuses on the economy as a whole

Macro-economic Stabilisation: Interventions on the economy to ensure that economic indicators (i.e. GDP, Inflation, Interest Rates, etc) improve

Micro-economic Policy: Economic policy that focuses on specific sectors or areas of the economy

Policy: Strategic intent or a plan aimed at achieving a predetermined agenda or outcome

5

Economic Empowerment

Introduction

The South African economy during apartheid colonialism was designed, through various laws and policies, to favour the white population. This chapter gives a brief overview of the various policies and laws instituted by the post-1994 governments to redress, in racial terms, the ramifications of apartheid colonialism. In addition, various institutions tasked with ensuring that the redress policies and programmes happen are discussed. There have been many policies, programmes and strategies aimed at empowering those that were previously disadvantaged (i.e. Africans or blacks in general). Among the main ones are: Black Economic Empowerment Strategy, National Youth Empowerment Strategy, Women Empowerment Strategy, the Promotion of Small, Micro- and Medium Enterprises as well as a plethora of policies and laws pertaining to racial redress. Notwithstanding the various initiatives and their positive effects, it would seem that there is still a very long way to go in empowering the previously disadvantaged people in South Africa.

As indicated in Chapter 4, the post-1994 governments led by the ANC inherited an economy that was in crisis. The South African economy had previously been shaped and influenced by apartheid capitalist policies which was characterised by a systematic exclusion of Africans from the means of production and key economic activities.

Economic Empowerment

The post-apartheid governments or the democratically elected administrations have enacted numerous legislative measures, policies and programmes aimed at overcoming the negative economic legacy of apartheid. The various legislative measures are primarily focused on broadening participation, equity and access for the previously disadvantaged people in South Africa.

In attempting to rectify the economic problems caused by both British colonial and Afrikaner apartheid regimes, the post-apartheid government has formulated strategic transformative policies and legislations. One of the more prominent policies is the Black Economic Empowerment (BEE). It is generally understood that BEE has been central to the South African government's economic transformation strategy, though many argue that BEE has only benefited a few.[119] The formulation of policies and legislation to achieve BEE were originally spearheaded by the Presidency together with the Department of Trade and Industry.

The South African Department of Trade and Industry (DTI)[120]defines BEE as a specific government policy that is aimed at economic transformation and increased economic participation by black people in the South African economy. However, as time progressed and the original policy of BEE developed, certain problems began to exist. These included the accrual of benefits to a select few individuals, the non-responsiveness of the private sector, the inability to address the majority of poor blacks, and the likes. Due to these and other reasons, BEE was modified to become Broad-based Black Economic Empowerment (BBBEE).

Despite the initial problems linked to BEE, numerous scholars and reports have explained that the original ethos of the policy were good and had firm historical grounding. Acemoglu, Gelb and Robinson[121] argue that BEE originates from the 1994 government's Reconstruction and Development Programme (RDP), which involves the transfer of equity from a white company to a black person or a company owned by blacks. It was one of the initiatives which were aimed at overcoming apartheid's legacy as well as ensuring that historically disadvantaged people are empowered. Kruger[122] interprets BEE as being the economic empowerment of black people, which altogether includes the empowerment of women, workers, youth, people with disabilities and people living in rural areas through integrated and diverse socio-economic strategies.

In a nutshell, BEE was conceived of as an integrated and coherent socio-economic process that was geared to directly contribute to the economic transformation of South Africa and to bring about significant increases in the numbers of black people that manage, own and control the country's economy, as well as significant decreases in income inequalities. In essence, BEE is about attempting to create a degree of economic equality which would not itself be a natural market outcome of the changed political environment. There are many countries that have had to pursue policies such as BEE. United States of America and Malaysia are often highlighted as specific examples.

Ertner[123] lists the following as the main aims of BEE, which were scheduled to be achieved by 2014:

- A significant increase in the number of black owned and managed businesses;
- A significant increase in the number of black people in top executive positions;
- A significant increase in the number of black people with capital share in companies;
- An increase in the number of black people with a share in factors of production;
- The expansion of economic activities in underdeveloped areas;
- Accelerated economic growth available equally to all segments of the population;
- A significant increase in the level of income for black people, resulting in the reduction in income differentials.

Arguments against BEE

There are many people in South Africa that argue that BEE has not succeeded. Moeletsi Mbeki,[124] the brother of the former president of South Africa, observes, as an example, that BEE has become both the core ideology of the black political elite, and it is the driving material and enrichment agenda which is to be achieved by maximising the process of reparations that accrue to the political elite. Mbeki[125] argues that BEE strikes a fatal blow against the emergence of black entrepreneurship by creating a small number of unproductive yet wealthy black crony capitalists, which is made up of ANC politicians who have become strong allies of the economic oligarchy.

Hamann, Khagram and Rohan[126] also argue that the BEE strategy has not worked well in redressing the legacies of apartheid because many of the challenges which the strategy was aimed at addressing remain or have become even more acute in terms of poverty, unemployment, housing and basic services, inequality, HIV and AIDS. Kovacevic[127] observes that the BEE programme has not really succeeded in eradicating poverty, increasing employment or fostering economic growth. Further criticisms includes: (a) rural communities, particularly black women, are denied access to affordable financial services; (b) millions of black people are unable to access any form of credit; and (c) small- and medium-sized enterprises, in particular, have not been able to secure sufficient funding from the formal financial sector.

Broad-based Black Economic Empowerment

Because of the criticisms levelled against BEE, the Broad-Based Black Economic Empowerment (B-BBEE Act) of 2003 was enacted, followed by the B-BBEE Codes of Good Practice. The Code of Good Practice includes, among other things, the indicators to measure BEE and the weighting to be attached to those indicators.[128] It formed the basis for measuring BEE 'Scorecard', which was to be used in assessing BEE compliance and performance. The Code of Good Practice takes into account critical issues such as ownership. Ownership is accorded 20 per cent of the points on the BEE Scorecard. The other elements are: management and control (10 per cent); employment equity (15 per cent); skills development (15 per cent); preferential procurement (20 per cent); enterprise development (15 per cent); and corporate social investment (5 per cent).

There are various Codes of Good Practice that have been published or gazetted by the DTI in terms of the BEE Act which deal with all of the different aspects of the scorecard. Some sectors took initiatives themselves in drafting the Codes of Good Practice for themselves.

Presidency's Twenty Year Review Report[129] outlines, in detail, the core elements that should be incorporated into sector- and enterprise-based charters, including the following:

- The BEE challenges in that sector/ enterprise;
- The sector's/enterprise's vision for achieving BEE targets and timetables;
- The specific mechanisms to be used to achieve BEE targets, including financing instruments, skills development and employment equity, preferential procurement and enterprise development, as well as any additional mechanisms appropriate to the specific sector/enterprise;
- An assessment of the financing required to fund BEE transactions;
- The institutional and management mechanisms that will coordinate, facilitate, monitor and evaluate the implementation of the charter.

Financing Economic Empowerment

The financing of the B-BBEE process is strategically important for the economy. It is understood that B-BBEE must have a credible financing component in order that set targets are met. The Presidency's Twenty Year Review Report[130] also indicates that dearth of the funding component results in two problems: the first is that the extent to which B-BBEE is implemented would be limited because of the lack of financial resources for support. Therefore, rate of economic empowerment will not be broad-based; secondly, investment funds will be diverted into asset transfers, with the danger of a flow of funds out of the economy from the sellers of assets.

In an attempt to improve funding of B-BBEE, the National Empowerment Fund was established to support and facilitate increased participation of black South Africans in the economy by providing financial and non-financial support. Other financing mechanisms include guarantees, grants, incentive schemes, loan and equity financing. However, despite the establishment of the National Empowerment Fund, the B-BBEE strategy has been confronted with serious financial constraints. It is generally agreed that one of the main challenges relating to the transfer of ownership and control to black investors is the low level of access to capital resources by black investors.[131]

In the first wave of economic empowerment deals, black investors relied heavily on external funding from institutional investors, and the repayment of borrowed funds depended on the growth in the equity value of the underlying investments. However, many of these ventures failed, and thus resulted in the equity ending up in the hands of the financial institutions. The current wave of BEE transactions is aimed at addressing the lack of finance as well as reducing transaction and finance costs through vendor financing mechanisms. This usually involves employing elaborate transaction structures which generally involve a combination of debt, equity and hybrid instruments (such as deferred shares, options and preference shares).

Promoting Small, Medium and Micro-Enterprises

To ensure a more broad-based economic transformation approach, there has been an increasingly stronger focus on the broad-based elements, support for small enterprises and cooperatives, and procurement from local producers, as per the B-BBEE codes. According to the Department of Trade and Industry,[132] the promotion of entrepreneurship and small business remains an important priority of the government of South Africa. According to the 1995 White Paper on National Strategy for the Development and Promotion of Small Business in South Africa,[133] Small, Medium and Micro-Enterprises (SMMEs) represent an important vehicle in addressing the challenges of job creation, economic growth and equity in the South African economy.

As argued in Gumede,[134] South Africa, like many other countries, is concerned with what constitutes SMMEs and the preoccupation to address constraints. A broad definition for SMMEs includes registered businesses that consist of less than 250 employees. However in practice, SMMEs are defined in different ways, generally with reference to either the number of employees or turnover. The National Small Business Act of 1996[135] acknowledges that SMMEs include a separate and distinct business entity, which consists of co-operative enterprises and non-governmental organisations, which are managed by one owner or more.

The Act further categorised SMMEs into distinct groups. First, survivalist enterprises are enterprises with a total income that is less than the minimum income standard or the poverty line. This category is also considered as pre-entrepreneurial, and it includes hawkers, vendors and subsistence farmers. Second, micro-enterprises should have a turnover that is less than the Value Added Tax (VAT) registration limit (which is, R150,000 per year). These enterprises usually lack formality in terms of registration, therefore they include enterprises such as spaza shops, minibus taxis and household industries, which employ no more than five people. Third, very small enterprises are enterprises which employ less than ten paid employees, except for the mining, electricity, manufacturing and construction sectors. Fourth, small enterprises are enterprises that are generally more established than very small enterprises and display more complex business practices. Lastly, medium enterprises have a maximum of 200 employees and are characterised by the decentralisation of power to an additional management layer.

According to the Department of Trade and Industry,[136] based on the Integrated Small-Enterprise Strategy, the vision for SMMEs is that:

> South Africa becomes an entrepreneurial nation that rewards and recognises those who recognise a business opportunity and pursue it, a South Africa with a vibrant and competitive small enterprise sector, with enterprises that grow in both size and success. Those who were once excluded from full participation in the economy will have access to support and development services and be fully integrated into the core of the South African economy, with access to local, national, African and international markets.

The Department of Trade and Industry[137] highlights the following as main objectives of the Integrated Small Enterprise Strategy:

- Increase the contributions made by small enterprises to the growth of the South African economy;
- Create an enabling environment for small enterprises, with a level playing field between big business and small enterprises that reduces the disparities between urban and rural enterprises and is conducive to entrepreneurship;
- Create sustainable long-term jobs in the small enterprise sector;
- Ensure equitable access and participation in term of race, gender, disability, age, geographical location and sector; and
- Increase the competitiveness of the small-enterprise sector and its enabling environment so that it is better able to take advantage of opportunities emerging in national, African and international markets.

Institutional Framework

There are mainly five different departments and their agencies that implement small business promotional activities:

Department of Trade and Industry

Small business development falls under the Minister of Trade and Industry and specifically under two of the Department's units, namely: the Enterprise Organisation and the Empowerment and Enterprise Development Division. The Department of Trade and Industry has various entities that operate under it, namely:

- Small Enterprise Development Agency (Seda): Primarily assigned to supporting small enterprises, Seda was formed out of a merger between Ntsika Enterprise Promotion Agency, National Manufacturing Advisory Centre (Namac) and the Community Public Private Partnership Programme (CPPP).
- National Empowerment Fund (NEF): This was established in 1998 and effectively began operating in the 2004. NEF aims at empowering and funding black-owned businesses (both big and small).
- National Small Business Advisory Council (NSBAC): This serves to advise the Minister on ways to boost support to small businesses and therefore reports to the minister of Trade and Industry.

Department of Economic Development

The Department of Economic Development (DED) was established in 2009 to coordinate the South African government's economic development programmes. The Department oversees various entities, including:

- Khula Finance Limited: This is government's small business finance organisation which was established in 1996 to help fund small businesses in both the public and private sector, through a network of channels which include South Africa's leading commercial banks, retail financial institutions and specialist funds.
- Industrial Development Corporation (IDC): This government's development finance institution was established in 1940, for the purpose of funding small businesses.
- South African Micro-finance Apex Fund (Samaf): This is a wholesale funding institution which is aimed at facilitating the provision of affordable access to finance by micro-, small and survivalist businesses for the purpose of growing their own income and asset base. The primary purpose of Samaf is to reduce poverty and unemployment as well as extend financial services deeper and broader to reach the rural and peri-urban areas.

Department of Science and Technology

Technology Innovation Agency (TIA): This was a new umbrella body set up in the year 2009 and launched in the year 2010 for funding innovations which include the Tshumisano Trust (which housed the technology transfer stations), the Innovation Fund, and the Council for Scientific and Industrial Research's (CSIR) Advanced Manufacturing Technology Strategy.

The Presidency of the Republic of South Africa

The National Youth Development Agency (NYDA) was established in 2009, emanating from a merger between the National Youth Commission and the Umsobomvu Youth Fund. The NYDA is aimed at assisting the youth with career skills and helping them start to their own businesses.

Department of Agriculture

Micro-Agricultural Financial Institute of South Africa (Mafisa) was established to contribute to the working poor's ability to run existing agricultural businesses; to start new ones and be able to develop these into fully commercial operations. Mafisa propels and facilitates the development of financial services intended to uplift very small and micro-level farmers, farm workers, farm tenants, small holders, landless emerging farmers and processes, and so on.

Conclusion

This chapter has discussed selected initiatives for the economic empowerment of the previously disadvantaged South Africans: (a) Broad-based Black Economic Empowerment Strategy; (b) National Youth Empowerment Strategy; (c) the Women Empowerment Strategy; and (d) the Promotion of Small, Micro- and Medium Enterprises. In the main, these selected initiatives have contributed to the economic transformation and empowerment of Africans. The various post-apartheid administrations have pursued numerous policies and programmes to economically empower black South Africans. However, there is still a long way to go.

Key Terms

Affirmative Action: Programmes and projects, as well as activities, undertaken to redress imbalances with regards to opportunities.

Broad-based Black Economic Empowerment (also called Economic Empowerment): Initiatives aimed at empowering the previously disadvantaged people, in an instance that those people are black, in order that participation of black people in an economy can be increased.

6

Industrial Development

Introduction

This chapter describes the industrial development initiatives – another important aspect of political economy – in post-apartheid South Africa. It also briefly discusses industrial development levels. The overall aim of this chapter is to contribute to knowledge regarding industrial development initiatives pursued since 1994. The discussion is linked to the performance of the South African economy as a whole, already discussed in Chapter 4. The chapter also investigates the extent to which industrial development strategies and policies pursued since 1994 have been effective in ensuring industrialisation in post-apartheid South Africa. In the main, industrialisation remains weak in South Africa.

The South African economy has, over several decades, been driven by inwardly-focused policies aimed at industrialisation and, particularly, import substitution.[138] This led to steady economic growth and also importantly diversified the economy to some extent, as the South African economy was largely based on mining and minerals. Industrialisation initiatives have played an important role in the growth of some non-traditional sectors such as tourism, automotive and the wine industries.[139]

Furthermore, most South African companies were highly protected from international competition and foreign market pressures.[140] The inward orientation allowed domestic industries to grow in such a manner that could not have been economically feasible in the absence of the import protection.

To be clear, industrialisation refers to the process of increasing manufacturing output or expanding the manufacturing sector broadly. Industrial development entails both enacting policies for industrialisation and ensuring the growth of the economy and manufacturing opportunities. Industrial policy or strategy involves a set of principles and actions in the pursuit of industrialisation. According to Lall,[141] industrial strategy refers to an action plan or method for achieving industrial outcomes such as manufacturing, steel production, beneficiation and other such heavy or light industry outcome; while Robinson[142] defines industrial policy as any government regulation or law that encourages the ongoing operation of, or investment in, a particular industry.

The chapter starts with describing the main objectives of an industrial policy in post-apartheid South Africa. This is followed by a discussion of the industrial structure, both before and after apartheid. Then there is a discussion of other industrial development initiatives, followed by a discussion of what has been achieved through or regarding industrial development in the post-apartheid era so far. Before conclusion, challenges and threats pertaining to industrial development are discussed.

Brief History of Industrialisation

Industrialisation is documented as having begun in Europe in the early eighteenth century. This occurred when there was a shift of the European countries' productive activities away from agriculture towards manufacturing. Engineers incorporating discoveries of scientific breakthroughs in the field of physics (mechanics) and similar areas worked together with labourers on the machines used for production. This brought about technological breakthrough and inventions in the textiles machinery, and the adoption of the steam energy which brought a significant change to industrialisation.

Industrialisation brought about rapid economic growth and the source of demand increased dramatically. The expansion of production was fuelled with increasing domestic demand associated with rising wages as larger sections of the population were incorporated into labour. Since people now had money to spend, this created a domestic market for all the local craftsmen who, for example, created tea sets for tea imported from China. This paved the way for the textile industries and increased the demand for manufacturing goods.

It should, however, be noted that the industrialisation or industrial development of Europe also happened through the colonisation of other continents, including Africa. Many Africans were shipped as slaves to work in Europe. Also, raw materials extracted in Africa were taken by Europeans in order to advance industrial development in Europe. This is still largely the case even though Africa has become politically independent. Lately, China is developing rapidly also through processing Africa's raw materials and precious metals into finished goods.

Industrial Development

It is clear from the Europe case that industrialisation plays a fundamental role in the economy of the country. According to Kiliçaslan and Taymaz,[143] industrial structures of industrialised countries consist mostly of medium and high technology production and exports. Thus, it is of importance that structural change occurs with regards to the industry to bring about economic development in developing countries. Structural change is marked by initial growth and eventual decline of industries. Steenkamp et al[144] indicate that structural change follows three stages: primary goods (mainly agricultural) production is the dominant economic activity, then industrialisation takes centre stage and, ultimately, a developed economy emerges.

Kaldor[145] proposed four ideal stages of industrial development that constituted the driver for rapid economic growth and the sources of demand that sustain industrial development. The first stage, in the early stages of industrial development, involves the expansion of a domestic wage/consumer goods sector fuelled by increasing domestic demand associated with rising wages as larger sections of the population are incorporated into the labour force. The second stage has to do with the continued expansion of the consumer goods sector through increasing export. The third stage, which is the stage of industrial development, is marked by a shift in the industrial structure as heavy industries, in particular capital goods industries, serve the demand for investment in other manufacturing sectors. The fourth stage, referred to as explosive growth, is epitomised by a fast rate of growth of external demand for products of heavy industries in combination with the self-generated growth of external demand caused by the economy's own expansion.

The apartheid government laws did not have an impact only on the society but also on the state. The government and state assisted the Afrikaner and British capital at the helm by imposing policies which were oriented with the strategic objectives of the apartheid regime.[146] Clark[147] argues that the state's involvement in the economy was one of the major tenets of the apartheid state. Furthermore, he explains that the state established corporations primarily to enhance government ownership and control of the key sectors of the economy. However, this approach started to change as the nation drew closer to the 1994 elections, as the last apartheid administration and the incoming government of the ANC began implementing a process of privatisation of State Owned Entities (SOEs), mainly because they wanted to raise capital, cut down on debt and other performance-related matters.[148]

Industrial Structure of South Africa

Industrial structure has at least three dimensions, according to Chabane et al.[149] First, economists use concentration ratios as summary measures of the number and relative size of firms in different sectors on the assumption that sectors include similar products. Second, structure takes into account vertical and conglomerate linkages (i.e. the extent to which firms control production at different levels of supply and in related and unrelated activities). Third, industrial structure can also be understood, at a more fundamental level, to do with the nature and orientation of big businesses in particular and the way they interact. To study an industrial structure or the structure of an economy, sectors are considered.

Primary Sector

The primary sector of the economy extracts or harvests products from the earth. The primary sector includes the production of raw material and basic foods. Activities associated with the primary sector include agriculture (both subsistence and commercial), mining, forestry, farming, grazing, hunting and gathering, fishing, and quarrying. The packaging and processing of the raw materials are also considered to be part of this sector.

Secondary Sector

The secondary sector of the economy manufactures finished goods. All of manufacturing, processing and construction lies within the secondary sector. Activities associated with the secondary sector include metal working and smelting, automobile production, textile production, chemical and engineering industries, aerospace manufacturing, energy utilities, engineering, breweries and bottlers, construction, and shipbuilding.

Tertiary Sector/Services Sector

The tertiary sector of the economy is the service industry. This sector provides services to the general population and to businesses. Activities associated with this sector include retail and wholesale activities, transportation and distribution, entertainment (movies, television, radio, music, theatre, etc.), restaurants, clerical services, media, tourism, insurance, banking, healthcare and law.

Industrial Regulation and Policies

As Bodibe[150] argues, it is important that South Africa designs and implements an industrial strategy that can support sectors that are most likely to create employment for the low skilled. This would require the state to play a more developmental and transformative role rather than merely creating a climate conducive for private accumulation. South Africa positons itself to have an industrial strategy that can 'build a diversified and competitive economy that can sustain higher levels of labour absorption by ensuring sufficient levels of industrial upgrading and moving manufacturing sectors towards higher value activities'.[151] In the main, the objectives of an industrial policy are to:

- Develop a diversified and dynamic industrial base;

- Build the tradable non-commodity sectors, which include manufactured and service exports as well as import replacement sectors;
- Foster cooperation and agreement by industry, labour and government on sector; and
- Recognise the necessity for greater prioritisation of sectors and sector specific approaches.

Bodibe further indicates that the motivation for an industrial strategy, from the ANC's point of view, arises from the recognition that:[152]

- Colonialism and apartheid shaped the economy to support mineral export with very concentrated ownership and control. These resulted in high levels of unemployment and underemployment, especially in the former homeland areas;
- The market will not lead to more equitable development or job creation unless the state intervenes to mobilise stakeholders to bring about change. In particular, the state must drive development, disciplining business where necessary;
- The most important interventions must support labour-intensive activities, more equitable ownership (especially collective ownership through the state, worker control and co-ops) and investment in people and communities through education skills development and social programmes like health, welfare and housing.

This strategy requires a greater balance between productivity for export and production to meet the needs of the poor in South Africa and the region.

National Industrial Policy Framework

In January 2007, the South African Cabinet adopted the National Industrial Policy Framework (NIPF), which sets out government's broad approach to industrialisation. The aim of the NIPF is to achieve the following:[153]

- To facilitate diversification beyond our current reliance on traditional commodities and non-tradable services;
- To ensure the long-term intensification of South Africa's industrialisation process and movement towards a knowledge economy;
- To promote a more labour-absorbing industrialisation path, with emphasis on tradable labour-absorbing goods and services, and economic linkages that create employment;
- To promote industrialisation, characterised by the increased participation of historically disadvantaged people and marginalised regions in the industrial economy; and

- To contribute towards industrial development in Africa, with a strong emphasis on building the continent's productive capacity.

The NIPF envisioned that this policy cannot be implemented in a vacuum. The policy introduces four main economic indicators that should be in place for implementation:[154]

- A stable and supportive macro-economic and regulatory environment;
- Skills and education for industrialisation;
- Traditional and modern infrastructure; and
- Innovation and technology.

Industrial Policy Action Plan

The Industrial Policy Action Plan (IPAP) aims to play an increasingly sophisticated and determinant role in South Africa's ongoing development, with its particular emphasis on producing a labour-absorbing industrial/manufacturing sector.[155] IPAP is derived from the South African government's objective of defending, supporting and nurturing the manufacturing sector. The state exercises leadership by 'steering but not rowing'. Thus, IPAP 'identifies a complex range of complementary, interlocking policies that require alignment….'[156]

The IPAP focuses on the following areas:

- **Economy-wide**: Pursuit of a stronger articulation of macro- and micro-economic policies, greater policy coherence and better implementation. Stronger alignment of industrial policies and programmes with investment and export-promotion programmes, such as the National Exporter Development Programme (NEDP), focused on widening and balancing SA's exporter base. Better policy alignment, both in general and in relation to specific sector strategies, focused particularly (but not exclusively) on those sectors where the domestic economy enjoys global competitive advantages.
- **Procurement:** A sustained effort to secure compliance with existing public procurement policies and strategic supplier development/sourcing measures, with the overall aim of supporting the manufacturing sector to raise domestic production and grow employment. This effort will be combined with further policy framework and institutional improvement measures flowing from the Public Procurement Review and strong persuasive initiatives to secure greater private sector support for local manufacturing – a contribution that large companies in particular are well placed to make, given their significant procurement spend. It also includes providing further support for broad-based black economic empowerment (B-BBEE)

and better alignment between B-BBEE and industrial development objectives – further discussed below in the section on 'Critical New Initiatives'.

- **Industrial finance**: Stronger alignment and progressive strengthening of industrial financing across all DFIs – and within the Industrial Development Corporation (IDC) in particular – in order to secure an optimal mix of public and private sector funding that can progressively strengthen investment in the productive, especially manufacturing, sectors of the economy.

- **Developmental trade policy**: Ongoing strengthening of developmental trade policies with the following key components: deployment of trade measures such as selective and strategic tariffs and their improved alignment with industrial policy objectives; working closely with the International Trade Administration Commission (ITAC) while recognising their independent role; closer and more detailed cooperation with the Customs Division of the South African Revenue Services (SARS) to combat the ever-present (and steadily growing) problem of illegal and fraudulent imports – one of the key pillars of the illicit economy; steady and incremental strengthening of the capacity and capabilities of the Standards, Quality Assurance, Accreditation and Metrology (SQAM) institutions, which provide an indispensable support framework for a modern and competitive economy.

- **Competition policy**: Strengthened interventions to combat anti-competitive and collusive behaviour in both the private sector and state owned companies – and in so doing, lower the cost of procurement to the national fiscus and of wage goods to working families.

- **Regulation and intellectual property**: An Intellectual Property Rights (IPRs) regime that seeks to create a supportive environment for South Africa's industrialisation objectives. The regime should provide broad terms of scope for protection and less stringent criteria for novelty. Thus, the recently signed Intellectual Property Amendment Bill enables the regime to strike a balance between encouraging incremental innovations, providing protection for indigenous knowledge and providing enough incentives for innovators to make the necessary research and development investments.

- **Innovation and technology**: New policies and programmes to ramp up competitive capabilities in the production and services sectors of the economy, taking advantage of every opportunity to leverage the quantum advances on offer in the sphere of digital and other globally emergent advanced technologies.

Other Industrial Development Initiatives

For the effective operation of industrial development, the post-apartheid government put in place industrial support institutions. The institutions and stakeholders include other government departments, particularly in the Economic Sector and Employment Cluster, the National Economic Development and Labour Council, and organised business formations, such as Business Unity South Africa (BUSA) and industry associations.

The following regulatory bodies have been put in place to assist in industrial development:

- National Regulator for Compulsory Specifications (NRCS) is responsible for the administration and maintenance of compulsory specifications and the implementation of regulatory and compliance systems for compulsory specifications.
- National Metrology Institute of South Africa (NMISA) is responsible for connecting the national measurement system to the international measurement system. The institute also provides reference analysis in case of measurement disputes and maintains primary methods for chemical analysis, to certify reference materials for South Africa, SADC and Africa.
- South African Bureau of Standards (SABS) is mandated to be the national institution for the development, promotion and maintenance of standardisation and quality related to commodities, and the rendering of related conformity assessment services.
- Industrial Development Corporation (IDC) is to contribute to the creation of balanced, sustainable economic growth in South Africa and the rest of Africa. This is aimed at IDC being ultimately the primary source of commercially sustainable industrial development and innovation for both South Africa and the rest of the continent. This is done by promoting entrepreneurship through the building of competitive industries and enterprises based on sound business principles.
- The South African National Accreditation System (SANAS) is an accreditation institution that deals with accreditation and laboratory practice compliance monitoring in order to accredit and monitor laboratory activities in South Africa.

Lastly, South Africa through the IPAP was determined to grow the competitiveness and labour absorbing capacity of the manufacturing sector, particularly the traditional and non-traditional tradable and value-adding sector in the economy. In this context, considerable emphasis was placed on reducing the current account deficit, by increasing exports and finding local substitutes for imports in these value-adding and labour-intensive sectors. On the other hand, Special Economic

Zones (SEZs) are geographically designated for specifically targeted economic activities supported through special arrangements (that may include laws) and systems that are often different from those that apply in the rest of the country.[157] SEZ may be sector-specific or general. The following categories of SEZs have been identified in the 2014 Special Economic Zones Act:[158]

- Industrial Development Zone: This is an industrial estate specifically built to leverage domestic and foreign fixed direct investment in value-added and export-oriented manufacturing industries and services;
- Free Port: This is a duty free area adjacent to a port of entry where imported goods may be unloaded for value-adding activities within the Special Economic Zone for storage, repackaging or processing, subject to customs import procedures;
- Free Trade Zone: This is a duty free area offering storage and distribution facilities for value-adding activities within the Special Economic Zone for subsequent export;
- Sector Development Zone: This is a zone focused on the development of a specific sector or industry through the facilitation of general or specific industrial infrastructure, incentives, technical and business services primarily for the export market.

Studies indicate that Industrial Development Zones (IDZs) are important vehicles used by developing countries to facilitate investment, create jobs and boost exports. In South Africa, the establishment of IDZs is a recent phenomenon intended to attract investment, increase exports and the competitiveness of South African products, and is part of a growing international Export Processing Zone (EPZ) phenomenon.[159] The South African government also shares this perception and IDZs are used as a policy tool for development and export-oriented growth. The South African IDZ programme is aimed at raising the competitiveness of the manufacturing sector through 'leveraging investment in export-oriented manufacturing industries and the export of value-added manufactured products'.[160] A new policy framework SEZ provides a clear guide for the development, operations and management of SEZs, including addressing challenges of the current IDZ Programme. The purpose of the SEZ programme therefore is to:

- Expand the strategic industrialisation focus to cover diverse regional development needs and context;
- Provide a clear, predictable and systemic planning framework for the development of a wider array of SEZs to support industrial policy objectives, the IPAP and the NGP;

- Clarify and strengthen governance arrangements, expand the range and quality of support measure beyond provision of infrastructure; and

- Provide a framework for a predictable financing framework to enable long term planning.

The benefit of operating within the SEZ is that a number of incentives will be available to ensure SEZs growth, revenue generation, creation of jobs, attraction of Foreign Direct Investment (FDI) and international competitiveness.[161]

Post-apartheid South Africa's Industrial Development

Although significant improvements have been noted with regards to policy interventions made, the interplay of state, wholesale and trade, manufacturing and finance, real estate and business sector interests contributed to the GDP growth of 0.7 per cent in 2014, which is very low when compared to the real GDP growth of 3.3 per cent recorded in 1994. Comparing the GDP by industry for the quarters of 1994 and 2014, there has been significant increase in the GDP figure with the highest contributor being the finance, real estate and business sector.

South Africa is said to be characterised by high unemployment, income inequality and poverty. This is as a result of small domestic markets, due to low incomes of the mass of the population coupled with systematic under-education and training, and an absence of a thriving layer of SMMEs, especially black-owned ones, resulting in the high job loss.[162] Another view is that the structure of the economy has not changed.

In addition, almost half of manufacturing exports come from these very same industries; basic iron and steel 17 per cent of manufacturing exports, vehicles 13 per cent, machinery 11 per cent and chemicals 7 per cent.[163]

Table 5.1: Gross Domestic Product by Industry

Industry	Quarter 1 1994 '000	Quarter 2 1994 '000	Quarter 3 1994 '000	Quarter 4 1994 '000	Quarter 1 2014 '000	Quarter 2 2014 '000	Quarter 3 2014 '000
Agriculture, Forestryand Fishing	3	7	6	4	16	36	22
Construction	4	4	4	4	34	37	34
Electricity, Gas and Water	3	4	4	4	29	38	33
Finance, Real Estate and Business Services	16	17	17	18	174	169	175
General Government Services	18	19	19	20	140	144	147
Manufacturing	22	23	25	26	108	109	116
Mining and Quarrying	8	8	8	8	68	67	76
Personal Services	6	6	6	6	46	49	50
Transport, Storage and Communication	11	10	10	10	78	84	87
Wholesale and Retail Trade, Hotels and Restaurants	15	15	16	19	119	122	124
Total	**107**	**113**	**116**	**118**	**812**	**855**	**864**

Source: Own Calculations from Statistics South Africa Data

Table 5.2: Employment by Industry

	Jan-Mar 2008 '000	Jan-Mar 2009 '000	Jan-Mar 2010 '000	Jan-Mar 2011 '000	Jan-Mar 2010 '000	Jan-Mar 2013 '000	Jan-Mar 2014 '000
Both sexes	**14 438**	**14 616**	**13 797**	**13 904**	**14 284**	**14 558**	**15 055**
Agriculture	838	778	683	627	694	764	709
Mining	353	361	324	335	363	393	424
Manufac-turing	2 111	2 031	1 846	1 906	1 838	1 856	1 804
Utilities	102	112	78	100	95	124	130
Construction	1 181	1 221	1 105	1 093	1 042	1 084	1 199
Trade	3 319	3 207	3 021	3 119	3 208	3 032	3 186
Transport	808	819	838	776	833	872	895
Finance	1 780	1 864	1 780	1 739	1 855	1 916	2 045
Community and social services	2 714	2 824	2 843	2 990	3 094	3 296	3 428
Private households	1 233	1 393	1 271	1 214	1 257	1 219	1 231

Source: Based on Statistics from South Africa Data

Table 5.2 shows the number of employees by industry during the first quarter of 2008– 2014. The table suggests that, overall, the number of those employed across various industries has slightly increased in some and slightly decreased in some industries. The industries that saw an increase include mining which increased from 353,000 to 424,000 employees; utilities from 102,000 to 130,000; construction from 1,181,000 to 1,199,000; transport from 808,000 to 895,000; finance from 1,780,000 to 2,045,000; community and social services from 2,714,000 to 3,428,000. Many jobs were created by the economy in the community and services industry and the finance industry but there is a decline in employment in the manufacturing sector.

Conclusion

This chapter has described the industrial development initiatives in post-apartheid South Africa. The industrial development levels are also briefly discussed and this was linked to the performance of the South African economy as a whole. The chapter also discussed the extent to which industrial development strategies and policies pursued since 1994 have been effective in ensuring industrialisation in post-apartheid South Africa. In the main, industrialisation remains weak in South Africa. One view is that, because the global economic context frequently and rapidly changes, South Africa's industrial policy should be within the context of regional integration and African unity.

Key Terms

Economy: The total output, expenditure, investments and savings as well as net trade (i.e. exports minus imports) in a country. The economy is measured by Gross Domestic Product.

Gross Domestic Product: Total sum of goods and services produced in a country.

Industry (also called Sector): Companies or business on similar or related products.

Industrial Development: Programmes, policies and other initiatives aimed at industrialisation.

Industrialisation: A process by which industries, particularly manufacturing, grow as measured by the number of companies in the sector or the output produced or number of jobs created.

Regional Integration: A process of blending different countries within the same region together economically, socially and culturally, in the pursuit of economic growth and development.

7

Public Enterprises

Introduction

This chapter explains how state ownership came into existence in South Africa during apartheid. It also gives an overview of other experiences and examples of state ownership in other countries. Relevant government departments and their roles are also discussed as far as state ownership is concerned. Most importantly, this chapter explores how and to what extent state ownership has been successful or otherwise in South Africa. The chapter also gives an overview of the types of state owned entities and companies that have been critical in the post-1994 South African economy.

South Africa has a long history of state ownership. State ownership refers to any form of ownership or majority shareholding by a government. The establishment of the Electricity Supply Commission (Eskom in Afrikaans language) in the 1920s is said to mark the beginning of state ownership in South Africa. State ownership has its merits, if undertaken properly. Broadly speaking, state ownership is critical for socio-economic development. There are two main institutions that entail state ownership: State Owned Entities (SOEs) and State Owned Companies (SOCs). This chapter clarifies the difference between SOEs and SOCs, which is important but often taken for granted. Also, the term 'public enterprise' is generally used to refer to both SOEs and SOCs. In the context of South Africa, there is also a notion of Development Finance Institutions, which include SOEs and SOCs as well as other institutions that are within the control of the government – as long as those institutions are said to be pursuing a developmental goal. This chapter uses public enterprises to include both SOEs and SOCs.

Historical Context

The history of the state intervening in the economy and business operations in South Africa started in the 1920s, when the Electricity Supply Commission (Eskom), Iron and Steel Corporation (Iscor), South African Railway (SAR), South

African Coal, Oil and Gas Corporation (Sasol), and South African Airways (SAA) were created. The logic for establishing SOEs was a politically motivated decision that stemmed from the political aspirations of the leadership of the National Party (NP) to advance Afrikaner Empowerment.

The 1920s and the 1980s are the phases that are important in understanding state ownership initiatives in South Africa. The initiatives of the 1920s stemmed from the basic notion that the state in the form of government should manage and establish large utilities like electricity, railway, water projects and companies. It is for this reason that the South African government created companies like Eskom and SAR. However, other SOEs such as Iscor, the Armaments Corporation of South Africa (Armscor) and the South African Broadcasting Corporation (SABC) came into existence to primarily meet the political objectives of the NP, namely to ensure the economic and human capital development of the Afrikaner population.

The 1980s and post-1980s period saw the creation of SOEs, first to counter the international sanctions the apartheid government had come under as a result of the crimes it committed against humanity, in the form of the subjugation of black people through apartheid laws and policies. It was during this time that SOEs like Sasol (this SOE was primarily created to offset the petroleum embargo imposed on South Africa), Telkom (a telecommunications company) and Transnet (a transportation infrastructure and logistics company) were established. During the 1980s in particular, SOEs also allowed for development into newer technologies and markets, such as the communications, rail and ports businesses.

Therefore, SOEs in South Africa began their existence as large state or government investment into large utilities but would later come to be used by the NP to establish an Afrikaner middle-class and skilled working community. As apartheid and NP rule began to unravel and the African National Congress (ANC) emerged as the leading political party to lead the Republic of South Africa, the role and nature of SOEs would change. South African SOEs, in the post-apartheid dispensation, would come to be characterised, first, by the privatisation of certain key entities such as Iscor (which would later become ArcelorMittal) and the Sasol (which would become a private business corporation); and secondly, inquiries into the performance management, or lack thereof, of the remaining SOEs or SOCs, such as SAA, SABC, Eskom and Alexkor.

Size Complexity of Public Enterprises

In establishing what and how many SOEs currently exist under the current government, it is important to start by defining what an SoE in post-apartheid legal terms means. The Public Finance Management Act (PFMA) of 1999[164] defines SOEs as:

Government business enterprises – juristic persons, under the ownership control of the national executive (the line minister), assigned financial and operational authority to carry on a business activity, as their principal business provides goods or services in accordance with ordinary business principles, and are financed fully or substantially from sources other than the National Revenue Fund or by way of tax, levy or other statutory money.

Two of the unforeseen consequences of new SOE laws and policies have been that (a) numerous and new SOEs have come into existence; and (b) a poor attitude to understanding how many SOEs exist has occurred. The National Treasury in 2006[165] explained that there were 38 SOEs or what it terms Government Business Enterprises (GBEs) and they operated in the following sectors: Transport (4), Defence (2), Telecommunications (4), Energy – Oil, Gas and Electricity (3), Development Finance Institutions (DFIs) (6), Others – Agriculture, Mining, Water, Research, etc. (19). Yet, the more recent 2012 Presidential Review Committee (PRC)[166] Report says that:

According to the PRC database, there are more than seven hundred public entities/SOES in existence in South Africa. These include subsidiaries. There is currently no official mechanism of keeping an accurate record of how many public subsidiaries exist.

What is particularly interesting about the propagation of SOEs is that, according to the Human Sciences Research Council (HSRC), the majority of new SOEs were established after 1997.[167] However, the PRC[168] explains that:

There has been a proliferation of SOEs, including commercial and non-commercial entities and their subsidiaries, across all spheres of Government. At the start of its investigation, the PRC received a list of recognised SOEs from National Treasury, comprising approximately 300 entities. This list did not include municipal entities and other forms of SOEs, such as trusts and Section 21 companies...the PRC compiled a consolidated national database of SOEs that includes subsidiaries, trusts and Section 21 companies. The PRC's consolidated database established that, as at end May 2012, there were approximately 715 SOEs (including Chapter Nine institutions).

What is important to note about South Africa's SOEs is that they are fairly numerous in size and that many of them are recent creations.[169] It therefore should be no surprise that the numerical size of SOEs has caused multiple problems related to how government SOE boards manage so many numerous and complex institutions.[170] An SOC refers to 'an enterprise that is registered in terms of the Companies Act as a company, and is either listed as a public entity in Schedule 2 or 3 of the PFMA or is owned by a municipality.'[171]

Brief Profiles of Selected Public Enterprises

State Owned Companies

Alexkor

Alexkor was established in accordance with the Alexkor Limited Act, No. 116 of 1992, and amended by the Alexkor Amendment Act, No. 29 of 2001. Alexkor is a listed Schedule 2 public entity wholly owned by the government through the Minister of Public Enterprises who acts as the shareholder representative. The company has two divisions or business units, which are the Alexander Bay Mining (Alexkor RMC JV) and the Alexkor Corporate Unit. The mining division is the core business of the company, exploiting a large land-based diamond resource and extensive diamondiferous marine deposits.[172]

Eskom

Eskom was established in South Africa in 1923 as the Electricity Supply Commission. In July 2002, it was converted into a public, limited liability company, wholly owned by government. Eskom is one of the top twenty utilities in the world by generation capacity (net maximum self-generated capacity of 41 194MW). Eskom generates approximately 95 per cent of the electricity used in South Africa and approximately 45 per cent of the electricity used in Africa. Eskom directly provides electricity to about 45 per cent of all end-users in South Africa. The other 55 per cent is resold by redistributors (including municipalities).[173]

SAA

SAA is one of the world's longest-established airlines. It was founded on 1 February 1934, when the South African government acquired the assets and liabilities of a private airline, Union Airways, to create a new national airline, South African Airways. On 1 April 1999, SAA ceased to be a division of what had by then become Transnet and was incorporated as a company in its own right, South African Airways (Pty) Limited.[174]

Denel

Denel is the largest manufacturer of defence equipment in South Africa and operates in the military aerospace and landward defence environment. Incorporated as a private company in 1992 according to the South African Companies Act (No 62 of 1973), Denel's sole shareholder is the South African Government. Denel is an important defence contractor in its domestic market and a key supplier to the South African National Defence Force (SANDF), both as original equipment manufacturer (OEM) and for the overhaul, maintenance, repair, refurbishment and upgrade of equipment in the SANDF's arsenal.[175]

State Owned Enterprises

SABC

The main object of the Corporation is to supply broadcasting and information services and services that are ancillary thereto, to the general public in the Republic of South Africa and beyond its borders, and to achieve the objectives as set out in the Broadcasting Act 4 of 1999 (as amended), and in accordance with the objectives set out in the Independent Broadcasting Authority Act 153 of 1993 (as amended) that are directly relevant to the Corporation.[176]

Armscor

The Armaments Corporation of South Africa Ltd (Armscor) is a South African state-owned entity mandated by the Armaments Development and Production Act, 1968 (Act 57 of 1968), and continues its existence through the Armaments Corporation of South Africa Limited Act (51) of 2003. The Minister of Defence and Military Veterans is the executive authority responsible for Armscor.[177]

Perspective Box: State Owned Entities

Pros	Cons
• Government is able to invest human capital and state tax in selected utilities for strategic and national security reasons.	• Governments use government taxes to compete with more nimble and smaller better operated private sector companies.
• Government can sometimes use public enterprises to create mass employment.	• Government resources are divverted from developmental sons, e.g. service delivery, road building, developing health facilities in order to sometimes compete in niche non-profitable industries.
• Government can shape and lead economic developmental imperatives through using policy and large institutional capabilities.	
• Government is able to use large amounts of resources to foster and grow niche human capital skills capabilities like engineering, artisan, science type skills.	• Public enterprises are prone to prevailing political dynamics or manipulations and may end up draining much needed tax.
	• Public enterprises can be prone to laziness as they understand that government resources are able to bail them out.

Internal and External Challenges

SOEs and SOCs in post-1994 South Africa have had to deal with numerous operating challenges stemming from not only internal dynamics but also external dynamics which made it hard to operate their businesses.

External
Thatcherism and Reaganomics

One of the biggest influences on how South African SOEs and SOCs operated post-1994 is how the then British Prime Minister, Margaret Thatcher, and the then United States of America President, Ronald Reagan, understood and approached SOEs. Both these leaders, and more precisely Prime Minister Thatcher, believed that SOEs should be privatised and that the market, and not the state in the form of government, should lead economic development initiatives. Chaves[178] explains that:

> The combined pressures of globalisation, liberalisation and marketisation unleashed by the market-driven dogmas of Thatcherism and Reaganomics had massively expanded the private sector and concurrently downsized the public sector. Corporate power was in the ascendancy and many state-owned companies had become a little more than second-rate government departments; and the underlying assumption was that, as the economy evolved, the government would close or sell them to private investors.

While Thatcherism[179] was a United Kingdom-based policy and operation, it did greatly influence how the government of South Africa went about operating its SOEs. It is important to acknowledge that certain nuances did influence the move towards privatisation of SOEs, given that the inherited debt from the apartheid government meant that the new government of the ANC had to rethink the role and existence of SOEs. One of the decisions taken in the early 90s, with regards to SOEs, was to follow the Thatcher model and privatise them; yet this decision, according to political entities like the South African Communist Party (SACP), was disastrous due to the large job losses that followed it.[180] It should also be mentioned that the privatisation of public enterprises was also influenced by the World Bank and International Monetary Fund within the context of Structural Adjustment Programmes. In short, Structural Adjustment Programmes were neo-liberal economic projects aimed at reducing the role of governments in socio-economic development and prioritising the market.

Changing Market Dynamics

Another factor influencing how public enterprises would perform and operate after 1994 was the influence of external competition and evolving competitors in various operating spaces of public enterprises. One SOC that has had to rethink how it works and operates its business is the South African Airways (SAA), within the aviation sector.

While SAA is one of the oldest operating aviation companies, the competition and competitors it has come up against in twenty years (1994-2014) has meant that it is constantly having to find new means to **(a)** stay profitable; **(b)** compete with foreign carriers; and **(c)** assist government to meet its developmental mandate. Yet, meeting these challenges has been affected, firstly, by the aviation sector experiencing mass privatisation in the early 1990s in the form of European carriers such as British Airways (BA), Lufthansa and Air France.[181] Secondly, the rise of newly established SOE carriers from the Middle East, in the form of Emirates and Etihad Airlines, has had a negative impact.[182] Thirdly, it has also been affected by the fluctuating role of operating inputs like fuel, as well as the geographical location where the airline operates.[183]

Alexkor too has not been able to compete with established Anglo-American, Ashanti-Gold, Anglo-Platinum and other privately owned mining firms, the role and future of South African mining continues to face the challenge of deteriorating labour relations between employers and employees.[184] Furthermore, while the established private sector companies have found some form of success within the twenty-year period, the success of Alexkor has yet to be properly assessed with regards to whether its structure and current mandate allow it to be considered a major asset in government's public enterprises plans.[185]

Internal Balancing Mandate

In the early formation and operational mandate of the SOEs, especially under NP rule, the Afrikaner economic development was the primary goal and objective. The SOEs were seen and operated in a manner that would (a) allow for skills development; (b) encourage Afrikaner entrepreneurship; (c) enable unskilled labour to have a decent income among Afrikaner and white minorities.[186] However, the post-1994 mandate of the SOEs and SOCs has been a rather complex and tougher one to establish. While the apartheid SOEs did not judiciously operate in a manner that sought to keep operation cost down, the post-1994 government has had to battle with the challenges of corporate governance and balancing the financial status of the SOEs.[187]

The post-1994 balancing mandate has become a rather tough prospect for SOEs to manage. Commentators, such as the SACP, complain that the SOEs have failed to learn from the NP government and re-skill the mass population of African and black people; while other commentators continuously call for SOEs and SOCs to act as private sector entities and ensure they keep their finances positive, and not operate as debt ridden entities.

Poor Leadership

The final internal factor that has seen public enterprises' existence being questioned and at times criticised is the issue of their leadership. Post-1994, the leadership of public enterprises has been cited as a major reason for their inability to deliver on either a mandate to grow jobs or create the necessary capital/service delivery outputs.[188]

Major indicators of the poor leadership of public enterprises like the SABC, SAA and Eskom are (a) bailouts by National Treasury; (b) constant or seasonal restructuring programmes; and (c) constant scandals over decisions or appointments made by their boards. While it is possible to sometimes quantify the mistakes of leadership, as in the case with the Eskom's rolling blackouts cost to the economy and the external funds sourced for developmental purposes, in most cases the full extent of the damage of poor leadership has yet to be estimated. However, it cannot be overstated how much poor leadership in some public enterprises has cost the South African taxpayer and hampered the government's intention of utilising public enterprises to meet South African socio-economic needs.

Performance of Selected Commercial Public Enterprises

The assessment of public enterprises is not straightforward, because as stated earlier, when observing the fact that Eskom has been mismanaged alongside other public enterprises like SAA and SABC, it would seem that public enterprises are underperforming if not mismanaged. However, it needs to be remembered that there exists numerous other public enterprises which this chapter has not analysed, such as Airport Company South Africa (ACSA), Public Investment Corporation (PIC) and Human Sciences Research Council (HSRC), to mention but a few. In some ways, some of these public enterprises are performing relatively well.

This then brings to question whether new measurements and metrics are needed to assess where and whether the numerous public enterprises are playing a positive socio-economic developmental role. On current evidence as has been outlined in this chapter, the performance in relation to not only present-day reports like the

HSRC 2006 and 2012 Reports explain, but also reports emanating from the apartheid government operational mandate of SOEs, the present day public enterprises are not doing enough to assist South Africa develop socio-economically.

Conclusion

This chapter has explained the difference between the State Owned Companies (SOCs) and State Own Enterprises (SOEs) and discussed selected SOEs and SOCs, such as the SABC, SAA and Alexkor, to ascertain how the post-1994 ANC governing party views and operates public enterprises. It would seem that the post-1994 government has not been able to learn or build on the models put forward by the NP government with regards to ensuring that SOEs and SOCs operate in a manner as to (a) strengthen a black skills base; and (b) use them to jumpstart black entrepreneurs and other mandates the NP government had used to uplift the white minorities. It might very well be that the challenge has to do with a non-racialism philosophy of the ANC that could be limiting the extent to which explicit affirmative action programmes can be pursued.

Key Terms

Development Finance Institution: Both State Owned Companies and State Owned Enterprises as well as government agencies implementing developmental programmes.

Public Enterprises: Companies or enterprises owned by government, both State Owned Companies and State Owned Enterprises.

State Owned Company: A company that is owned by government or in which the government has majority shareholding, and is listed as a public entity.

State Owned Enterprise: An enterprise that is either wholly owned by government or the government is a majority shareholder.

8

Land and Agriculture

Introduction

This chapter discusses land and agriculture before and after apartheid. South Africa has endured a long history of colonisation, racial domination and land dispossession that has resulted in the bulk of its agricultural land being owned by a white minority. According to Pottinger,[189] land has played a significant role in defining political power and position in South Africa. This chapter deals with this issue and others, looking at the different views, perspectives and challenges relating to land and agriculture in post-apartheid South Africa. Furthermore, the policies and programmes that have been implemented, since 1994, to pursue land and agrarian reforms in South Africa are also presented. In the main, land reform has not been properly or satisfactorily implemented in South Africa. Therefore, the chapter will look at the social and economic strands of land or agricultural reform programmes as well as the sustainability of the land reform policy.

The chapter starts by providing a brief historical background of land dispossession in South Africa, identifying the systematic processes through which Africans were dispossessed of their land. It then discusses land and agrarian reforms by the post-apartheid government, including the progress (or lack thereof), and then presents the different views and perspectives on land and agrarian reforms since 1994. Before concluding, the chapter discusses the sustainability of land and agrarian reform as a measure of addressing progressive transformation related issues, such as rural development and the alleviation of poverty.

Historical Context

The Centre for Development and Enterprise[190] opines that the land claimants get frustrated by the delays, and sometimes resort to land invasions. Furthermore, politicians hear from their constituencies that land reform is not working, while existing farm owners are unable to sell land once it has been gazetted as under claim. Banks do not accept gazetted land as collateral for loans. Incumbent farmers therefore lack the incentives and/or the money to continue working with the land and it is sometimes taken out of production or allowed to deteriorate. This lack of confidence and motivation among farmers gets exacerbated in many areas by the introduction of municipal rates in respect of farm land, sometimes at levels exceeding those applicable to residential properties, and potentially costing individual farmers significant funds.

A lot has been said and written about the historical context of land dispossession. However, what is worth highlighting is that from the seventeenth century, white settlers in South Africa, through a systemic process of colonialism and land dispossession, ended up legally appropriating more than 90 per cent of the South African land, a process that was later formalised with the passing of the Natives Land Act of 1913. According to Pottinger,[191] the position of land played a critical role in defining political, social and economic power of the colonial people as it did for Africans. Therefore, the impact of expanding white power in Southern Africa negatively shaped the lives of black people and finally relegated them to the Bantustans where they became reservoirs of cheap labour removed from productive land.

The 1913 Land Act became the culmination of efforts to exclude blacks from their own land. According to Pepeteka,[192] the 1913 Land Act played a major role in restricting Africans to buying, leasing and selling land only in the 'scheduled areas' which were referred to as 'reserves' while whites were prohibited from owning land in those areas. The scheduled areas amounted to about 21 million acres, which was only 7.3 per cent of South Africa while the area, set aside for the white minority, was ten times larger than that of the African majority. The land that was made available to Africans was later increased by 5 per cent through the Native Administration Act (No. 38) of 1927 and the Bantu Trust and Land Act (No. 18) of 1936, which provided for the conversion of the reserves into Bantustans or self-governing-territories. As a consequence, Pepeteka[193] acknowledges that African people were restricted to owning land in the overcrowded 'Bantustans' which constituted only 13 per cent of the total area of South Africa.

According to Rugege,[194] the extent to which black people were dispossessed of their land by whites in South Africa as well as other parts of Africa during the colonial apartheid era is also an important point of departure. After the National Party took over government in 1948, the Group Areas Act of 1950 was passed and used by the apartheid state to carry out the forceful removal of black people from land declared to be white areas and to complete the policy of racial segregation by removing 'coloured' and Indian people from the so-called white areas. Ramphele[195] argues that the apartheid government deliberately and institutionally limited the African people to implicitly contribute to the growth of the economy. The institutionalised underdevelopment of black people by the apartheid government is the major cause of unemployment and poverty among black people.

Pockets of black farmers who had escaped the 1913 Land Act because they had title deeds to their land were, according to Rugege,[196] removed under the Group Areas Act in a process that was called 'cleaning up the black spots'. Land is a major source of livelihood for Africans. So, land dispossession meant that many black people were forced to migrate towards white-owned mines and farms to work as cheap labour under appalling working conditions. Workers had no rights, were paid very low wages, housed in compounds, controlled by pass laws and separated from their families.

Land and Agrarian Reforms Since 1994

Ntsebeza[197] acknowledges that while colonialism and apartheid systematically undermined African agriculture, white farmers, on the other hand, benefited from substantial state subsidies. Land reform is in this regard 'South Africa's way of redress, social justice and reconciliation.'[198] It is necessary in order to undo the injustices of the past by giving black people opportunities to meaningfully participate in the economy. The White Paper on Land Reform (not yet adopted by Parliament) and the 2011 Green Paper on Land Reform are additional attempts by government to expand access to resources in an equitable manner which could also offer prospects for economic development in the country.

According to Partridge,[199] the issue of land goes beyond its use as a means of production. It is a source of livelihood through which people can obtain substances for survival. Land reform is underpinned by both ethical considerations and development. Ethical consideration refers to land reform being seen as a redress concern, which is aimed at correcting past inequalities. According to the Green Paper on Land Reform and Rural Development,[200] it is the 'democratic and unbiased allocation of land across race, gender and class' that can redress the injustices of the past. It is also a development concern which is aimed at the prospect of shared economic growth and participation. Land redistribution is, in the words of Binswanger-Mkhize et al,[201] an attempt by governments to alter the distribution of land ownership, often utilised to reverse ownership patterns stemming from unfair past practices.

The Reconstruction and Development Programme (RDP) in South Africa was one of government's first policy documents that served as a guideline for managing the land issue in the country. According to Partridge,[202] land reform was one of the key features of the newly elected ANC's[203] policy, as reflected in the Reconstruction and Development Programme (RDP):

> Land is the most basic need for rural dwellers. Apartheid policies pushed millions of black South Africans into overcrowded and impoverished reserves, homelands and townships. In addition, capital intensive agricultural policies led to the large-scale eviction of farm dwellers from their land and homes. The abolition of the Land Acts cannot redress inequities in land distribution. Only a tiny minority of black people can afford land on the free market. The RDP must implement a fundamental land reform programme. This programme must be demand-driven and must aim to supply residential and productive land to the poorest section of the rural population and aspirant farmers. As part of a comprehensive rural development policy, it must raise rural incomes and productivity and encourage the use of land for agricultural and other productive or residential purposes.

In 1997, the government adopted the White Paper on South African Land Policy to inform land reform in South Africa. According to the 1997 White Paper on South African Land Policy,[204] the land policy was pronounced with four objectives, namely: to correct past injustices; to engender reconciliation and stability; to promote economic growth; and to improve lives through the alleviation of poverty. In order to meet these objectives, the White Paper on South African Land Policy[205] had three aspects, namely, (a) Land Redistribution; (b) Land Restitution; and (c) Land Tenure Reform. Land redistribution seeks to facilitate the right of access to land for residential and farming purposes. According to Kahn,[206] it is conceived as a means of opening up the productive land for residential and agricultural development. The national government set itself a target of redistributing 30 per cent of the country's commercial agricultural land (about 24 million hectares) by 2014. Land restitution on the other hand forms the second pillar of the land reform programme. It seeks to compensate and restore land to those who lost land because of colonial and apartheid laws.

According to the Restitution of Land Rights Act of 1994,[207] the nature of restitution is determined by three broad categories of the effects of land dispossession, namely, dispossession leading to landlessness, inadequate compensation for the value of the property, erosion of human dignity and hardships that cannot be measured in financial or material terms. Lastly is Land Tenure Reform. According to the Constitution,[208] the tenure reform programme seeks to validate and harmonise forms of land ownership that evolved during colonialism and apartheid. Weideman[209] argues that it is an attempt to redress the dual system of land tenure in which whites owned land as private property as opposed to communal land allocation among blacks. According to Kloppers and Pienaar,[210] a large number of rural blacks lived and still live on communal land, registered as the property of the state under the erstwhile South African Development Trust. The White Paper on South African Land Policy[211] argues that government could ensure poverty reduction by tackling the land question.

Similarly, Section 25(5) of the Constitution[212] introduced the second pillar of land reform, which Kloppers and Pienaar[213] referred to as the land redistribution programme. According to the Constitution,[214] the state must take 'reasonable legislative and other measures, within its available resources, to foster conditions which enable citizens to gain access to land on an equitable basis'. In the Constitution, land rights are viewed and protected in the context of property rights. According to the Global Strategy for Shelter for the Year 2000,[215] property rights, particularly land rights, are closely connected to the problem of housing. Therefore, a person or a community that lost property post-1913 due to discriminatory laws is entitled to restitution or redress.

Nonetheless, despite the issue of land reform continually taking up a central position in policy since 1994, the post-apartheid government is still unable to achieve its desired targets. By 2000, 63,455 claims had been lodged since 1994, and only 4,925 had been settled with most of the settlements being cash payments and only 162 involving restoration of land. According to the Centre for Development and Enterprise,[216] by 2006, validated land claims for restitution numbered nearly 80,000, with 81 per cent of the claims being urban land and 19 per cent of the claims being rural land. According to Gumede,[217] government had imposed on itself a 2008 deadline to finalise all the land restitution claims. However, even though most of this land was urban land which could easily be settled with cash payment, government still failed to meet this deadline due to the legal processes, where current owners of the land would take government to the Land Claims Court for determinations.

In addition to this, there are other institutional barriers which seriously hinder the progress of reaching the land reform goal. These barriers, according to Partridge,[218] include market failures undermining the willing buyer-willing seller requirement for land transactions; conflicting agendas in the policy setting process; monetary instability; barriers to land subdivision and finally the lack of post-transfer support for farmers.

Willing Buyer- Willing Seller

According to Partridge,[219] the 'willing buyer-willing seller' (WBWS) requirement is the most criticised requirement of the South African land redistribution programme. It requires that a seller has to submit a formal agreement to sell his/her land at a price which must be validated as market-related by an independent valuator, generally retained in the Department of Land Affairs. If the estimated market value is below the seller's asking price, Lahiff[220] argues that the negotiations that take place between the seller and valuator will enable the seller having to opt out if necessary. Therefore, Partridge[221] argues that the seller determines his own selling price with no contribution from the beneficiaries; and even though prices have to be approved by an independent valuator, evidence of negotiations breaking down over the prices being minutely less than the asking prices suggests poor negotiating skills from the valuators.

Conflicting Agendas

According to Partridge,[222] there are many actors who are actively involved in shaping South African land policy, hence putting different forces on the policy process. Lahiff[223] argues that the first group of actors include groups and individuals who argue for the preservation of the current commercial farming sector. Although they challenge radical reform, this group generally accepts the notion that measures need to be put in place to ensure the increase of African farmers in the sector, which will consequently suppress social tensions. Partridge[224] identifies the second group of actors as groups such as the World Bank as well as proponents of Black Economic Empowerment who encourage land reform through the market; while the third group of actors are those who push for a more radical reform process, calling for the state to play a more direct role in redistributing land to the disadvantaged, with minimal or no compensation. According to Greenburg,[225] this group includes the Landless Peoples Movement; grassroots ANC members, in particular the ANC Youth League; the Economic Freedom Fighters (EFF), led by former ANC Youth League Leader Julius Malema, and various other NGOs, all of which call for direct expropriation against white farmers. According to Lahiff,[226] all of these conflicting political forces have led to 'a messy compromise that has proven to be extremely slow and has failed to deliver on its key policy objectives'.

Economic Issues

According to van der Merwe,[227] inflation has generally been high and unpredictable in the South African economy, despite inflation-targeting measures being adopted since 2002 to keep inflation between 3 per cent and 6 per cent (van der Merwe 2004). Therefore, according to Nieuwoudt and Vink,[228] the primary reason for the poor black minority not being able to gain access to land in developing countries is high rates of inflation.

Partridge[229] argues that the failure to allow the subdivision of land is arguably the single largest contributor to the failure and general underperformance of land reform projects, because not only does it foist inappropriate sizes of farms on people, but it also forces them to work in groups, whether they want to do so or not. Although the Subdivision of Agricultural Land Act doesn't restrict subdivision entirely, getting permission from the government brings in uncertainty and delays in the process, effectively increasing the cost of acquiring small areas of land. Therefore, according to Partridge,[230] this means that given the small size of the grants offered under land reform, beneficiaries are forced to pool together with other beneficiaries in order to make up the full amount needed to buy a piece of land.

The main causes for land reform failure in South Africa, as Partridge[231] puts it, is the fact that policies that have succeeded in transferring land have not been supplemented with support to the beneficiaries to enable them to make productive use of the land. According to Jacobs,[232] there are five key functional areas of support for farmers receiving land through the land redistribution programme. These include extension services, infrastructure support, skills development and capacity building, financial assistance, and access to markets. In response to the lack of agricultural support, the Comprehensive Agricultural Support Programme (CASP) was launched in 2004. According to Partridge,[233] the primary purpose of this programme was to make provision for agricultural support to targeted beneficiaries of the land reform as well as agrarian reform programme within six specified priority areas. The six priority areas referred to are 'information and knowledge management', 'technical and advisory assistance, and regulatory services', 'training and capacity building', 'marketing and business development', 'on-farm and off-farm infrastructure and production inputs' and 'financial assistance'. However, despite the added effort to support post-transfer, the post-1994 government has failed to deliver on its targets. The South African government made very big promises with its land policy targets. Trying to achieve these targets has put serious financial constraints on government and, in particular, the Department of Land Affairs.

Sustainability of Land and Agrarian Reform

It is important that a discussion of land and agrarian reform takes into account rural and agricultural development as measures for addressing poverty. According to Twala and Selesho,[234] land and agrarian reform programmes are the most important rural development strategies employed by the post-apartheid government. This is primarily because land remains a major source of livelihood for people in rural and peri-urban communities, as well as communal farmers. According to Twala and Selesho,[235] agricultural growth is the best way to reduce rural poverty at farm level, in the rural economies.

Liversage[236]acknowledges evidence that reveals 'that agricultural growth and development, through land and agrarian reform, may lower food prices and thus provide cheaper wage goods which stimulate industrial growth, thus recognising the use of land as a productive resource and an integral part of the economic growth'. According to Gumede,[237] if there is anything to be distilled from the Zimbabwean land reform process, it is the model where new land owners are given small plots of between two to five hectares for them to be able to practise subsistence farming and petty commodity production. Such could be achieved by subdividing large farms into smaller units to act as a multi-functional farm that will benefit more people. Therefore, rural, peri-urban communities as well as communal farmers should be given adequate land in order for them to practise subsistence farming because land reform goes hand in glove with a restructuring of the rural economy.

Moyo[238]also argues that land reform in South Africa should result in agrarian transformation which must ensure food security and environmental sustainability for the country. The apartheid government has equated national food security with large scale commercial farming – a sector dominated by the white minority. According to Gumede,[239] the potential for millions of South African smallholders to increase production, raise income and create much needed jobs was overlooked, even in the post-apartheid dispensation. The post-apartheid government prioritised grafting the redistributed land onto existing communal units, and much of this land was deemed as no longer productive. Now, because of this, there is no doubt that successful large farmers will always have a key role in South Africa's agricultural economy. It would seem that the current model is not compatible with a critical need to transform the rural economy and to create more rural jobs.

A progressive transformation process should benefit smaller farmers and emerging African commercial farmers. In Mozambique, for example, Liversage[240] argues that land and natural resource are used by commercial farmers to occupy a central position in their livelihoods, contributing to food security within the country and regions. Therefore, by strengthening land reform process, it is hoped that people will invest more in the land and agricultural development. However, it is also recognised that a range of other inputs would also be required and that land reform in itself will not necessarily lead to increased economic activity and poverty reduction. According to the National Planning Commission,[241] these inputs may include:

- Converting some under-used land in communal areas and land reform projects into commercial production; and
- Choosing and support those farmers that have the highest potential for growth and employment.

Furthermore, the National Planning Commission[242] proposes a model for a more feasible land reform which is to be achieved through the following:

- Enabling a fast transfer of agricultural land to black farmers without interfering on the land markets or business confidence in the agricultural sector;
- Making sure that targeted human population groups is trained and developed through programmes such as learnerships and apprenticeships, in addition to training and agricultural science, to ensure the production that will take place on the transferred land will be sustainable;
- Developing institutions of monitoring to safeguard small and emerging farmers from corruption and speculation arising in the market;
- Aligning fiscal targets with government expenditure to make sure that land is transferred successfully; and
- Establishing cooperation between white farmers and black farmers to facilitate skills transfer and chain integration.

Furthermore, the southern Africa region is confronted by a number of challenges. Not only is the region faced by the problem of racially skewed land distribution and poorly resourced land administration, the region is also confronted with unsustainable land utilisation, leading to a decline in the ability of our land resources to provide goods and services. It is therefore important that land users be provided with adequate skills, knowledge and other resources to be able to optimally and sustainably utilise the land for income generation and poverty reduction. There is a need to enhance and deepen skills development, infrastructure development, service provision and credit access to ensure the better use of existing irrigation facilities, to extend irrigation schemes and enhance water access by rural dwellers. There is now a renewed emphasis, which is placed on overcoming food insecurity through support for smallholder farmers and by stimulating the market opportunities for smallholder farmers. The ANC's goal of creating a million agriculture-related jobs by 2030 might suggest that it is recognising the opportunities associated with the agricultural sector.

Conclusion

This chapter has provided a brief historical background of land dispossession, and identified the systematic processes through which Africans were dispossessed of their land in South Africa. It also discussed land and agrarian reform since 1994, including the progress (or lack thereof) regarding land and agrarian reforms by the post-apartheid government. It also briefly covered experiences of other countries. As argued in Gumede,[243] South Africa can learn a lot from land reform processes in Zimbabwe in terms of what worked and what should be avoided.

However, although the land question for South Africa appears similar to that of Zimbabwe from a historical sense, it might very well be that the current contexts require different kinds of intervention.

Key Terms

Colonialism: A practice of acquiring full or partial political control over another country, occupying it with settlers, and exploiting it economically.

Land Redistribution: The process of reversing land ownership patterns.

Land Reform: The changing of laws, regulations or customs regarding land ownership.

Land Tenure: Ownership of land through title deed or similar past practices.

Willing Buyer-Willing Seller: A process whereby someone selling land sets the price for land and the buyer agrees with the price given.

9

Education and Training

Introduction

The provision of quality education in South Africa has always been the goal of the post-apartheid government and other education stakeholders in the country. The main reason for this is that, as Gumede[244]puts it, if the democratic South Africa is to produce informed, productive and progressive citizens who not only value, but also practise the principles treasured in the Constitution, then it must have an educational system that matches the goal. A lot has been achieved since the dawn of democracy, especially in the first decade. According to Kraak,[245] this is evident in the increased number of school-going adults and children in South Africa, increased number of investments by both government and the private sector in education, as well as the improvement in the institutionalisation processes and regulations. However, the provision of quality education is still facing many challenges.

While access to education in South Africa has significantly improved, the quality of education is a hotly debated issue. Education in South African, as it is in so many parts of the developing world, is continuously being confronted by extreme pressures to change. This is attributed to the need to address the continuously changing social and economic dynamics of the world. The failures in education in South Africa are in primary school literacy, mathematics and science education which are the cornerstone for the development of modern economies. In addition, poor school management systems, inappropriate curriculum changes as well as poor performing teachers, which have consequently resulted in low academic standards, are some of the critical issues confronting education in South Africa.

The quality of primary, secondary and tertiary education has an inevitable effect not only on the job markets, but also on the prospect of the country emerging as a democratic developmental state. This chapter contends that serious challenges remain, especially with regard to those brought about by the implementation of the policy reform. Also, it identifies and discusses a few of the qualitative challenges that are found in South Africa's education, namely that while primary and secondary enrolment has greatly improved and teacher-pupil ratio decreased, the lack of performing and happy teachers and the constant changing of education curriculum has led to a decline in the quality of education provided.

The chapter begins with a background on the history of South Africa's education system. It then discusses education in the post-1994 dispensation, identifying the inherent challenges faced by the post-1994 government in developing an education system that ensure that human resources are developed to their full capacity. Before concluding, the chapter explores the policy reform measures that can be undertaken to address the quality of education in South Africa.

Background

During the nineteenth century, an ever-increasing number of foreign missionary societies began arriving in South Africa, and by the twentieth century they all had considerable impact on both church and society. It is reported that the first European school to be founded in South Africa was by the Dutch Reform Church in the Cape Colony during the 1970s, for the sole purpose of establishing biblical instruction and salvation; civilisation was simply an impor tant by-product and a sign of redemption.

Missionaries facilitated a cultural re-orientation by undermining traditional customs and structures through evangelisation and education. Missionaries rejected African cultures not only because of their own sense of European supremacy, but primarily through the reading of the Bible, convincing Africans that they are heathens and they need to turn away from superstition and unevangelical lifestyles, and embrace an entirely new way of life. So, education was not simply a matter of literacy but it was also part of a comprehensive strategy to reconstruct African culture (see works of Ngugi waThiong'o, for instance). They separated converts from their cultural roots and traditional structures which had previously supported and controlled their lives, by introducing new agricultural techniques and technologies, and fostering entrepreneurial skills consistent with the emerging capitalism of the mining and industrial revolution and its urban setting. Missionary stations were rapidly becoming centres of education where literacy and numeracy skills necessary for economic progress in colonial society could be learned, while simultaneously taming the wilderness of African communities.

Nonetheless, missionary education provided the only access into broader society; however, even so, the doors of opportunity were limited, based on the assumption that Africans were culturally not prepared to participate as adults in the society. By the mid-1900s, the education system was characterised by strong British influence, following the victory of whites in the South African War. Language soon became a sensitive issue in education, which saw the installation of the English language and cultural values across the country.

Hungwe[246] argues that British settlers were influenced by a persistent and deeply held belief in white supremacy. This therefore resulted in the development of a complex educational policy which sought to guarantee white privilege, while promoting limited and segregated African development. Fundamental to the educational policy of the colonial authorities and the missionaries, then, was a social Darwinism which assumed that Africans were culturally unprepared yet to take their place as adults in society. This placed African communities in a dependent position on the education offered by the missionaries as the only access into the new colonial order. They increasingly believed in the dignity of labour and laziness as a form of positive sin, thereby fitting and contributing to the economic expansion of the empire. The decision to focus on education encouraged Africans to work for white societies rather than their own African communities. This, Hungwe[247] argues, not only established clear boundaries of social behaviours between blacks and whites but also reinforced the racism which was so inherent in settler society, providing a new ideological basis for the redefining of the missionaries' role. Based on this, Ruddell[248] argues that 'concepts such as racial superiority were primary influences which were at work in the formation of colonial education policies'. Evangelisation and education of Africans did not imply immediate social equality; their aim – so they claimed – was more long-term. Africans, it was argued, were members of an adolescent race in need of missionary guidance and discipline in order to reach their potential. The missionaries were in this regard, the creators of a new class of Africans.

Before the Bantu Education Act of 1954, Africans were subjected to what was known as 'Native Education'. This, as Tabata[249] puts it, meant inferior institutions, poor conditions and pitifully low allocations. Throughout the colonial regime in South Africa, the Missionaries, the Dutch and the British used colonial powers in institutions of education to drive and uphold patterns of domination and exploitation. For centuries, the education system was not only segregated based on racial differences to the advantage of whites, but rather, Gumede[250] argues, also deprived Africans of equal access to educational opportunities, and subjected them to inferior systems which were designed to perpetuate the oppressive power relations. Therefore, it would be a big mistake to assume that educational marginalisation of African only began with the introduction of apartheid. The system of segregation and unequal education was already in place long before the National Party (NP) assumed power in 1948. By the 1990s, the South African education system was characterised by an educational policy that further entrenched racial fragmentation into the education system.

Brian Lapping[251] quotes a speech outlining the policy on Bantu Education by Hendrik Verwoerd, stating that:

> There is no place for the African in the European community above the level of certain forms of labour…. Until now he has been subjected to a school system which drew him away from his own community and misled him by showing him the green pastures of European society in which he was not allowed to graze. Therefore, My Department's policy (i.e., the Department of Native Affairs) 'is that education should stand with both feet in the Reserves and have its roots in the spirit and being of Bantu society…. The basis of the provision and organisation of education in a Bantu Community should, where possible, be the tribal organisation.

Furthermore, according to Tabata,[252] a report of the Departmental Committee on Native Education (1935) sums up the policy on Bantu Education as follows:

> The Education of the White child prepares him for life in a dominant society and the Education of the Black child for a subordinate society…. The limits (of Native Education) form part of the social and economic structure of the country.

Indeed, the apartheid government formulated a system to separate all races, creating a form of educational hierarchy with whites assuming supremacy. The adoption and implementation of the Bantu Education Act created untold damage to the African. On the one hand, white schooling was free, compulsory and growing while, on the other hand, education for Africans was severely neglected. And such neglect manifested in financial under-provision and urban influx, which then led to insufficient schooling facilities, teachers and educational materials, and student absenteeism or non-enrolment. In addition to this, Tabata[253] highlights that, the curriculum of Bantu Education was also altered and separated from that of whites. According to Tabata,[254] an excessive amount of time is given to religious instruction and devotional activities as well as manual training.

Post-apartheid Dispensation

According to Ali-Dinar,[255] the education and training system under apartheid was characterised by three key features: first, a system fragmented along racial and ethnic lines, which was also saturated with the racial ideology and educational doctrines of apartheid. Second, it was characterised by unequal access to education and training at all levels of the system. Ali-Dinar[256] argues that extreme educational inequalities existed between black and white and large numbers of people, in particular, adults, out-of-school youth and children of pre-school age, had little or no access to education and training. Lastly, it was characterised by a lack of democratic control within the education and training system. Students, teachers, parents, and workers had been excluded from decision-making processes.

The post-apartheid government of 1994 inherited one of the most unequal societies in the world. According to Jansen and Taylor,[257] decades of social and economic discrimination against black South Africans left a legacy of not only income inequality, but also educational inequality along racial lines. The challenge faced by the post-apartheid government was to create an education and training system that will ensure that the human resources in our society were developed to their full capacity. According to Ali-Dinar,[258] this is the challenge posed by the vision of the Freedom Charter: to open the doors of learning and culture to all.

The number of school-going children in South Africa has increased. As Table 9.1 shows, there has been an increase in enrolment ratio of Africans from 115.4 in the year 2010 to 117.2 in the year 2013. According to Twenty Year Review,[259] the gross secondary school enrolment improved from 51 per cent in 1994 to 89 per cent in 2012, and the gross primary school enrolment in 2012 was high, at approximately 98 per cent. The Twenty Year Review[260] also acknowledges that the learner-teacher ratio also improved from 33:1 in 2000 to 30:1 in 2012 and as a result the number of schools has also increased with improved infrastructure and higher proportions. Furthermore, South Africa's education has seen more and more matriculates passing their exams. This is illustrated in the matriculation pass rate of 78.2 per cent in the year 2013 – this being the highest pass rate in the history of post-1994 education in South Africa, after the 2012 rate of 73.9 per cent. The government also implemented a number of programmes, such as Adult Basic Education and Training (ABET) and mass literacy campaigns which were all geared towards eradicating illiteracy, and have been made available to adults seeking to finish off their basic education by offering learning tools, knowledge and skills under nationally recognised qualifications.

There are still challenges regarding literacy, numeracy and enrolment rates in general. To measure progress on literacy and enrolments, certain calculations are done. Literacy refers to the ability to read and write while the Gross Enrolment Ratio is calculated as total enrolment in a specific level of education, regardless of age, expressed as a percentage of the eligible official school age (i.e. 7–18 years) population. As Table 9.1 shows, looking at 2010–2013, there are about 7 per cent of South Africans who cannot read and write at all and the gross enrolment ratios suggest that there are either a large number of those outside the standard schooling years that are at school or that repetition of classes is high.

According to the National Department of Education,[261] a policy to transform the education sector was effected in 2001 through the publication of the Education White Paper on Special Needs Education, all of this being in line with the ANC's

Table 9.1: Literacy and Gross Enrolments

	Literacy				Gross Enrolment Ratios			
	2010	2011	2012	2013	2010	2011	2012	2013
Male	94.1	94.3	95.0	94.9	113.8	115.4	115.6	115.6
Female	91.7	92.1	92.6	92.6	111.5	113.2	112.0	113.7
African	91.3	91.6	92.4	92.3	115.4	117.1	116.3	117.2
Coloured	95.9	96.3	96.8	96.9	99.2	99.3	102.0	101.0
Indian/Asian	98.5	98.4	98.6	98.2	101.8	101.7	103.5	107.5
White	99.8	99.7	99.8	99.9	98.5	100.8	98.4	100.7
Western Cape	97.2	97.7	98.0	97.9	102.5	101.6	102.8	106.3
Eastern Cape	90.9	91.3	92.1	91.9	117.6	120.8	118.0	118.1
Northern Cape	85.5	86.4	88.7	89.6	109.3	108.8	107.9	108.5
Free State	92.6	92.1	94.2	93.9	109.2	113.3	115.8	113.2
KwaZulu-Natal	91.8	92.5	92.5	92.1	113.2	116.6	114.9	117.4
North West	89.2	87.9	89.4	89.2	108.3	115.9	112.1	113.0
Gauteng	98.0	97.3	98.0	97.9	105.4	107.5	107.2	108.0
Mpumalanga	88.5	89.3	89.0	89.4	114.4	116.1	117.7	115.1
Limpopo	87.1	88.7	89.3	90.1	127.8	122.0	124.1	125.0
Total	**92.9**	**93.1**	**93.7**	**93.7**	**112.7**	**114.3**	**113.8**	**114.7**

Source: Own Calculations Using Statistics South Africa's General Household Surveys (2010–2013)

commitment to improve access to public education as well as being on track with Millennium Development Goal (MDG) of achieving universal primary education by 2015.

According to Pottinger,[262] education in South Africa may have improved quantitatively; however it has not improved qualitatively, either in absolute terms or in comparison with other developing countries. Despite the fact that South Africa spends 18.5 per cent of its annual budget on education, Modisaotile[263] acknowledges that the education system remains largely in a poor state of affairs. South Africa has a high-cost, low-performance education system that does not compare favourably with education systems in other African countries, or in similar developing economies.

There are many who argue that the quality of education is a challenge in South Africa. So, even though access has significantly improved, the quality of education is not satisfactory.[264] Modisaotsile[265]argues, like many others, that more attention needs to be focused on the quality of education. Quantity should, however, also be considered when the majority of those learners who pass matric do not meet the minimum requirements for university entrance. In addition, Modisaotsile[266] identifies that only half of the number of learners enrolled in Grade 1 eventually makes it to Grade 12.

Without a doubt, the purported poor quality of South Africa's education has had a knock-on effect on skills creation. Just as South Africa's education might be swamped with ideological over-reach, so too is the workplace skills crisis infinitely compounded by the worst administrative decisions: the imposition of costly, ideological, corrupt, bureaucratic and ineffectual skills development processes on South African industry.[267]

The other significant intervention in the education and training sector in the post-apartheid dispensation are the Sector Education and Training Authorities (SETAs). According to Pottinger,[268] SETAs are seen as the central mechanism for mediating the relationship between training (supply side) and economic and social requirements (demand side). According to the Twenty Year Review,[269] SETAs were established with the aim of linking skills development more closely to the needs of economic sectors and providing opportunities for experiential learning through learnerships. SETAs are, according to Brown,[270] central to interpreting the skills requirements in the context of economic demand, but they do not create demand. There are 23 SETAs, each funded by 1 per cent levy on the national payroll.

Many argue that SETAs have not worked well. According to the Twenty Year Review, [271] the number of unemployed people completing learnerships reached over 22,000 per annum in 2013, but there have been challenges in placing learners in experiential learning and sustainable employment. Furthermore, the funds that have been accumulated for the purpose of identifying and meeting sector specific scarce and critical skills have either not been spent or have been spent inappropriately. Also, most private sector companies are reported to have simply discounted the SETA levy as another tax and have gone back to doing their own internal training. A report by the Construction Industry Development Board (CIDB), for instance, found that most SETA trainees were only at basic levels of training, and this made no significant contribution to the specialised skills required by industries. It is therefore not surprising that there is so-called mismatch between the skills potential employees possess and the skills expected by the employers. It would be important that a robust conversation takes place between government and industry, as well as organised labour and the broader civil society, in order to find ways to reduce unemployment.

Perspective Box: Skills Development

Pros	Cons
SETAs provide work experience and nationally recognised qualification within the national qualifications framework	The challenge of placing learners in experiential learning and sustainable employment.
Develop skills of SA workforce	Require a large amount of *paperwork*
Increase global economic competitiveness	Companies with staff payroll of over R500 000
Promote self-employment and entrepreneurship	Monitored and controlled by government – no education and training priority
Improve delivery of social services	Many service providers are not SAQA accredited
Increase investment in education and training	Many organisations do not support this
Improve the return on investment on education	Difficult to monitor and control
Improve employment opportunities for new entrants	Many people who go through SETAs do not readily find work

Another notable education sub-sector is Further Education and Training (FET), whose transformation is articulated by the National Department of Education[272] as the desire for 'coordinated, comprehensive, interlocking sectors that provide meaningful experiences to learn at a post-compulsory phase'. A clear role was identified for the FET sector with the economy, which was soon followed by the introduction of the FET Act (No. 98) of 1998.

The South African FET sector is also confronted by a number of challenges. These challenges, Hoekel[273] argues, include the perception that FET colleges are inferior institutions producing low-status qualification. According to Akoojee and McGrath,[274] despite significant attempt by DHET to recapitalise and turn around the FET college sector, the uncertainty remains in the country about the extent to which FET colleges should be viewed as suitable alternatives to higher education. Another challenge that facing the FET sector is that a significant number of teaching staff at FET colleges are either 'under-qualified or unqualified.'[275]

Much has been said about the various education and training policies and relevant pieces of legislation since their introduction and during their years of implementation. Suffice it to say here that the argument that government has made progress in the expansion of the educational opportunities is persuasive. This, according to Kraak,[276] is evident in the increase access, headcount enrolment, investment by government and other private sector, and institutional rationalisation processes and regulations respectively. However, there is also literature pointing to a correlation between the quality of educators and students and, by extension, the quality of the education system.

Another area worth highlighting in the context of South Africa's education and training landscape is the Technical Vocational Education and Training (TVET) College system. Given the challenges with education in general in South Africa, the TVET colleges have also had to undergo numerous reforms, in the main, in order to prepare the youths in South Africa for the world of work. However, the unemployment challenge remains pronounced, especially for the youth, and there is a phenomenon of large numbers of the youth that are not in employment, not in education or not getting training. Kgobe and Baates (2014) estimate that 3.4 million youths between the ages of fifteen and twenty-four were neither in employment or education or training (otherwise known as NEET).[277] Although the President Jacob Zuma government maintains that the TVET colleges are better placed to train young school leavers, providing them with the skills, knowledge and attitudes necessary for employment in the labour market, others argue that government's view perpetuates unrealistic and false hopes.[278]

Policy Reforms

Since 1994, the vision for a transformed education system that would reflect the values and practices of a democratic South Africa have been clearly articulated in a number of policy documents. According to the 1997 Education White Paper, the structure of educational institutions should create conditions that ensure the development of coherent and flexible national systems that redress past inequality, eliminate inequalities through the use of policy resources and ensure an improvement in the quality of education across the system.

The National Development Plan[279] provides the vision for South Africa's future as well as useful ideas that will guide us towards the attainment of that vision. The NDP[280] takes forward government's commitment to seeing education as an apex priority. It recognises that the South African education system needs urgent action. It suggests that building national capabilities requires focus on early childhood development, basic education, further and higher education. Therefore, priorities such as human capacity, school management, infrastructure and results-oriented mutual accountability between schools and communities are, according to the NDP,[281] critical for the improvement of South Africa's education system.

Teacher development

One of the keys to a successful education system is the recruitment of quality teachers. According to Pottinger,[282] the South African education systems has ceased to recruit quality teachers and quality teachers that remain in the education system are uncertain about their own future in education as well as the future of education in South Africa. Some of their fears and concerns emanate from the political and economic climate in the country, changes in policies, changes in the curriculum, high rates of teacher attrition, unsafe school environments and unsatisfactory working conditions. This has therefore resulted in poor teacher morale and declining quality of education. According to Lumby,[283] 'if motivation and morale are low, then teaching and learning suffer'. Therefore, in order to achieve educational progress, van der Berg et al[284] argue that South Africa needs an institutional structure that consists of teacher pay, bursary programmes and other interventions aimed at promoting good teaching as well as attracting and retaining the best teachers.

In addition to this, teacher development is also critical in ensuring high quality education in South Africa's education system. According to the National Education Collaboration Trust,[285] improving the quality of education can also be achieved through pre-service and continuous teacher development. Teachers need to be developed to deal with the school, classroom and community challenges effectively. According to the National Education Collaboration Trust,[286] teacher development can be achieved if the following conditions are put in place:

- The appointment of principals and school management teams based on merit;
- Development of coordinated training plans;
- Integration of professional development time into the school calendar and timetables;
- Improved quality of teacher training, including more practical on-the-job training;
- Teaching techniques that keep up with the latest trends to meet the demands of the twenty-first century, including the use of technology in teaching;
- Acknowledgement of good performances by school and district officials;
- Performance measurement and development of teachers by linking academic success of learners directly with teacher success.

Leadership

According to Pottinger,[287] South Africa's education system is characterised by weak school management. Van der Berg[288] further argue that effective schools require well selected individuals as principals, together with management teams that understand and fulfil their roles as leaders of the curriculum, towards ensuring that an organised environment conducive to learning is present. Therefore, in order to ensure effective leadership in schools, the National Education Collaboration Trust[289] suggests the following:

- Delivering widespread training on good governance at school, district and provincial levels;
- Assisting leaders to set examples and provide models of behaviour for officials and learners to follow;
- Reviewing the institutional governance framework which includes school principals, school management teams (SMTs) and school governing bodies (SGBs).

Textbooks and Infrastructure

Even though it's not a new phenomenon, the Limpopo textbook crisis in the year 2012 placed a much needed national spotlight on systematic difficulties in the delivery of resources that ensure quality education. This is one of the many operational inefficiencies which contribute to poor teacher capacity and ultimately the continued weaknesses in the South African education system. It goes without saying that school infrastructure, in its various facets, is critical.

Community and Parent Support

The community has an influence on what is happening at school and the school is a mirror image of the community within which it is situated. According to Ngqela and Lewis,[290] it is crucial that the focus should be on positive relationships and that issues of better security measures, parental roles and community involvement in schools should be addressed. Indeed, the involvement of parents and the wider community in schools is very important.

Learner Support and Wellbeing

The National Development Plan recognises the importance of learner wellbeing to achieve quality learning and teaching.[291] The holistic approach to learning would include such aspects as health, nutrition, psychosocial support, sport and culture, and catering for children with special needs. The government of South Africa has many initiatives regarding learner support and advancing learners' wellbeing. However, more can be done to eliminate the challenges, such as very long distances to schools.

Access to education has improved, but education remains untransformed

Bloch[292] is of the view that although many challenges still remain, there were significant achievements in turning apartheid education around in the first decade of democracy. This has, according to Kraak,[293] been evident in increased access to education, headcount enrolment in schools, investment by government and the private sector in education, and institutional rationalisation processes and regulation.

The changes pursued in the education sector have resulted in great strides. Government has made some progress in the expansion of education access, particularly improving access for disadvantaged groups. Progress is also visible in the different sectors, as presented in the 2008 Review of National Policies for Education in South Africa by the OECD.[294] For instance, the OECD noted that what government had been able to achieve in the space of fourteen years is commendable and that it is understandable that some of the policy goals had not yet been realised.

In this instance, data from the Towards a Fifteen Year Review[295] indicates that education participation has increased since 1994, especially in the case of primary schooling. This is attributed to those interventions geared towards increased access. In terms of the growth in enrolments for the age group 7–15 years between 2002 and 2007, the enrolment of 6-year-olds had improved from 40 per cent to 60 per cent; for 6-year-olds the improvement was from 70 per cent to 88 per cent, and for 15-year-olds the improvement was from 96 per cent to 98 per cent.

Data from the Department of Basic Education's 2010 Education Statistics in South Africa report,[296] according to Table 9.2, show relatively high gross enrolment rates: 94 per cent for the foundation phase (Grades 1–7), 86 per cent for the senior phase (Grades 8–12) and an overall 91 per cent for Grades 1–12. In essence, South Africa has been successful in facilitating access to primary and tertiary education, particularly for the girl child. Based on the Millennium Development Goals (MDGs) target for 2015, the country has achieved its goal.

Table 9.2: Gross Enrolment Ratios by Gender and Level of Education

Gender	Primary phase (Grade 1 – 7) %	Secondary phase (Grade 8 – 12) %	Total (Grade 1- 12) %
Female	92	89	91
Male	96	83	91
Total	**94**	**86**	**91**

Source: Department of Basic Education (2012) in Gumede (2013b, p. 73)

Further corroborating this point, the OECD report[297] (referred to above) indicates that South Africa is close to achieving universal basic education with 96.6 per cent enrolment for the age group 7–15 years, with almost all children of school-going age entering school and the majority reaching the end of Grade 9.

In support of the OECD report and others, Table 9.3 shows improved access to education between 2001 and 2011. Although the number of those not attending school is still high, the percentage of those attending has increased from 71.5 per cent in 2001 to 73.4 per cent in 2011, while the percentage of those not attending school has decreased from 28.5 per cent in 2001 to 26.6 per cent in 2011. There are also increases in percentage shares, in terms of attendance, for all types of educational institutions except pre-school, as Table 9.3 shows. In the ten-year period 2001–2011, there has been an increase of about 100,000 attendance for universities. This reiterates the point that the number of those seeking higher education increases over time in any society and, as such, more universities are needed.

Table 9.3: Access to Education in South Africa (2001–2011)

Education	2001		2011	
	Number	%	Number	%
School attendance				
Yes	13,727,893	71.5	13,837,961	73.4
No	5,463,823	28.5	5,023,110	26.6
Type of educational institution				
Pre-school	575,936	4.2	128,719	0.9
School	12,584,818	91.7	12,862,961	92.9
FET College	191,234	1.4	359,228	2.6
University/ Technikon	315,592	2.3	410,063	3.0
ABET	26,505	0.2	22,730	0.2
Other	33,809	0.2	57,883	0.4
Public or Private				
Public	13,028,486	94.9	11,924,285	92.7
Private	699,407	5.1	934,480	7.3

Source: Statistics South Africa (2012) in Gumede (2013:71)

Other important areas are literacy and numeracy. Various datasets and publications show a steady increase in the literacy rate in South Africa. Development Indicators[298] show that, according to General Household Surveys, literacy rate has increased from 70.7 per cent in 2002 to approximately 80 per cent in 2009. Although there are improvements, there is still a long way to go in ensuring that the 20 per cent that is classified as illiterate may be literate. Bloch[299] shows that despite the fact that South Africa has high levels of educational spending than most countries, it is amongst the worst performing countries internationally on literacy and numeracy.

Despite improved literacy rates and access to education, it remains evident that key historical factors have continued to constrain and limit the successful transformation of the education sector. Over the past year and a half, it has become increasingly evident that South Africa's education institutions remain untransformed. There is emerging consensus that the quality of education is poor and the curriculum is not well structured as part of the legacy of the Bantu education system.

Data from the latest census highlights the reality that access to education, not to mention the quality of the education system, remains a challenge. For instance, the number (at above five million) and the share of those not attending school remains very high. Also, there is slow progress with rolling out early learning. Lastly, although the enrolment of Africans in higher education institutions has increased, detailed analysis of data reveals historical disparity in participation rates among population groups. The total gross participation rate remains more or less the same, at approximately 15.7 per cent, in early to mid-2000 and it increased marginally to 16.18 per cent in 2007. The number of those enrolled in higher education has been increasing. However, participation rates for the African student population do not seem to be increasing at any significant rate.

Of concern is that even qualified graduates are struggling to find employment. Moleke[300] found that the majority of the unemployed fall under the categories of Africans, females, graduates of humanities and the arts, and graduates from the so-called historically black universities. The unification of the education system and standards also remains an issue. The two-tier education system is accentuated by an increasing share of those attending the private education system. Also, it remains to be seen whether the approach adopted while restructuring the higher education landscape was appropriate or not. The Higher Education Monitor of the Council on Higher Education reflects on a number of issues pertaining to the challenges confronting the South African higher education landscape. Overall, the picture looks bleak but there is some progress, especially in the context of proposals contained in the 2012 Green Paper for Post-School Education and Training.[301]

The higher education sector has also gone through (and continues to go through) transformation. Education White Paper Three: A Programme for the Transformation of Higher Education[302] outlines a framework for transforming the higher education system to serve a new social order, meet pressing national needs, and respond to new realities and opportunities. In line with the vision in the National Plan on Higher Education,[303] achieving equity and diversity in the South African higher education system; producing graduates needed for the social and economic development of South Africa; promoting research; and restructuring the institutional landscape are important objectives. Again, this mirrors the objectives of government's broader PSRs described above. The most recent thinking on further transforming the higher education sector (and perhaps correcting errors committed earlier) is contained in a Green Paper for Post-School Education and Training.[304]

Similar to other education sub-sectors, Breier and Mabizela[305]argue that the higher education system inherited from the apartheid era was one characterised by inequity, fragmentation and inefficiency, with 36 public higher education institutions (21 universities and 15 technikons), separated along racial lines. For some reason, government opted for restructuring the higher education landscape through merging institutions. Two phases of restructuring occurred between 2004 and 2005, which saw the emergence of new terms of reference and institutional arrangements for the institutions. For instance, universities not required to merge with any other institution remained 'universities' (like those that merged with or rather incorporated other universities); some technikons were transformed into 'universities of technology'; some universities were merged with technikons and became 'comprehensive institutions'; and two national institutes for higher education were established in Mpumalanga and Northern Cape. The Green Paper for Post-School Education and Training[306] recommends, among other things, that the two national institutes for higher education in Mpumalanga and Northern Cape should be converted to two new universities.

In terms of enrolments, it is noted by Breier and Mabizela[307] that the extent to which the higher education system can actually produce highly skilled graduates is predicated on three important factors: the number of school 'graduates' that qualify for entry into higher education institutions, the number that choose to enter higher education institutions, and the number that complete their qualifications. However, as discussed in the schooling section above, the quality of Grade 12 school-leaving passes is questionable. Bloch[308] elaborates the issues bedevilling the education system in South in detail.

Although the enrolment of Africans in higher education institutions has increased, detailed analysis of data reveals historical disparity in participation rates among population groups. Table 9.4 illustrates, from the latest data available, participation rates in the years 2002, 2004 and 2007. The total gross participation rate remained more-or-less the same in early to mid-2000, at about 15.7 per cent, and it increased marginally to 16.18 per cent in 2007. The number of those enrolled in higher education has been increasing. However, participation rates for African student population do not seem to be increasing in any significant rate – it was 11.4 per cent in 2002, 11.5 per cent in 2004 and 12.29 per cent in 2007. These improvements, however pedestrian, suggest that government plans – though seemingly farfetched – are yielding some results.

Table 9.4: Gross Participation Rates in Higher Education

Year	Population Group	Enrolment in Higher Education	Gross Participation Rate (per cent)
2002	African	405 914	11.4
	Coloured	38 965	11.0
	Indian	48 717	47.7
	White	181 999	61.9
	Total	**675 595**	**15.7**
2004	African	453 639	11.5
	Coloured	46 090	12.1
	Indian	54 315	50.2
	White	188 957	59.5
	Total	**743 001**	**15.7**
2007	African	478 146	12.29
	Coloured	49 211	12.99
	Indian	52 748	45.38
	White	180 985	56.77
	Total	**761 090**	**16.18**

Source: Kraak, A. (2008:283) and Steyn, A. (2009:67)

However, on the other hand, Breier and Mabizela[309] also note that graduation rates have recently been declining. Although strides in encouraging access are yielding some positive results, graduation numbers and rates show a continual decline. This is starkly reflected in graduation ratios by field of study in relation to national targets. Breier and Mabizela[310] estimated that if 2004 graduation targets were to be consistent with enrolment targets, the percentage ratio of graduates for human sciences, commerce and science, and engineering and technology should have been 40:30:30. However, the ratio was 48:25:27.

The declining trend with regard to graduation rates is largely attributed to the difficulty of subjects, depending on the preparedness of individual students by the schooling system. Importantly, however, it has been noted that higher education faces a serious challenge of student attrition. It is reported that 30 per cent of the year 2000 first-time entrants into the system dropped out within the first year while 20 per cent dropped out after two or three years of study. Of the group, 50 per cent was out of the system before attaining their qualification. This is obviously worrisome, in the light of the country's unemployment challenge. Also of concern is that even qualified graduates are struggling to find employment. For instance, Moleke[311] found that the majority of the unemployed fall under the categories of Africans, females, those who studied humanities and art, and those who studied at so-called historically black universities.

Overall, it remains to be seen whether the approach adopted with restructuring the higher education landscape was appropriate or not; South Africa, during the early years of democratic government, collapsed many tertiary education institutions to a few. There remains an imbalance between the numbers in universities and those in technical universities and FET colleges. It could be argued that further education will not flourish and benefit society until appropriate structural features have been put in place. The issue of access to higher education remains one of the major challenges too.

Conclusion

Reforms that have taken place in South Africa's education system since 1994, in the context of reforms in the public sector, were necessary for a newly democratic country that had inherited a racially segregated and dysfunctional education system. These reforms have happened at many levels, such as early learning and development, general schooling, further education and training, basic education and training, and higher education. Although the reforms undertaken since 1994 have accomplished some of their intended objectives, they have not gone far enough. The quality of education in South Africa is one of the most hotly debated issues in the post-apartheid dispensation.

Key Terms

Experiential Learning: A process of learning through experience.

Further Education and Training (FET): Vocational or occupational by nature implying that the student receives education and training with a view to getting a specific range of jobs or employment possibilities.

Learnerships: A work-based learning programme.

Literacy: Ability to use written language actively and passively; ability to 'read, write, spell, listen, and speak'.

Numeracy: Ability to work with numbers.

Sector Education and Training Authorities (SETAs): Training and education institutions aimed at developing and improving the skills of the South African workforce.

10

Poverty and Inequality

Introduction

This chapter deals with poverty and inequality which are among South Africa's most intractable development challenges linked to high unemployment. The concepts of poverty, inequality and related terms are explained. The evolution of policies and programmes aimed at reducing poverty and inequality is also discussed. The chapter starts by providing a brief background on poverty and inequality, before and after apartheid. A broad analysis of poverty and inequality in South Africa implies that race remains a key marker of inequality (and poverty) in South Africa – this has to do, in the main, with the ramifications of apartheid colonialism and a structure of the South African economy that negatively affects the labour market. Furthermore, the chapter discusses the various types of inequalities; and lastly, the levels of poverty and inequality in democratic South Africa.

Indeed, poverty and inequality are among the most contested issues in the post-1994 South Africa. This is largely because poverty and inequality, particularly income inequality, remain very high in South Africa. For a country with over 350 years of apartheid colonialism, there is cause to worry that if poverty and inequality are not reduced, the affected people can revolt. This is even more likely, given the character of income inequality in South Africa: inequality is not only a class character but also racial and political character. Barrera[312] describes racial inequality as where race and inequality meet. Political inequality, on the other hand, according to Verba,[313] refers to 'the extent to which citizens have an equal voice over governmental decisions.' Although this chapter cannot do justice to the notion of political inequality, it is important to briefly reflect on this important issue, especially given the history of apartheid colonialism.

Historical Context

There is a general consensus in South Africa that poverty and inequality, particularly income inequality and income poverty, are persistent. These two development issues are primarily linked to the legacy of apartheid colonialism, as well as the structure of the economy. As argued in Chapter 1, apartheid colonialism relegated Africans, or black South Africans in general, to low skill and unskilled sectors by systematically ensuring that Africans received inferior education (as discussed in Chapter 9). Inequality is entrenched in a particular structure of the economy. On the other hand, the structure of the economy perpetuates inequality by benefitting those with certain skills or political connections, while keeping the rest of society, within the African community, at lower levels of economic or financial wellbeing.

According to Townsend,[314] drawing from the World Bank perspective, poverty can be defined as the inability to attain a minimal standard of living measured in terms of basic consumption needs or income required to satisfy those needs, while inequality is defined as the unequal or unevenness of social disparities, characterised by the existence of unequal opportunities and rewards within a group or society. Poverty and inequality are also political concepts because, according to Meth,[315] they relate to the allocation or distribution of resources, and reflect the impact of past and present policy choices.

The roots of poverty and inequality in the post-apartheid dispensation can be traced back to both the pre-colonial era as well as the apartheid colonial dispensation. According to Wilson,[316] the first steps in shaping poverty and inequality in South Africa's political economy can be traced back to the arrival or the settlement of Europeans in the most southern tip of Africa. Even though the ownership of land did not necessarily imply acquisition of wealth, Wilson[317] argues that the ownership of land by the dominant population group enabled a process of accumulation to begin which placed resources in the hands of some individuals, families and groups, mainly white settlers, which could then be used for investment into human capital in the form of education and training for their sons and daughters.

Furthermore, land as a basis for accumulating wealth for 200 years was overtaken by the discovery and exploitation of minerals at the end of the nineteenth century. According to Frye et al,[318] a developed industrial capitalism was super-imposed on settler colonial land and mercantile socio-political domination. This capitalism – colonial and apartheid capitalism – was based on 'wage slavery' more typical of advanced capitalist societies.

Since 1994, successive democratic governments have pursued numerous initiatives to redress the ramifications of apartheid colonialism as far as poverty and inequality are concerned. Chapter 5 discussed some of the programmes, policies and legislation aimed at reducing income inequality. With regards to poverty, government has experimented with various anti-poverty initiatives.[319]

Perspectives on Poverty and Inequality

To start with, there are many definitions and many aspects of poverty. Similarly, there are many definitions and/or aspects of inequality. Someone is said to be poor if the person's income is below a predetermined poverty datum line. There are also aspects of poverty that relate to access to basic services and assets, hence some talk of poor–poor-service or poor-asset. Similarly, there are different aspects of inequality: income inequality, asset inequality, educational inequality, gender inequality, political inequality, social inequality, and so on.

Normally, poverty and inequality are measured in monetary terms – the term used is 'money metric measures'. In other words, measurements or calculations take into account the amount of money a person has. It is in this context that a poverty datum line should first be calculated before the people classified as poor are determined. With regard to poverty, economists talk of absolute poverty, relative poverty, subjective poverty and intensity of poverty. In a nutshell, with regard to measuring poverty, through money metric measures, (a) a Headcount Index (notated as P_0) measures the proportion of the population whose consumption (or other measures of standard of living) is less than the poverty line; (b) Poverty Gap Index (notated as P_1) is the average, over all people, of the gaps between poor peoples' living standards and the poverty line, and it indicates the average extent to which individuals fall below the poverty line (if they do) – P_1 can be interpreted as a measure of how much (income) would have to be transferred to the poor to bring their expenditure up to the poverty line – and (c) Squared Poverty Gap Index (notated as P_2) is a weighted sum of poverty gaps (as a proportion of the poverty line), where the weights are the proportionate poverty gaps themselves – P_2 takes inequalities among the poor into account, for instance, a (cash) transfer from a poor person to an even poorer person would reduce the index and a transfer from a very poor person to a less poor person would increase the index. It is important to note that money metric measures of poverty are known as Foster-Greer-Thorbecke (FGT) family measures of poverty, named after those who came up with money metric measures of poverty.

Table 10.1, indeed, shows very high levels of poverty although the share of those below the various poverty lines is declining in South Africa. For instance, for an income poverty line of R551.78 per person per month, there are about 46 per cent of people living below the poverty line.

Table10.1: Income Poverty in South Africa (2005-2009)

	Percentage of population living below various poverty lines (in 2009 constant Rand)	
	2005	2009
Expenditure Poverty Line [R551.78 per person per month]	70	65
Income Poverty Line [R551.78 per person per month]	59	46
Expenditure Poverty Line [R298.17 per person per month]	54	49
Income Poverty Line [R298.17 per person per month]	40	27
Expenditure Poverty Line [R149.08 per person per month]	31	25
Income Poverty Line [R149.08 per person per month]	23	12

Source: Development Indicators (2012) in Gumede (2014b:287)

The main point is that income poverty remains very high in South Africa. Other aspects of poverty can be said to be high as well. Bhorat et al confirm that service- and asset-poverty are still very high in South Africa, though declining.[320] There are also measures of poverty that relate to the 'voices of the poor', the work that is originally associated with Nanak Kakwani and Ravi Kanbur, which the World Bank sort of appropriated. The voices of the poor relate to whether people are able to freely express themselves. Lastly, Amartya Sen[321] developed what came to be known as capability measures of poverty. These have to do with an ability of individuals to pursue the kinds of life that they value.

It should be noted t hat there is no single widely accepted or best way to measure inequality – although the Gini Coefficient is the most popular measure. In economics, there is an understanding, if not acceptance, that inequality measures perform differently under different kinds of income transfer. The Gini coefficient ranges between 0.0 and 1 – the highest inequality being 1 and the lowest being 0. Another used economic measure of inequality is the Lorenz Curve which is a graphical representation of the relationship between the cumulative percentage of income and the cumulative percentage of (ordered) population. The Gini Coefficient, for instance, is much less sensitive to income transfers between households if they lie near the middle of the income distribution, compared to the tails. The Atkinson Index, on the other hand, is strongly correlated with the extent of poverty; therefore, it is more 'bottom-sensitive' than other measures. The Robin Hood Index is insensitive with respect to income transfers between households on the same side of the mean income.[322]

In the context of South Africa, there is discourse relating to what is called 'Two Economies' which, as a metaphor, is a short form of socio-economic dualism: 'first economy' and 'second economy'. The First Economy is a part of the South African economy that is at developed and it is globally integrated while the Second Economy is a part of the economy that is marginalised, exists at the edges, consists of large numbers of the unemployed and the 'unemployable', and does not benefit from progress in the first economy. Lastly, the second economy is characterised by underdevelopment, contributes little to gross domestic product and has weak social capital. It is also characterised by poor skills, incorporates the poorest of the rural and urban poor, is structurally disconnected from both the first and global economies, and is incapable of self-generated growth.[323] Like measuring poverty and inequality, there is no standard measure of the second economy or the first economy. Using a measure of persons aged fifteen years and above whose level of completed education is primary (grade seven/standard five) or below, Gumede (2008) estimated that there were about 9.5 million South Africans in the second economy.[324]

Another important issue of measurement, linked to poverty, is human development. The Human Development Index (HDI) is a composite index that measures human development based on three aspects: longevity, knowledge and a decent standard of living. It is important that the HDI improves so as to advance the wellbeing of people. Besides the commonly known HDI, there is also a Human Poverty Index, which, for developing countries, combines measures of life expectancy, child nutrition status and access to improved water sources, and income. Then, there is a Gender-related Human Development Index, which reflects differences in HDI for women compared to men; while the Gender Empowerment Measure combines measures of equality in political and economic power for men and women.

South Africa's HDI has been increasing, albeit marginally, in the past few years. As Table 11 shows, in 2010 the HDI for South Africa was 0.604, and this has steadily increased to 0.629 in 2012.

Table 10.2: Human Development in South Africa (1980-2012)

	Life Expec- tancy	Expected years of Schooling	Mean years of Schooling	GNI per capita (2005 PPP$)	HDI
1980	56.9	11.1	4.8	8,399	0.57
1985	59.8	11.1	4.8	7,892	0.581
1990	61.5	11.4	6.5	7,671	0.621
1995	59.9	13.1	8.2	7,350	0.65
2000	54.8	13.1	8.2	7,462	0.622
2005	51.1	13.1	8.2	8,420	0.604
2010	52.2	13.1	8.5	9,307	0.621
2011	52.8	13.1	8.5	9,463	0.625
2012	53.4	13.1	8.5	9,594	0.629

Source: 2013 Human Development Report

As Table 10.2 shows, per capita incomes have been increasing, so also is life expectancy although the increase in life expectancy has effectively been negligible. Other useful numbers in the 2013 Human Development Report relate to schooling: data implies that South Africans, on average, school five years less than expected. Since 1995, according to the 2013 Human Development Report, the expected period of schooling in South Africa are 13.1 years; however, the mean period of schooling have remained 8.5 years since 2010.

Perspective Box: Human Development Index (HDI)

Pros	Cons
It is a wider measure of ' 'development' and GDP alone	HDI fails to takeaccount of qualita- tive factors, such as cultural identity and political freedoms, human securityand gender opportunities
The additional indicators used are objective and measurable	HDI does not include dimensions, ranging from gender equity to environmental biodiversity.
It gives a sense of the level of human development	HDI does not take into account the inequalities in income distribution

When it comes to inequality, there are different theories. With regard to racial inequality, according to Barrera,[325] the theories of racial inequality are classified into the following categories: deficiency theories, bias theories and structural theories. Deficiency theories are based on the perspective that social, political and economic inferiorities of the racial minority are a result of the biological, structural and cultural deficiencies of the minority groups. Bias theories, on the other hand, are often used to explain racial inequalities by expanding on racial differences. As opposed to deficiency theories, bias theories assert that racial inequality is a result of the injustice of dominant groups. Structural theories find explanations of racial inequality in sub-cultural groups. They can be divided into two categories: class and colonial. The class model is essentially a Marxist approach to inequality while the colonial model draws attention to political oppression, self-determination and liberation of the geographically restricted group.

There are also various theories and models of ethnic and racial inequality, as captured in Hirschman.[326] Gunnar Myrdal,[327] for instance, argued that racial inequality was an act of discrimination which was a consequence of prejudice behaviour by dominant groups. Myrdal described racial inequality as a vicious prejudice-discrimination cycle on the minority group, where the 'effects' of discrimination by the dominant group encourage further discrimination on the minority group. Although Myrdal[328] was writing about the American society, his hypothesis bears relevance to the case of South Africa. In addition, from the menu of racial inequality theories, the bias and colonial theories have relevance to South Africa because discriminatory policies and legislation, for over three centuries, have created racial inequality in South Africa.

Poverty, Inequality and the Labour Market

According to van der Berg,[329] South Africa consists of high levels of inequality, with especially large and persistent inequality in income distribution. It is common to ascribe South Africa's high levels of inequality and poverty to racial discrimination and, in particular, apartheid colonialism. This is primarily because racial discrimination under, first British colonial rule and then apartheid distributed the spoils of economic growth along racial lines, which, according to van der Berg,[330] laid the foundation for patterns of further development and privilege in a society stratified by race. At least from a theoretical perspective, racial inequality in South Africa is a function of the political history which has transcended over three centuries and which is characterised by whites treating Africans as inferior and subhuman.

From an economic point of view, income inequality is a function of the labour market – South African poverty and inequality are strongly rooted in the labour market (see, for instance, Leibbrandt et al).[331] Van der Berg[332] demonstrates that South Africa is a country with infamously skew distribution of income and, consequently, high poverty levels for an upper-middle-income developing country. Bhorat et al[333] argue that income inequality in South Africa have to do with the structure of the economy. According to Narayan and Mahajan[334] the South African economy is characterised by high unemployment rates, where the narrowest measure places unemployment rate at about 25 per cent and the wage differentials in the labour market account for the high income inequality in South Africa.

Leibbrandt et al[335] illustrate that education affects the propensity of black people participating in the labour force, as well as their probability of being employed and earning some income. According to Bhorat and Hodge,[336] the South African labour market demand patterns reflect an increasing demand for highly skilled labour and decreasing demand for low-skilled workers, thus increasing the inequality. The labour market is influenced by the structure of the economy in South Africa – it might be in this context that Frye et al[337] characterise South Africa's inequality as 'structural inequality'.

The restructuring of the South African economy, by implication, would redress income inequality. To restructure the South African economy, sectors would need to be configured and articulated differently, the financialisation and internationalisation of the economy would need to be tampered with and Mineral Energy Complex (MEC) would need to change, as Chapters 4 and 6 have indicated. The restructured South African economy should create more jobs, and in particular employ Africans, especially the youth.

It is important to acknowledge that many economists in South Africa conclude that economic/income inequality has increased during the first twenty years of democracy because intra-inequality, within the African group, has increased. Seekings and Natrass[338] were first to publish a book arguing that the nature of income inequality in South Africa relates to class; that 'race had given way to class' and or the 'the basis of disadvantage shifted from race to class' (p.4). However, others have argued – see for instance Bhorat et al[339] – that the character of economic inequality in South Africa should be understood along racial lines.

Table 10.3 actually demonstrates that all population groups have experienced some increase in (in-group) inequality – it is not convincing that the African population group accounts for the significant increase in income inequality that post-apartheid South Africa is reported to be experiencing. In fact, income inequality for the African population group appears to be relatively steady from 2005 to 2011 (for the latest available data).

Table 10.3: Gini Coefficient by Population Group

	1975	1995	2005	2009	2011
African	0.47	0.49	0.56	0.54	0.55
White	0.36	0.39	0.45	0.39	0.42
Indian	0.51	0.45	0.53	0.49	0.45
Coloured	0.45	0.49	0.58	0.52	0.53

Source: Gumede (2015b:97)

In a ten-year period, from 1995 and 2005, as Table 10.3 shows, there was a relatively significant increase in income inequality within the African population group (from 0.49 in 1995 to 0.56 in 2005) but income inequality within the African population group has remained similar to the 2005 level, at least until 2011. Table 10.3 suggests that it is within the white population group that a significant increase in income inequality has occurred.

In addition to racial inequality and other inequalities in South Africa, there is a challenge of political inequality. While racial inequality concerns the gap between different population groups, political inequality refers to differences with regard to influence over governmental decisions particularly within the same population group.[340] In the case of South Africa, political inequality can be found within the African population group. Because political inequality is fuelled by political patronage, South Africa has increasingly experienced service delivery protests.

Conclusion

This chapter discussed poverty and inequality which are among South Africa's most intractable development challenges. The evolution of policies and programmes aimed at reducing poverty and inequality was also discussed. A broad analysis in this chapter confirms that race remains a key marker of inequality (and poverty) in South Africa; this is linked, in the main, to the ramifications of apartheid colonialism. There is a general consensus in South Africa that poverty and inequality, particularly income inequality, remains high. These two development issues are primarily linked the negative legacy of apartheid colonialism, as well as the structure of the economy.

Key Terms

Absolute Poverty: A condition where a person does not have the minimum amount of income needed to meet the minimum requirements for basic living needs.

Gini Coefficient: A measure of the inequality of income distribution, a value of 0 expressing total equality and a value of 1 expressing maximal inequality.

Human Development Index: A summary composite index that measures human development based on three aspects: longevity, knowledge and a decent standard of living.

Income inequality: Unequal distribution of household or individual income across the various participants in an economy.

Inequality: Social disparities, characterised by the existence of unequal opportunities and rewards within a group or society

Labour Market: A market where workers and employers interact for a wage or salary.

Political Inequality: Differences with regard to influence over governmental decisions, particularly within the same population group.

Political Patronage: The use of state or governmental resources or political power to benefit one's acquaintances.

Poverty: A state or condition in which an individual or a community cannot enjoy the minimal basic standard of living due to financial constraints.

Racial Inequality: The unequal distribution of opportunities and rewards along racial lines.

Relative Poverty: A situation whereby a household income level is below a given proportion of average national income.

Social Inequality: The existence of unequal opportunities and rewards for different social positions within a social group or society.

Structural Inequality: A condition where one category of people is attributed an unequal status in relation to others.

11

Spatial Planning

Introduction

This chapter discusses the concept of spatial planning, starting with the role that British colonialism and the Afrikaner apartheid system played in spatial planning during apartheid colonialism. It also outlines the main policies, laws and other initiatives that have been pursued, with regards to spatial planning, since 1994. In that context, the chapter also explores how and whether the new policies and legislation for spatial planning are redressing the colonial apartheid geography. In the main, it would seem that South Africa is still largely characterised by apartheid geography.

Spatial planning in South Africa has predominantly been influenced and, in most instances, shaped by racial laws and policies dating back to British and Afrikaner white minority rule. One of the main laws that began the process of systemic spatial planning in South Africa is the 1913 Land Act, discussed in detail in Chapter 8. The 1913 Land Act forcibly put into place mechanisms and tools to displace African indigenous peoples from their ancestral land and economic base. Furthermore, in enacting the 1913 Land Act and its subsequent legislation, white minorities were allowed the opportunities to develop their rural economies and urban development into world class centres of living and education while Africans, and later on blacks in general, were relegated to the peripheries of underdevelopment.

The chapter begins by giving a brief background and a historical context on spatial planning in South Africa, before and after democracy. It then discusses the various spatial planning laws and policies. That is followed by a discussion of the characteristics of post-1994 spatial planning and the principles guiding post-apartheid spatial planning.

Historical Context

Spatial planning is both a theoretical and practical governance challenge, as well as a detailed field of study. Spatial planning is a contested concept and one that varies according to different regions and countries.[341] As both a concept and a practice, spatial planning is very diverse and, in many instances, it is concerned with trying to interpret how socio-economic development in form of policies and laws (at both regional and national government levels) within a country can be better planned and executed. Spatial planning is a government's development tool which also assists government's planners and citizens to interpret and implement effective socio-economic development initiatives. In simple terms, spatial planning refers to processes aimed at better use of land for socio-economic development.

South Africa's first encounter with both the concept and execution of spatial planning occurred in two ways or waves: the first was the colonial period in which European settlers began to trade and encroach more and more on African kingdoms. The second and more legally binding action of spatial planning occurred when 'the Native Land Act of 1913 prohibited Africans from purchasing or leasing land outside the reserves, from people who were not Africans. It also prohibited share-cropping in the Orange Free State. The Act listed areas totalling about 22 million acres, or about 7 per cent of the area of the Union of South Africa.'[342]

The legal and policy decision of what was then known as the Union of South Africa set in place the future of how South Africa's spatial planning history would (a) operate; (b) create socio-economic inequity; (c) set in place homeland operations; and (d) create a conglomeration of 'small South Africas' based on race. As time went on, the National Party majority in parliament began formulating more spatial planning laws and policies that created homelands (otherwise known as Bantustans) and ensured that the white minority received the best and most productive land.

Thomson[343] explains that:

> In 1936, fresh legislation created the South African Native Trust, managed by whites, and empowered it to buy more land for Africans from funds provided by parliament....Those areas, which were destined to be treated as the Homelands of all the African inhabitants of South Africa in the apartheid era, were scattered throughout the eastern half of the country. The land thus proclaimed as African formed a small proportion of the territory that African mixed farmers had occupied before the Mfecane and the white conquest.

It is due to this aforementioned history that the post-1994 South African government, the African National Congress (ANC) has sought to put in place numerous policies and legislation to redress spatial planning injustices emanating from apartheid colonialism. Numerous initiatives have also been undertaken to change the apartheid economic geography, as discussed below.

Spatial Planning Laws and Policies

As indicated above, the first major legal and policy considerations in relation to spatial planning in South Africa is the Land Act of 1913, which created a socio-political and socio-economic environment that: (a) allocated a white minority with the best available land; (b) stripped the majority of the African population of the economic means of sustaining themselves; and (c) ensured that the government would decide who resides where and who receives the best government aid in socio-economic development.

The other policy that greatly influenced how South Africa's spatial planning would function is the Group Areas Act of 1950. The Act can be said to have been an upgrade of the practice of apartheid in that it sought to create personal and business areas in urban centres for each racial grouping.

According to the South African History Archives, the Group Areas Act of 1950...[344]

> ... had the effect of entrenching the NP [National Party] policy of separate development, or 'apartheid', by assigning group areas to different racial groups. People were not free to choose where they wanted to live. The majority of both urban and rural land was allocated to the minority white population. The Act also cleared the way for nation-wide forced removals that ruined countless lives. One of the focal points, in opposition to the apartheid regime, was bringing an end to the system of influx control sanctioned through the Group Areas Act. Over the years, the system evolved and changed, but it retained the fundamental principle of separate development.[345]

Other laws and policies that were aimed at entrenching apartheid include the Black Homeland Citizenship Act of 1970, the Reservation of Separate Amenities Act of 1953 and other policies and laws which had a profound effect on African and black people's lives. In the post-apartheid dispensation, the main policies that have reshaped spatial planning include the Constitution, which repealed most of what apartheid rule implemented. The other important policy initiative pursued since 1994 is the National Spatial Development Perspective (NSDP).

The NSDP set in place firm spatial plans to attempt to reverse the colonial apartheid economic geography. As the NSDP [346] explains, 'the spatial reorganisation of a country can induce the release of tremendous physical and mental energies, whose practical outcome is certain to give rise to the socio-economic transformation necessary to launch a country on to a path of self-centred, self-reliant and self-sustaining development'. It is for this reason that the NSDP of 2006 is such a crucial and important post-1994 policy document, as it actively attempts to systemically engage with the spatial planning policies and laws of the previous era.

Characteristics of Post-1994 Spatial Planning

Although there are many, seemingly informal, initiatives to redress the ramifications of the colonial and apartheid spatial planning, the discussion here is limited to the NSDP. The NSDP[347] explains its mandate and the identification of the main characteristics of spatial planning as follows:

> The ultimate purpose of the NSDP in the South African setting is to fundamentally reconfigure apartheid spatial relations and to implement spatial priorities in ways that meet the constitutional imperative to provide access to basic services and economic opportunities to all, to alleviate poverty and inequality.[348]

Principles Guiding Post-apartheid Spatial Planning[349]

The NSDP, in an effort towards achieving what it terms its core mandate or ultimate purpose, is guided by five principles:

- **Principle 1:** Rapid economic growth that is sustained and inclusive is a prerequisite for the achievement of other policy objectives, among which poverty alleviation is key.
- **Principle 2:** Government has a constitutional obligation to provide basic services to all citizens (e.g. water, energy, health and educational facilities) wherever they reside.
- **Principle 3:** Beyond the constitutional obligation identified in Principle 2 above, government spending on fixed investment should be focused on localities of economic growth and/or economic potential, in order to gear up private-sector investment, stimulate sustainable economic activities and create long-term employment opportunities.
- **Principle 4:** Efforts to address past and current social inequalities should focus on people, not places. In localities where there are both high levels of poverty and demonstrated economic potential, this could include fixed capital investment beyond basic services to exploit the potential of those localities. In localities with low demonstrated economic potential, government should, beyond the provision of basic services, concentrate primarily on human capital development by providing education and training,

social transfers (such as grants and poverty-relief programmes). It should also reduce migration costs by providing labour-market intelligence to give people better information, opportunities and capabilities, to enable them to gravitate – if they choose to – to localities that are more likely to provide sustainable employment and economic opportunities.

- **Principle 5:** In order to overcome the spatial distortions of apartheid, future settlement and economic development opportunities should be channelled into activity corridors and nodes that are adjacent to or that link the main growth centres. Infrastructure investment should primarily support localities that will become major growth nodes in South Africa and the SADC region to create regional gateways to the global economy.

The principles found in the NSDP[350] can be said to ensure that South Africa's spatial planning character, post-1994, is one that: (a) has local government at its core; (b) aims to rectify human settlement or living conditions of the previously disadvantaged people' and (c) desires development to occur within the ambit of local or municipal areas.

As indicated earlier, spatial planning is a multidimensional tool of analysis and also a practical socio-economic development framework. Therefore, when measuring how far democratic South Africa has come with regards to spatial planning, especially as laid out in the five NSDP principles, judging South Africa progress is very challenging but important. One of the key issues this chapter could raise in challenging whether spatial planning is occurring to the level needed to socio-economically grow all South African provinces is found in the fact that

> Gauteng generated 35.6 per cent or an estimated R675 billion of the gross domestic production last year, consolidating its position as a single largest contributor to the economy of the country. Thus, even though Gauteng has the smallest land area of 1.4 per cent in the country, its economy is more than twice that of KwaZulu-Natal or the Western Cape. Gauteng also contributed 7.7 per cent to the gross domestic product of Africa, an indication of the province's importance as one of the economic hubs of the continent.[351]

While it is understandable that Gauteng, as the economic hub of not only South Africa but also of the African continent as a whole, would generate such high GDP percentages, it is critical to remember that the history of Gauteng is closely entwined with the history of mining, manufacturing and subsequent economic development phases. Therefore, large numbers of Gauteng's citizens in the past migrated to South Africa from other south African provinces and neighbouring countries.

However, in democratic South Africa, this has created new problems and raised new questions. For instance, with Gauteng being the financial capital of South Africa, can its provincial and municipal governments be able to service all incoming citizens? Secondly, how will continuing influxes of people be catered for within the national and provincial budgets if numbers keep streaming in an undocumented fashion? Thirdly, how has the exodus of people from rural areas like Limpopo, KwaZulu-Natal and Eastern Cape affected those areas and South Africa's rural land dynamics?

Perspective Box: Spatial Planning

Pros	Cons
• Good spatial planning ensures basic amenities, e.g. housing, sewerage, transport services are better incorporated into planning for cities.	• Executing spatial planning could that mean having to work against the wishes and rights of people, in order to assist them.
• Spatial planning, when thoughtfully done, ensures that the quality of life of people is well catered for.	• It can be dangerous when left to untrained and unskilled bureaucrati personnel.
• Spatial planning in the modern era, when executed in a forward thinking manner, can and does assist in saving natural environment and resources of state.	• Spatial planning procedures and systems work in a world that is dynamic and ever changing; means certain mistakes are likely to be made in an attempt to apply hard spatial planning goals and objectives.

Explaining Development Dynamics

There remain many spatial challenges in South Africa. The case of Gauteng, as aa example, represents three key spatial planning challenges:

- Large unplanned migration numbers from South Africa and other African states: Gauteng, over the last two decades, has experienced large influxes of people from rural provinces such as Limpopo, Eastern Cape, KwaZulu-Natal and other provinces. In addition to this, due to numerous socioeconomic problems in countries such as Zimbabwe, Democratic Republic of Congo and Mozambique, other African citizens have also come to Gauteng, making the province a melting point of culture in South Africa, and Africa as a whole.

- Physical strain on housing, healthcare and treasury resources: The large number of people that have come into Gauteng, has meant that the Gauteng government has to spend vast resources to ensure that the system works. Over the last five years, various service delivery strikes and protests have shown how challenging managing the province is despite large influxes of differing peoples.

- Transport challenges and movement: Due to the large numbers of people and also the Apartheid spatial planning (where townships and cities are spread apart), the province has had to invest large amount of capital on ensuring that buses operate, roads are maintained, new roads are built, new transport systems are delivered, and so on. These developing challenges clearly illustrate why Gauteng, as a province, is one of the most spatially challenging regions to work and live in.

The North West province, and Rustenburg in particular, illustrates the challenges rural areas and non-dynamic economies (Rustenburg and North West, rely heavily on mining royalties) in South Africa face. The North West therefore provides three key interesting points for discussion relating to spatial planning:

- Non-traditional migration patterns: Due to the job-specific industries such as mining, the North West, especially Rustenburg, has migration that is purely predicated on people mining. It is therefore no surprise that in areas such as Marikana and its surroundings, the major problem has been housing, basic amenities and other developmental problems.

- Challenges of fast-paced development: The economy of Rustenburg and North West faces the challenge of having to develop while being predicated on a non-dynamic economic entity like platinum. While it has helped the province and city to have this entity, it does make it difficult to develop using an entity that has its value firstly in the stock exchange and private sector-led companies.

- Managing smaller resources: While the Rustenburg area is served by a single municipality, the municipality does not derive its capital directly from the mining houses and entities, but from the national government. This means that smaller non-metro municipalities have to contend with the challenges of migration, housing shortages, and stagnant socio-economic and other problems with limited resources, as these smaller municipalities lack additional sectors to add additional capital to their revenue streams.

Conclusion

This chapter sought to briefly discuss key phenomena affecting spatial planning in a country that has been severely affected by unjust spatial planning which favoured a white minority at the expense of indigenous African and black population. The chapter merely discussed and described what has previously taken place. The post-apartheid administrations have pursued various policies to correct apartheid spatial planning. However, although many initiatives have been undertaken to reverse apartheid spatial relations, there is still a very long way to go.

Key Terms

National Spatial Development Perspective: The post-apartheid policy aimed at addressing some of the problems caused by British colonialism and Afrikaner apartheid rule in the areas of spatial planning and economic development in South Africa.

Spatial Planning: How land (or even space) is utilised for purposes of development.

PART III

TOWARDS A DEVELOPMENTAL STATE

12

Post-apartheid South African Society

Introduction

This chapter describes the evolution of democratic South Africa, starting with processes that brought about democracy in South Africa through the 27 April 1994 elections. Chapter two has already covered some of the relevant issues in detail. However, this chapter discusses different views and perspectives regarding the transition from apartheid to democracy. It highlights linkages between some aspects of the apartheid dispensation and the democratic period, at least for the first two decades of democracy. It also deals with main socio-economic fissures and discusses power dynamics in post-apartheid South Africa. Overall, although apartheid policies and legislation have been repealed and new policies and legislation put in place, South Africa still remains a deeply divided society; and from the perspective of nation building, it seems South Africa is still very far from being characterised as a nation.

When speaking about a post-apartheid society, it is critical to understand that one is referring to a very broad and sometimes complex analysis of society. In simple terms, the post-apartheid South African society broadly refers to the formal ending of the separate development and oppression by the National Party (NP) and British Imperial rule. We can talk of a post-apartheid South African society as far as the laws such as the 1913 Land Act, 1950 Group Areas Act, 1953 Bantu Education Act and many others no longer obtain, or that formal discrimination and racism have been abolished.

This chapter focuses on how government, business and civil society interact with one another and the rest of society since political independence, and discusses where political power lies. It begins with a brief background and historical context regarding the making of the South African society. This is followed by a discussion of changes and shifts that have taken place since 1994 in the processes of creating a post-apartheid South African nation. The chapter pays particular attention to (a) major shifts in society since the end of apartheid; (b) narratives of unity; and (c) divergent points of the new South Africa, and attempts to define what the major power dynamics are. Before concluding, the chapter characterises post-apartheid South African society by highlighting salient factors that define South Africa since political independence.

Historical Context

When discussing a post-apartheid South African society and what power relations look like, it is critical to first understand three key periods in the history that have shaped the society to date, namely: 1652-1795; 1795-1870 and 1948-1994. The first period (1652-1795) represents colonial exploits of the Dutch kingdom and its particular type of colonialism, which used commercial entities like the Dutch East Indian Company (DEIC). It was during this time that the Cape of Good Hope (present-day Cape Town) slowly began to be used as a place of trade and stop-over on the way to get to Asian colonies and spice markets.[352] Although the periods (i.e. 1652-1795; 1795-1870 and 1948-1994) are said to be the most important in understanding the making of what is now known as South Africa, there are many other important historical moments, dating before 1652, that are worth acknowledging.[353]

The period 1795-1870 represents the ascent and eventual colonialism of the British Empire of the Cape, which eventually became what we now know as South Africa. It was during this period that the development of mining, financial institutions and other activities evolved.[354] The years 1948-1994 formally represents the period in South Africa's history when the Afrikaner nationalists were in power and formally installed a system of apartheid. It was during this period that the majority of Afrikaner people would, like the English citizens of South Africa, benefit from the use of the state to gain not only political but also economic power.[355] The end result of the white minority rule was that, eventually, African peoples' land was confiscated (through the Land Act of 1913), their movement across the country was restricted and they were legally forced to live in Bantu areas, based on their ethnic classification (through the Population Registration Act of 1950, Group Areas Act of 1950, Prohibition of Mixed Marriages Act of 1949, Black Homeland Citizenship Act of 1970 and Reservation of Separate Amenities Act of 1953). The education system of South Africa was configured to favour white (through Bantu Authorities Act of 1951 and Bantu Education Act 1953).[356]

It is therefore important to understand that when discussing post-apartheid South Africa and South African society, the focus is on 350 years of systematic oppression and dispossession. The era of apartheid, its legislation and institutions through which the ideology was implemented, produced and left a legacy of persistent poverty and extreme inequality that spans 300 years. So, the society is confronted with massive 'accumulated disadvantages', particularly for the majority of South Africans, which can only be addressed collectively.[357]

Therefore, any change to formerly oppressive laws and ways of thinking was bound to be an exercise in the creation of something not only new but also significantly new to both victims and oppressors. Mamphele Ramphele, a South African politician, characterises transforming South Africa as equivalent to changing an aeroplane engine while the airplane is airborne.[358]

Changes and Shifts in the South African Society

As discussed in Chapter 2, it is important to bear in mind that early African kingdoms and socio-economic development were interrupted by European colonialism and apartheid rule. However, when outlining what constitutes major shifts in South African post-apartheid society, this chapter mainly discusses (a) unbanning of anti-apartheid political parties; (b) the Convention for a Democratic South Africa (Codesa); and (c) the creation of a new Republic of South Africa.

Unbanning of Anti-apartheid Political Activisms

F.W. De Klerk, the last apartheid president, announced the unbanning of the African National Congress (ANC), Pan-Africanist Congress of Azania (PAC) and other liberation movements like the Black Consciousness Movement (BCM) and the United Democratic Front (UDF) in 1990, and also the unconditional release of Nelson Mandela from 27 years in jail.[359] The unbanning of political activism dramatically changed what and how South African whites and blacks would interact and relate, firstly at a political level and secondly at a social level. Another important historical moment was the 17 March 1992 Referendum for white South Africans on – the majority of whites voted in favour of democratic elections, but almost 32 per cent were not in favour of political reforms towards a democratic South Africa.

The unbanning of political parties ushered in a new era from legal and political perspectives. While numerous events would transpire that would slow down the pace at which apartheid as a system was dismantled, the unbanning of liberation parties/movements began a new era for post-apartheid South African society.

Convention for a Democratic South Africa

Some of the key defining features of a post-apartheid South Africa emanate from the Convention for a Democratic South Africa (Codesa). The first and second Codesa pivotal points: (a) South Africa's future political stability rests on an understanding that no one party won the battle, but rather negotiations set South Africa's post-apartheid narrative and system;[360] and (b) the transition from dictatorial and oppressive apartheid NP rule would be done in a manner that sought to maintain certain institutions and rights of the minorities, while also recognising the historical injustices of apartheid colonialism. The Codesa negotiations were therefore an attempt to systemically create a decision making environment where a new South Africa could be agreed upon.

However, although Codesa meetings seemed like a series of smooth interactions, it is important to highlight the fact that two years before the negotiations and interactions began on 20 December 1991, many tragic and challenging events had occurred.[361] For example, the South African Communist Party's General Secretary, Chris Hani, was assassinated by right-wing elements (i.e. Janusz Waluce and Clive Derby-Lewis). Also, not all liberation movements participated in the negotiations.

New Constitution

One of the lasting legacies of the Codesa meetings was that an interim South African Constitution was drafted which later in 1996 became the Republic of South Africa's Constitution. The 1996 Constitution of the Republic of South Africa is one of the hallmarks of the post-apartheid South African society: it is a document that has numerous nuances such as Chapter 2 which contains the Bill of Rights, and caveats such as Chapters 4 and 10 which explain how the President and National Executive, Public Administration function as well how South African citizens should interact with one another and government.[362]

The 1996 Constitution of the Republic of South Africa has been important in the making of the post-apartheid society as it constitutes the 'foundations' on which citizens interact with the state and other democratic institutions of government and also find recourse for other non-political matters. It is the Constitution that best captures the aims and objectives of a post-apartheid society, as it states:

> We, the people of South Africa, recognise the injustices of our past; honour those who suffered for justice and freedom in our land; respect those who have worked to build and develop our country; and believe that South Africa belongs to all who live in it, united in our diversity. We therefore, through our freely elected representatives, adopt this Constitution as the supreme law of the Republic so as to: Heal the divisions of the past and establish a society based on democratic values, social justice and fundamental human rights; Lay the foundations for a democratic and open society in which government is based on the will of the people and every citizen is equally protected by law; Improve the quality of life of all citizens and free the potential of each person; and Build a united and democratic South Africa…[363]

Hence, any discussions about a post-apartheid South African society should begin or include the Codesa negotiations and the eventual end product of that era and time – the 1996 Constitution of the Republic of South Africa. These two landmarks exhibited the drive of numerous ordinary people and leaders, as well as political and non-political desire to become citizens of the first republic of South Africa, despite the numerous problems that would need to be dealt with, going forward.

Narratives of Unity

A part of the early post-1994 narrative of trying to unify South Africans, for them to see one another as joint owners of the Republic of South Africa, was the investment in soft-power politics by government and other non-government entities. Key defining moments in this regard were: (a) sporting events like the 1995 Rugby World Cup, 1996 African Nations Cup and subsequent sporting events; and (b) active creation of new symbols of unity like the national anthem and flag.

Sporting Events

Sporting events like the 1995 Rugby World Cup (RWC) helped create a new narrative of what it means to be South African. While in the past rugby was viewed and used as a sport to advance the interest of the white minority, by the end of the RWC, images of the new President of the Republic of South Africa, Nelson Mandela, and Springbok (South African rugby team) captain, Francois Pienaar, standing together wearing the same Number 6 green jerseys came to symbolise the soft-power effect of sport in South Africa.[364]

Subsequent sporting events like the 1996 African Cup of Nations' victory by Bafana-Bafana (South African national football team) in South Africa, led by a white South African captain, Neil Tovey, again with Nelson Mandela present, are testaments of the soft-power techniques used. Events such as this would further show how South African post-apartheid political leaders, especially Nelson Mandela, would leverage sports to gain soft-power for future government works and policies.[365] This approach of using soft-power to 'unite South Africans' would continue even into the late 2000s as exemplified by South Africa's hosting of the FIFA Football World Cup™ in 2010.

Creation of Unitary National Anthem and Flag

The adoption of new symbols of unity such as the South African flag and national anthem did not just arise from the higher echelons of power (i.e. political parties) but included ordinary civil servants like Frederick Brownell (State Herald), who designed the new South African flag. And in the case of the South African national anthem, it was a compromise between the original 'NkosiSikelel' iAfrika' written by Enoch Sontonga in 1897 and 'Die Stem van Suid-Afrika' composed by C.J. Langenhoven in 1918.[366]

Divergent Points and Defining Major Power Dynamics

The first half of this chapter began by outlining key historical events and defining certain key soft-power events like the creation of a national flag and anthem, the following segment will outline how such events were necessary in order to foster positive power dynamics. The power dynamic in question first relates to 'moral capital'. While the apartheid government and rule came to be reviled and rendered obsolete by the Anti-Apartheid Movement and other forces in the late 1980s, one of the greatest weapons or powers gained by post-Apartheid government of the ANC was moral capital which Kane describes as 'moral prestige – whether of an individual, organisation or a cause – in useful service.'[367]

This capital was best exemplified by the Nelson Mandela Presidency, which received much international and local support premised on the late president's moral capital. This aspect of power hinges on the fact that society, first voters and then non-political actors, trust government or non-governmental institutions. This form of power has been cited as being needed for building trust among society or institutions.[368] It hinges on citizens' ability to trust that government, civil service or business entities will do things for their best interest, and would not simply take them for granted.

As part of moral capital, the wisdom of the late president, Nelson Mandela, to establish a Truth and Reconciliation Commission, should be acknowledged. The TRC, established through the 1995 Promotion of National Unity and Reconciliation Act, was aimed at a process whereby victims and perpetrators discussed the harm that perpetrators of apartheid crimes caused, towards obtaining the victims' forgiveness.

Divergent Points due to Non-moral Capital

The post-apartheid South African society was initially characterised by the national government and political leaders being the primary custodians of both moral and non-moral capital. However, as South Africa entered its second decade of democracy, numerous signs of the bonds between citizens and political institutions (government and political parties) were breaking down. Some cite the declining number of eligible citizens who are not voting, service delivery protests, and growing number of concern about the enrichment of politicians at the expense of citizens, failure of government institutions to deliver quality education and health services, and other problems that create distrust in government authority.[369]

Second Power Dynamic

The second power dynamic that exists within the post-apartheid society is a two-fold one: namely, that of capital/financial resources and governmental power in the form of public policy.

- Capital/financial resources: While political power might have become more democratised, post-1994 elections and period, many commentators point out that financial or capital power still resides with white minority business and middle class. While this understanding of power has greatly been challenged by the ascent of a black middle class, the nature and ability of this middle class to effect wider socio-economic development has cast much doubt on whether white financial capital was affected in any manner, post-1994.[370]

- Public (government) policy: Government power, post-1994, has largely resided in its ability to do one of two things: Firstly, create/formulate socio-economic policies to advantage; or (b) attempt to improve the material condition of black (Africans in particular), key among which has been Black Economic Empowerment (BEE), which later became Broad-Based BEE or Reconstruction and Development Programme (RDP), Growth, Employment and Redistribution (GEAR), and other national laws/policies. Secondly, utilise national resources gained from individual and businesses' tax to affect socio-economic change, that is, build state-provided houses, invest in educational facilities and resources.

Divergent Points due Capital/Fnancial Resources and Public Policy

The inability to create a democratised form of shared capital/financial resources has meant that relations between white and black South Africans are not relations of equals. With financial resources still being the preserve of white South Africans, unequal power relations still characterise the working, living and even social environment.[371] The inability to ensure that blacks (Africans in particular) are able to share in the riches of the country means that they still depend largely on the ability of the government to provide quality education at primary and secondary level.

Furthermore, poor relations between a largely white private sector and largely black government have fostered a situation where neither party trusts each other enough to work together and invest in the wellbeing of South Africa. It is for this reason that the prime characterisation of financial/capital resource exploits for many citizens now stands as the 16 August 2012 Marikana Massacre, which was a result of the inability of private capital to pay fair wages for dangerous undertakings, yet pay executive management exorbitant salaries/bonuses.

South Africa's government continued failure to deliver much needed social and economic services (e.g. housing, poor electricity services, healthcare), crime problems and non-conviction of corrupt individuals, and the inability of the post-1994 to deliver much needed services, have created a growing situation where citizens no longer believe that government agencies and departments have their best interest at heart.

Perspective Box: Democracy

Pros	Cons
• South Africa is legally free of racially constructed legislation	• The plight of South Africa's African and coloured population seems not to be getting better
• The South African state has pursued processes to ensure that everyone has a voice	• There is no visible black middle class being developed, beyond a small clique of well-connected peoples
• South Africa's democratic institutions and culture is relatively well entrenched and developing	• Politics has come to be seen as a means of attaining better socio-economic standings
• The country has visible and known symbols that make it a multi-cultural nation	• There is a proliferation of political parties and no driving national ethos

Post-apartheid South African Society

There are many questions worth fleshing out when considering the post-apartheid South African society: Is it possible, as the democratic government continues, to grapple with numerous socio-economic challenges as more citizens are prone to move their trust from government institutions to non-governmental entities? Where do South African business, especially large private sector entities, rank in the eyes of South Africans? It is questions such as these that currently define the post-apartheid South African society. These and other questions highlight three important characteristics about the post-apartheid South African society:

Race still Matters

Despite major strides made since 1994 by both government and other role players, the unfortunate issue of race still permeates the South African society. Chapter 10 goes into a lot of detail on this issue. The recent report by the Institute for Justice and Reconciliation explains that:

> The relationship between race and class in South Africa paints a picture of class segregation with racial inflections. Majority of the poor continue to be black and segregated from the multiracial, urban middle class. This pattern is witnessed on the geographical landscape of South Africa, where our cities may demonstrate increasing racial integration, but townships and rural settlements continue to be poor, black and segregated as was intended by apartheid planners. This finding is important for racial reconciliation in South Africa and points to the need to address the relationship between material and social exclusion that results in the segregation of many poor black South Africans from inter-racial middle-class city spaces.[372]

What is important to glean from recent report of the Institute for Justice and Reconciliation, along such literature as that of Gumede,[373] is that the post-apartheid society has yet to properly deal with the phenomenon of race at both social and economic levels. While it cannot be denied that the legal, and in some sense tangible, racism aspects began by British Imperialism and accentuated by Afrikaner nationalism have been addressed to some extent, the real effects of racial inequality and systematic racism have yet to be properly attended – Afrikaner nationalism has to do with pride in the identity of being an Afrikaner and looking down on other population groups while imperialism refers to subordination and domination by countries considered imperial powers over the countries considered to be in the so-called periphery.

Economic Democratisation/Reconciliation: A Non-event

It is also clear that the South African government has not yet properly developed economic and social policies that address youth unemployment, poor entrepreneurial support and financial assistance, non-usage of rural areas for rural development, poor spatial planning to develop township economic development, and other variables of much needed development.

More pressingly, the economic opportunities that have arisen due to South Africa's reintegration into global economy have not gone round all South Africans. Despite interventions like GEAR and the RDP, the economic development needed by the vast majority of South Africans is still a work-in-progress. If the government and the private sector are able to combine their monetary and human capital, perhaps the problem of economic development will be better addressed.

Yet, for the last twenty-one years, the defining characteristic of the post-apartheid society with regards to economic development is a society that has been unable to compete with other developing nations, create good jobs for its youth and use its natural resources to conclusively deal with poverty and inequality. This development experience, twenty years since political independence, appears similar to the development experiences of many other post-independent African countries.

Government Losing Moral or Societal Trust

One of the fast developing characteristics of a post-apartheid South Africa, especially after the 1994 elections is the phenomenon of citizens rapidly losing trust (moral and social) in majority governing party of the ANC and various government institutions, as evidenced by:

- decreasing numbers of voters voting for the ANC
- frequency of violent protests against local and national authorities/institutions, due to poor service delivery record
- ever-increasing spectre of the ANC spawning or experiencing new breakaways, for example, the United Democratic Movement (started by ex-ANC members in 1997), Congress of the People (started by ex-ANC government ministers in 2008) and, more recently, the Economic Freedom Fighters (started by former ANC Youth League leaders in 2013).

These and other examples of how citizens, whether in civil society or ordinary citizens' protests, paint a picture of a society that is deeply at odds with the majority party in power. Furthermore, it shows a picture of a society that is quickly beginning to believe that government is not the protector and agent of their socio-economic aspirations. There are also increasing signs that South Africa might be drifting further away from becoming a society that was envisaged by the liberation movement.[374]

Conclusion

This chapter has highlighted main characteristics of the post-apartheid South African society, starting with critical moments that brought about democracy in 1994. It also dealt with main socio-economic fissures and discussed power dynamics in post-apartheid South Africa. The chapter sees the post-apartheid South African society as one that is fundamentally different from the one crafted using draconian laws and policies described in Chapter 2. Yet, while the draconian laws and policies of the British Empire and National Party have been done away with in the post-1994 period, the South African post-apartheid society is one that is still grappling with the socio-economic effects of over three hundred and fifty years of systemic racism and abuse of blacks (and Africans in particular), and is yet to fundamentally change in order to be considered a just and equitable society.

13

Conclusion

Introduction

As indicated in Chapter 1, this book has been informed by the notion of developmental state. It is therefore apt that its conclusion discusses the extent to which South Africa could be characterised as a developmental state. As already indicated, the concept of developmental state is associated with socio-economic development in Asian states, such as the Republic of Singapore, Malaysia, South Korea and Hong Kong. The socio-economic rise of countries like Singapore and Malaysia was largely premised on the fact that these states were able to socio-economically develop to very high levels due mostly to their economic policies, government institutions and pragmatic leaders. There are those, however, who argue that the notion of developmental state dates farther back than the rise of Asian economies, and even that some of the countries in the early years of political independence had aspects of developmental states. Bagchi,[375] for instance, suggests that modern-day Netherlands (formerly northern parts of the Spanish Netherlands) epitomises the first 'developmental state' which emerged in the sixteenth century while Mkandawire[376] has argued that some countries in Africa during the early years of the post-independence period could be viewed to have been 'developmental states'.

The post-1994 South African government became attracted to the notion of developmental state, influenced by experiences of the Asian countries mentioned above as well as some Scandinavian countries. Although South Africa explicitly stated, in 2007 in particular, that it aspires to be a developmental state, the desire for a developmental state in South Africa dates back to the 1955 Freedom Charter and later the 1992 Ready to Govern discussion document of the African National Congress and its Tripartite Alliance.

This chapter begins with a brief discussion of the concept of developmental state, followed by the strides South Africa has taken towards attaining this goal. It concludes with a discussion of policy options that can assist in addressing the socio-economic challenges that face South Africa twenty years since the dawn of democracy, so that South Africa can truly become a developmental state.

South Africa and the Developmental State

As indicated earlier, the developmental state concept has come to be identified with the rise of Asian states, in terms of high economic growth and ability to deliver societal development for their citizens during the early 1980s and late 1990s. The ability of Asian governments such as South Korea and Japan to formulate economic development policies that (a) coordinate government institutions and human capital development; (b) direct private sector investment and planning; and (c) have citizen and societal buy-in or trust, even if undemocratic decisions are taken; came to characterise the Asian developmental states.[377] Chapter 1 – Introduction – presents different scholars' views on the concept of 'developmental state'. For instance, Chalmers Johnson, who is said to be a pioneer on the study of developmental states, analysed the socio-economic development in Japan and characterised the country as a developmental state.[378]

As indicated in Chapter 1, a developmental state can be defined as 'a state that has prioritised economic development in its policies, designing policies that effectively enable the promotion of such a goal.'[379] This definition captures the essence of what has come to be known as the main characteristics of a developmental state, that is, placing socio-economic development at the core of its agenda through the use of pragmatic policies and institutions in partnership with other role players.

Among the main characteristics of a developmental state are:

- developmental ideology
- developmental elite
- embedded autonomy
- institutional capacity
- meritocratic recruitment
- insulated/neutral public servants

Developmental ideology has to do with views and perspectives that prioritise socio-economic development while developmental elite implies a political elite, in particular, that considers socio-economic development very important. Embedded autonomy, a phrase coined by Peter Evans, refers to a context where the government works with the rest of society but is still able to be autonomous so as to take informed and independent decisions. Institutional capacity refers to various capacities needed to successfully design and implement policies shaped by a long-term socio-economic vision. Meritocratic recruitment means that people that get employed in government are recruited on the basis of merit or their skills and training. Lastly, insulated or neutral public servants imply that those employed in government can be politically neutral or that politicians do not victimise them in instances of disagreements.

The success of the Asian developmental states as epitomised by (a) the rise of living standards of numerous citizens in South Korea, Singapore and Taiwan; (b) development of Asian companies such as Samsung, Sony, Toyota, and so on; and (c) high human capital development and innovation[380] has had a profound effect on how the first democratic government of South Africa, under the guidance of the African National Congress (ANC), came to be drawn into the notion of developmental state as a worthwhile concept to pursue.

Although the ANC mentions its desire for a developmental state in many documents before 1994, one of the clearest examples of the ANC's attempt to pursue the path of becoming or experimenting with the concept of a 'Development State' is found in its *2007 Strategy and Tactics*. The document indicates that the ANC intends to:

> ... build a developmental state shaped by the history and socio-economic dynamics of the South African society. Such a state will guide national economic development and mobilise domestic and foreign capital and other social partners to achieve this goal. It will have attributes that include: having the capacity to intervene in the economy in the interest of higher rates of growth and sustainable development; effecting sustainable programmes that address challenges of unemployment, poverty and underdevelopment with requisite emphasis on vulnerable groups; and mobilising the people as a whole, especially the poor, to act as their own liberators through participatory and representative democracy.[381]

The drive to make South Africa a developmental state also needs to be understood as different from the Asian experience,[382] in that it occurred in the context of a post-apartheid environment. Therefore, the developmental state of South Africa had to be constructed in a manner that takes into consideration the country's democratic aims and objectives. Mkandawire[383] explains that Asian developmental states worked and functioned due to their unique historical circumstances. In fact, Castells[384] identifies three cultural areas in the case of East Asia: the Japanese communitarian approach, the Korean patrimonial logic and the Taiwanese patrilineal logic. A case study exhibiting this point is the developmental state of Japan, which Johnson[385] explains was a 'plan rational state', where the state shaped economic development as it intervened in the development process and established substantive social and economic goals.

The point that Castells[386] makes is important in understanding the South African developmental state initiative. Castells[387] implies that, even in Asia, a developmental state comes about and exists within a particular context or circumstance. The issue of context and circumstance thus becomes very important in analysing any country, whether it is a developmental state or not. Edigheji[388] explains that South Africa, unlike certain Asian developmental states, has had to contend with numerous contexts and circumstances, the two most pressing being its historical racial circumstance and the ethos and operations of its constitution, which prizes democracy and human rights. The South African context, according to Edigheji,[389] suggests a creation of a 'democratic development state' which principally embodies the following four principles: electoral democracy, popular participation in the development and governance processes, economic growth, and state driven socio-economic development.

The long history and numerous complexities associated with the notion of 'developmental state' means that every country has attempted to implement it in one way or another within specific circumstances and contexts. The South African government, under the auspices of the ANC, has had to contextualise and attempt to pursue a developmental state against its unique democratic principles, as Edigheji[390] explains.

Political Economy Interventions

This chapter as a conclusion merely highlights the various initiatives and interventions pursued towards creating a democratic developmental state in South Africa because Part II of the book has already covered many relevant issues in detail. The circumstances and context in which the democratic government of South Africa found itself had to do with numerous challenges, such as gross racial inequality, poverty, low human capital development, end of the Cold War, rise of the doctrine of liberal economics and a bankrupt economy. Because many initiatives have been covered in detail, especially in Part II, this chapter only briefly presents some of the major policy and or programmatic interventions that were meant to assist in the creation of a South African developmental state.

Reconstruction and Development Programme (RDP)

This intervention attempted to create a developmental state in a uniquely South African manner. Like most developmental states, the Reconstruction and Development Programme (RDP) aimed to use the state to achieve economic development and societal change. As Terreblanche[391] explains:

> The RDP originated in an attempt by labour to produce an accord that would tie a newly elected ANC government to a labour-driven development programme…

the RDP envisioned as priority at the beginning to meet the basic needs of people: jobs, land, housing, water, electricity, telecommuni-cations, transport, a clean and healthy environment, nutrition, healthcare, and social welfare.

The RDP intended to create an institution that would attempt to ensure its implementation. According to Webster and Adler,[392]

> ... the RDP soon became the paradigm within which all development policies were to be discussed – an extended wishlist in which the homeless, the landless, workers, and even international bankers could take equal comfort. From 1994 to 1996, the RDP became ostensibly the guiding document of the Government of National Unity, located in an RDP Office within President Mandela's Office.

Even though the RDP did not remain as South Africa's key socio-economic development programme, it introduced the blueprint that served as a guide for subsequent socio-economic policies in South Africa, namely: government-driven economic development policy process, establishment of policy implementation institutions, and prioritisation of economic development, to effect societal change.

Growth, Employment and Redistribution Programme

The economic policy following on from the RDP was known as the Growth, Employment and Redistribution Programme (GEAR). It attempted to deal with South Africa's macro-economic context in a rather sophisticated and technical manner. As Visser[393] explains:

> In order to calm domestic capital and foreign currency markets, the government embraced a conservative macro-economic strategy – Growth, Employment and Redistribution (GEAR). It was developed by a technical team of 15 policy makers that comprised officials from the Development Bank of Southern Africa, the South African Reserve Bank, three state departments, academics and two representatives of the World Bank.

Despite GEAR slanting towards having a reduced role for government, it attempted to use the private sector in much the same way as the Asian developmental states did. This paradox or problem is captured in Visser:[394]

> ... perhaps the most important difference between the RDP and GEAR was that, while the former expected the state to conduct a people-orientated developmental policy, the latter saw South Africa's economic 'salvation' in a high economic growth rate that would result from a sharp increase in private capital accumulation in an unbridled capitalistic system. The government's task in this was to refrain from economic intervention and concentrate on the necessary adjustments that would create an optimal climate for private investment.

While GEAR as a policy framework can be said to have been a counter to the state-driven developmental state model, as witnessed in Asia, it needs to be remembered that the private sector in South Africa was envisioned by the very state itself and that the private sector was also seen as critical by Asian developmental states.[395] The major problem that the South African government of the ANC can be said to have run into is that it allowed the private sector too much power and privilege without guiding it accordingly.

Industrial Policy Action Plan

The later rise of Asian developmental states such as the Peoples Republic of China (PRC), which came to the fore in the late 1990s due mostly to its becoming 'the manufacturing factory'[396] of the world, inspired South Africa to attempt creating a developmental state premised on the country's industrial policies. The lead agent in attempting to ensure this has been the Department of Trade and Industry (DTI), through its Industrial Policy Action Plan (IPAP) which has undergone five stages of development. The DTI explains that:

> The overriding goal of the IPAP in this policy context is to prevent industrial decline and support the growth and diversification of South Africa's manufacturing sector. The balance of international evidence is that manufacturing is the engine of growth and employment of all economies that have achieved high gross domestic product (GDP) and employment growth. Manufacturing can generate significant job creation directly as well as indirectly in a range of primary and service sector activities.[397]

IPAP therefore can be seen as further evidence that the democratic government still views itself, and wants to be seen, as an active and real developmental state.

New Growth Path
In order to achieve the New Growth Path's stated goals and objectives a standalone ministry known as the Ministry for Economic Development[398] was set up. Through the New Growth Path (NGP) the government intended to amalgamate South Africa's previous economic development policies and produce an all-encompassing economic vision for the State.[399] The NGP[400] explains that it will...

> ... place jobs and decent work at the centre of economic policy. It sets a target of 5 million new jobs to be created by 2020. It sets out the key job drivers and the priority sectors that we will focus on over the next few years. It is based on strong and sustained, inclusive economic growth and the rebuilding of the productive sectors of the economy. Infrastructure development in particular is a foundation for creating more jobs and addressing rural under-development.

The overarching goal of the NGP can be said to be consistent with the aspirations of the ANC's *2007 Strategy and Tactics* document in that it still desires the South African state to become a functional developmental state and sees the economic development benefits of previous developmental states as being the only way in which South Africa can overcome its socio-economic problems.

National Development Plan

The vision of the National Development Plan (NDP), 'Vision 2030', though not a clear policy document, is the South African government's attempt to coordinate its planning processes in order to better achieve economic development. It aims to replicate some of the core characteristics of previous developmental state by (a) producing more science and engineering human capital; (b) having a single ministry coordinate planning in government; (c) leading both public and private sector dialogue and planning on economic development; and (d) creating policy unity/cohesion between the IPAP, NGP and other related government economic development policies.[401]

The National Planning Commission (NPC) explains that the NDP's central goals are:

> ... expanding employment and entrepreneurial opportunities on the back of a growing, more inclusive economy. This will require far greater commitment to deepening the productive base, whether in agriculture, mining, manufacturing or services. By 2030, South Africa should have a more diversified economy, with a higher global share of dynamic products, and greater depth and breadth of domestic linkages. Intensified stimulation of local and foreign markets will be needed, as well as strong conditions to promote labour-absorbing activities. Traded activities will act as a spur to growth, as will active stimulation of domestic opportunities and the linkages between the two.[402]

The NDP could be said to be South Africa's first real attempt at planning for a developmental state that has many of the technical attributes found in other developmental states like Singapore and Japan. One of the most important technical attributes the NDP has is a Planning Commission, which in theory is said to coordinate the planning aspects of economic development policy in most developmental states.[403] It will, therefore, be interesting to note whether the South African government's NPC will be able to replicate the success of the Singapore Planning Commission, or even the Indian Planning Commission, in how they were able to steer economic development process in their respective nations.

Pursuit of a Developmental State

The goal of trying to become a developmental state can be said to exist in part due to South Africa's colonial and apartheid history, more poignantly the effects of these two catastrophic events in history. The Asian developmental states have not only brought coordination to how states like South Korea, China and Singapore plan economic development but they have also assisted in ensuring their respective populations move from being formerly poor nations to middle income nations[404].

As Fritz and Menocol[405] explain:

> Success stories of developmental states in Asia provide powerful symbols, showing that poor countries can become considerably wealthier in a generation or two. Turning Malawi, Kenya, Bangladesh or Nepal into prosperous, well-governed countries may remain a daunting challenge, but the vision of such a trajectory is potentially a powerful one, which may indeed have a broader appeal and greater traction than one focused narrowly on 'poverty reduction'.

South Africa, since 1994, has pursued numerous initiatives aimed at making the country a developmental state. Of course, a South African developmental state cannot be exactly as any of the Asian developmental states because of many differences in circumstances and contexts. It might be still too early to conclude, firmly, whether South Africa would become a fully-fledged developmental state.

Way Forward

South Africa requires a new mix of policy instruments that would ensure that the economy grows substantially and, most importantly, creates jobs. In other words, over and above robust social policy, South Africa needs an economy that works better for society – not a society that adjusts to the so-called needs of an economy. To achieve this, South Africa needs to be an agile and capable developmental state. South Africa's greatest threat would be government and policy failures to transform the structure of its economy. The question of structural transformation of the economy therefore remains central to the debate on its developmental trajectory.

Chapter 4 discussed the structure of the South African economy and indicated what is involved in changing the structure of an economy. The South African economy has, in the recent past, been the main obstacle to social and economic transformation on two levels. First, its structure has remained relatively unchanged from the predominantly Mineral Energy Complex (MEC) bias as well as in terms of ownership patterns. Second, the economy, after stabilising in the 1990s, has not been able to emulate those of its peers (such as India, Brazil, Malaysia and Mauritius) with regards to economic expansion, and job creation in particular.

Policies for the economy – including a robust industrial policy – should make up the vision, as an explicit socio-economic development approach that would be agreed upon by all relevant role players. It is not enough, anymore, to have a mixed and capitalist economy, but rather South Africa should have used the opportunity presented by the global economic recession to craft its own socio-economic development model.

The second most important issue for social and economic transformation is jobs. South Africa needs to resolve the challenge of unemployment broadly, and youth unemployment, which has since reached crisis proportions, in particular. This is another broader economic policy issue, and more narrowly a labour market one. The restructuring of the economy should alleviate the unemployment challenge. To fully address the unemployment challenge, however, the labour market should function differently. The demand side of the labour market, firm behaviour in particular, requires more attention. The requirements on experience, especially for graduates, should be revised. Graduates, in particular, should receive in-service training and there should be a set of effective active labour market type of interventions to increase the probability that graduates in particular are absorbed by the labour market.

At a broader level, the informal economy should not be discouraged. South Africa's peers (India, for instance) have an informal economy that is effectively above the formal economy. As a temporary cushion, the informal sector plays an important role in alleviating unemployment and poverty. Similarly, the minimum wage proposals that have been tabled should be concluded as soon as it is feasible – that would also, among other things, need that South Africa agrees on a poverty line. To address unemployment, a consensus is needed on the vision for the economy.

As indicated earlier, the gains on social development and social welfare in the post-apartheid South Africa are commendable. However, such gains are not enough, so far. Besides challenges of wider reach, the country is confronted with the challenge of the quality of social services. Therefore, implementation of programmes for social upliftment should be improved. Education and skills development, as well as healthcare services should also be improved.

To successfully transform society, as Mkandawire[406] argues, collective interventions directly affecting transformation in social welfare, social institutions and social relations are critical. In other words, social policy should transform social welfare, social institutions and social relations. It can be argued that social policy – if it exists in South Africa – has not been successful in transforming social institutions and social relations. The labour market is one of critical social institutions that remain significantly untransformed. Broadly speaking, there is merit in the argument that social relations remain largely untransformed too.

It is in this context that South Africa needs to rethink its social policy. Social policy should work in tandem with economic policy towards advancing wellbeing – both subjective and objective. Therefore, rethinking social policy should be undertaken jointly with improving economic policy. These policies can only work with a clear vision for the economy and the society at large.

The answer to South Africa's woes, from a policy perspective, is reform of the economy in particular. The strategies and programmes that have been introduced since the mid-2000s have not addressed the policy constraints that needed reform; but rather, programmes and strategies not informed by policy have been followed. Therefore, more policy thinking should be exercised for both social and economic transformations. Most importantly, policy should be pursuing the vision for the economy agreed upon through national consensus.

Conclusion

This chapter has broadly summarised, from a political economy point of view, the state of South Africa since 1994. Taken together with Part II chapters, it is concluded that many initiatives have been pursued to transform South Africa. However, there remains many challenges, most of which have to do with the historical experience of apartheid colonialism – and some might have to do with global power relations. Although there are significant interventions that are necessary if South Africa is to be a fully fledged developmental state, there are some policy initiatives that can be undertaken in order to ameliorate most of the socio-economic challenges facing post-apartheid South Africa, hence the proposed mix of policies.

Notes

1. Mandela, N., 1994, 'The State of the Nation Address', National Assembly, Cape Town, 24 May 1994.

2. Mohammed, S., 2010, 'The State of the South African Economy', in J. Daniel, P. Naidoo, D. Pillay and R. Southall, eds., *New South African Review 1: 2010: Development or Decline?* Johannesburg: Wits University Press.

3. Mhone, G., 2004, 'Organisational and Institutional Implications of a Developmental State', Human Sciences Research Council paper, Pretoria: HSRC.

4. Wai Yip So, B., 2007, *Does China Follow the Path of Taiwan's Developmental State Model? The Rise of Hsinchu Science Park and Zhongguancun Science Park,* Department of Public Policy and Management, Taiwan: I-Shou University.

5. Gumede, V., 2008a, 'Public Policy Making in a Post-Apartheid South Africa – A Preliminary Perspective', *Africanus: Journal of Development Studies,* 38 (2), p. 9.

6. Evans, P., 1995, *Embedded Autonomy: States and Industrial Transformation,* Princeton: Princeton University Press.

7. Leftwich, A., 1995, 'Bringing Politics Back In: Towards a Model of a Developmental State', *Journal of Development Studies,* Vol. 31(3), pp. 400-427.

8. Cummings, S. and Nørgaard, O., 2004, 'Conceptualising State Capacity: Comparing Kazakhstan and Kyrgyzstan', *Policy Studies,* 52(4), pp. 685–708.

9. Luiz, J., 2002, 'South African State Capacity and the Post-apartheid Economic Reconstruction', *International Journal of Social Economics,* Vol. 29(8), pp. 594-614.

10. Ibid.

11. Swilling, M., Breda, J., Van Zyl, A. and Khan, F., 2006, 'Economic Policy-making in a Developmental State: Review of the South African Government's Poverty and Development Approaches, 1994-2004', *Economic Policy and Poverty Alleviation Report Series,* Research Report 3.

12. Edigheji, O., 2007, *The Emerging South African Democratic Developmental State and the People's Contract,* Johannesburg: Centre for Policy Studies.

13. Dikeni, L., 2012, *South African Development Perspectives in Question,* Johannesburg: Real African Publishers, p. 37.

14. Hirsch, A., 2013, 'Aspirations to an Elusive Developmental State: The Obstacles to Deep Reform', in B. Ngcaweni, ed., *The Future We Chose: Emerging Perspectives on the Centenary of the ANC,* Pretoria: AISA Press, p. 308.

15. Mathekga, R., 2013, 'State Evolution and Sovereignty; The Case of South Africa', in M. Ndletyana and D. Maimela, eds., *Essays on the Evolution of the Post-Apartheid State: Legacies, Reforms and Prospects,* Johannesburg: Real African Publishers, p. 226.

16. Ibid, p. 45.

17. Mkadawire, T., 2001a, 'Thinking About Developmental States in Africa', *Cambridge Journal of Economics,* Vol. 24, pp. 289-313.

18. Marais, H., 2010, *South Africa Pushed to the Limit: The Political Economy of Change,* Claremond: UCT Press, p. 346.

19. Turok, B., 2008, *Wealth Doesn't Trickle Down: The Case for a Developmental State in South Africa,* Cape Town: New Agenda, p. 4.

20. Bagchi, K.A., 2000, 'The Past and the Future of the Developmental State', *Journal of World Systems Research*, Vol. XI(2), pp. 398-442.

21. Robinson, M. and White, G., eds., 1998, *The Democratic Developmental State: Political and Institutional Design,* Oxford: Oxford University Press, p. 22.

22. Ibid, p. 56.

23. Ibid.

24. Op.cit.

25. Johnson, C., 1982, *MITI and the Japanese Miracle: The Growth of Industry Policy 1925-1975,* Stanford: Stanford University Press, p. 152.

26. Onis, Z., 1991, 'The Logic of the Developmental State', *Journal of Comparative Studies,* Vol. 24, no.1, pp. 109-126.

27. Castells, M., 1997, *The Rise of the Network Society, Volume I,* London: Blackwell.

28. Ibid.

29. Ibid, p.9.

30. Ake, C., 2000, *Democracy and Development in Africa,* Maryland: Brookings Institution.

31. Sen, A., 2009, *The Idea of Justice,* London: Allen Lane.

32. The United Nations Educational, Scientific and Cultural Organization (UNESCO), 1977, *The Historiography of Southern Africa,* Proceedings of the Experts Meeting held at Gaborone, Botswana, 7 – 11 March.

33. Ibid.

34. Op.cit.

35. Thompson, L., 2000, *A History of South Africa,* Cape Town: Jonathan Ball Publisher.

36. Boahen, A., 1985, *General History of Africa VII,* Paris: UNESCO.

37. Op.cit.

38. Ibid.

39. Le Fleur, A. and Jansen, L., 2013, *The Khoisan in Contemporary South Africa,* Berlin, Germany: Konrad-Adenauer-Stiftung.

40. Barnard, A., 2003, *Diverse People Unite: Two Lectures on Khoisan Imagery and the State,* University of Edinburgh: Centre of African Studies.

41. Lee, R. and Hitchcock, R., 2001, 'African Hunter-gathers: Survival, History and the Politics of identity', *African Study Monographs*, Suppl. 26, pp. 257-280, March.

42. Ibid.

43. Ibid.

44. The United Nations Educational, Scientific and Cultural Organization (UNESCO), 1977, *The Historiography of Southern Africa,* Proceedings of the Experts Meeting held at Gaborone, Botswana, 7 – 11 March.

45. Ibid.

46. Boahen, A., 1985, *General History of Africa VII,* Paris: UNESCO.

47. Ibid.

48. Ajayi, J., 1989, *General History of Africa VI,* Paris: UNESCO.

49. Underwood, P., 2007, *An Overview of South Africa,* Cape Town: University of Cape Town, Centre for Information Literacy.

50. Mofuoa, K., 2011, *The Ethical Leadership of King Moshoeshoe 1 of the Basotho of Lesotho in the Nineteenth Century Southern Africa,* Australia: Charles Sturt University, Centre for Applied Philosophy and Public Ethics.

51. Ibid.

52. Ramoroka, M., 2009, '*The History of the Barolong in the District of Mafikeng: A Study of the Intra-Batswana Ethnicity and Political Culture from 1852 to 1950',* Doctor of Philosophy in the Department of the IsiZulu Namagugu, The University of Zululand.

53. Sarkin, J. and Cook, A., 2010, 'The Human Rights of the San (Bushmen) of Botswna', *Journal of Transitional Law and Policy.*

54. Ibid.

55. Op.cit.

56. Ibid.

57. Beach, D., 1974, Ndebele Raiders and Shona Power, *Journal of African History XV,* No. 4, pp. 633-651.

58. Op.cit.

59. Op.cit.

60. Op.cit.

61. Boahen, A., 1985, *General History of Africa VII,* Paris: UNESCO.

62. Ibid.

63. Op.cit.

64. Setumi, S., 2002, The Kingdom of Mapungubwe, http://policyresearch.limpopo.gov.za/bitstream/handle/123456789/535/theper cent20kindom%20of%20mapungubwe.pdf?sequence=1, Accessed on 20 October 2015.

65. Ramsey, S., 2011, 'Mapungubwe Rising', *Africa Geographic.*

66. Moffat, A., 2014, 'Iron Age Mining Links Ancient SA to the World', *Mail and Guardian, South Africa,* http://mg.co.za/article/2014-08-15-iron-age-mining-links-ancient-sa-to-the-world, Accessed on 27 November 2014.

67. Op.cit.

68. Gumede, V., 2011a., 'Policy Making in South Africa', in C. Landsberg and A. Venter, *South African Government and Politics* (4th ed), Pretoria: Van Schaik, p. 166.

69. Ibid.

70. Stewart, J. and Walsh, K., 1992, 'Change in Management of Public Services', *Public Administration*, 70(4), pp. 499-518.

71. Ibid.

72. Ferlie, E., Pettigrew, A., Ashburner, L. and Fiztgereld, L., 1996, *The New Public Management in Action*, Oxford: Oxford University Press.

73. Bale, M. and Dale, T., 1998, 'Public Sector Reform in New Zealand and Its Relevance to Developing Countires', *The World Bank Research Observer,* 13(1), p. 103.

74. Op.cit.

75. Gumede, V., 2008a, 'Public Policy Making in a Post-Apartheid South Africa – A Preliminary Perspective', *Africanus: Journal of Development Studies,* 38 (2): 7-23.

76. Morse, K. and Struyk, J., 2006, *Policy Analysis for Effective Development*, Colorado: Lynne Reinner Publisher.

77. Cohen, M., March, J. and Olsen, J., 1972, 'A Garbage-can Model of Organisational Choice', *Administrative Science Quarterly*, 17 (1), pp. 1-25.

78. Weick, K.E., 1979, *The Social Psychology of Organising Reading*, United States: McGraw-Hill Humanities.

79. Dye, T.R., 2002, *Understanding Public Policy*, New Jersey: Prentice Hall, p. 20.

80. Mitchell, B., 2002, *Resource and Environment Management,* Harlow, England: Prentice Hall.

81. Howlett, M. and Ramesh, M., 2003, *Studying Public Policy: Policy Cycle and Policy Subsystems.* Toronto: Oxford University Press.

82. Ibid.

83. Mégie, A., 2004, 'Mise en ceuvre', in Boussaguet, L., Jocquot, S. and Ravinet, P. *Diaitionnaire des Poltiques Publiques,* Paris: Presses de le Foudation Nationale des Science Politiques.

84. Constitution of the Republic of South Africa, 1996, Act 108.

85. See for instance, Gumede, V., 2011a, 'Policy Making in South Africa' in Landsberg, C. and Venter, A. *South African Government and Politics* (4th Ed.), Pretoria: Van Schaik.

86. The chapter also draws from Gumede, V., 2015, 'Economic Policy in Post-apartheid South Africa', in N. De Jager, Ed., *South African Politics,* Oxford: Oxford University Press.

87. The World Bank, 2014, *South Africa Economic Update: Fiscal Policy and Redistribution in an Unequal Society,* Washington, DC: World Bank.

88. Hanival, S. and Maia, J., (n.d.), *An Overview of the Performance of the South African Economy since 1994*, Pretoria: The Presidency of the Republic of South Africa.

89. African National Congress, 'The Freedom Charter', http://www.anc.org.za/show.php?id=72, Accessed on 28 December 2014.

90. Bodibe, O., 2007, 'Rethinking South Africa's Development Path: Economic Policy in the Era of Liberation', ANC Economic Transformation Policy Proposal, Centre of Policy Studies, Vol. 20 No. 10.

91. African National Congress, 2007, 'Economic Transformation', African National Congress Policy Discussion Document, http://www.anc.org.za/docs/discus/2012/economic_transformations.pdf.,Accessed on 31 December 2014.

92. Bodibe, O., 2007, 'Rethinking South Africa's Development Path: Economic Policy in the Era of Liberation', ANC Economic Transformation Policy Proposal, Centre of Policy Studies, Vol. 20 No. 10.

93. The 'Ready to Govern' discussion document of 1992 spelt out – upfront – very specific goals of a democratic South Africa. The points quoted in the paragraph come from what was said, in the Ready to Govern discussion document, to be the ANC's Vision for the Future.

94. African National Congress, 1998, 'State Property Relations and Social Transformation', Available on: http://www.anc.org.za/show.php?id=306, p. 01., Accessed December 2014.

95. Op.cit.

96. Op.cit.

97. Ibid.

98. World Bank, 2014, *South Africa Economic Update: Focus on Export Competitiveness.* Washington, DC: World Bank.

99. Op.cit.

100. Evans P., 2007, 'Rethinking South Africa's Development: Expanding Human Capabilities as a Strategy of Economic Transformation', *21st Century Agenda for the Developmental State*, Centre of Policy Studies Vol. 20(10).

101. The Presidency of South Africa, 2007, Accelerated and Shared Growth Initiative (ASGISA), Pretoria: The government of the Republic of South Africa, June.

102. Op.cit.

103. The National Planning Commission, 2012, 'The National Development Plan: Vision 2030', Pretoria: The Presidency of the Republic of South Africa.

104. OECD, 2013, *OECD Economic Surveys: South Africa 2013*, Paris: OECD Publishing.

105. Van Aardt C.J., Ligthelm, A.A. and van Tonder, J., 2011, *A Broad Review of the New Growth Path Framework with Specific Emphasis on the Feasibility of Its Proposed Targets*, Pretoria: University of South Africa, Bureau for Market Research.

106. OECD, 2013, *OECD Economic Surveys: South Africa 2013*, Paris: OECD Publishing.

107. Kie-Song, M.R., 2009, *The South African Expanded Public Works Programme (EPWP)*, Conference on Employment Gaurantee Policies 2004-2014, June.

108. Ibid.

109. Ibid.

110. The Department of Public Works, 2011, *Annual Report: 2010/2011.*

111. The Presidency of the Republic of South Africa, 2008, *Joint Initiative on Priority Skills Acquisition.*

112. Ibid.

113. Fedderke, J., 2014, 'South Africa's Growth Performance', in R. Kanbur et al, ed., *Oxford Companion to the Economics of South Africa,* Oxford University Press.

114. Industrial Development Corporation, 2013, *South African Economy: An Overview of Key Trends Since 1994, Department of Research and Information,* Sandton, Johannesburg: IDC.

115. Op.cit.

116. Ibid.

117. Mayer, M. and Altman, M., 2006, *South Africa's Economic Trajectory: Implications for Skills Development,* Cape Town: HSRC Press.

118. Bhorat, H. and van de Westhuizen, C., 2010, 'Poverty, Inequality and the Nature of Economic Development in South Africa', DPUR Working Paper 12/151, Cape Town.

119. Gumede, V., 2015, 'Economic Policy in Post-apartheid South Africa', in N. De Jager, ed., *South African Politics,* Oxford: Oxford University Press.

120. Department of Trade of Industry, 2007b, *South Africa's Economic Transformation: A Strategy for Board-Based Economic Empowerment,* Avalable at https://www.environment.gov.za/sites/default/files/legislations/bbbee_act.pdf.

121. Acemoglu, D., Gelb, S. and Robinson, J.A., 2007, *Black Economic Empowerment and Economic Performance in South Africa,* Johannesburg: The EDGE Institute.

122. Kruger, L.P., 2007, 'The Impact of Black Economic Empowerment (BEE) on South African Businesses: Focusing on Ten Dimensions of Business Performance', *Southern Africa Business Review,* 15(3), pp. 207-233.

123. Ertner, R.M., 2013, 'Broad-based Black Economic Empowerment', Available at www.INTO_SA_eINFO-_Black_Economic_Empowermenr_South_Africa_2013_PDF.

124. Mbeki, M., 2009, *Architects of Poverty: Why African Capitalism Needs Changing,* Johannesburg: Picador.

125. Ibid.

126. Hamann, R., Khagram, S. and Rohan, S., 2008, 'South Africa's Charter Approach to Post- Apartheid Economic Transformation: Collaborative Governance on Hardball Bargaining' *Journal of South African Studies,* 23(1), pp. 21-37.

127. Kovacevic, N. 2007, 'Righting Wrong: Affirmative Action in South Africa', *Harvard International Review,* 6.

128. Bowman, G.A., 2012, 'Black Economic Empowerment Boucher' Available at www.bowman.co.za/BEE/BEEBrochure-Ir.pdf

129. South African Presidency, 2014, *Twenty Year Review South Africa,* Pretoria: Government Print.

130. Ibid.

131. Op.cit.

132. Department of Trade and Industry, 2005, *Integrated Small-Enterprise- Development Strategy: Unlocking the Potential of South African Entrepreneurs,* Pretoria: Department of Trade and Industry.

133. Department of Trade and Industry, 1995, *White Paper on National Strategy for the Development and Promotion of Small Business in South Africa,* Pretoria: Government Print.

134. Gumede, V., 2006, 'Small and Medium Manufacturing in South Africa: Constraints and Opportunities', in Roberts, S., ed., *Sustainable Manufacturing,* Cape Town: Juta Academic Press.

135. South African Presidency, 1996, *National Small Business Act of 1996, No. 102,* Pretoria: Presidency.

136. Department of trade and Industry, 2005, *Integrated Small-Enterprise- Development Strategy: Unlocking the potential of South African entrepreneurs,* Pretoria: Department of Trade and Industry.

137. Ibid.

138. Clark, N.L., 1994, *Manufacturing Apartheid State Corporations in South Africa,* Yale: Yale University Press.

139. South Africa Info.Key Sectors, http://www.southafrica.info/business/economy/sectors/, Accessed on 29 December 2014.

140. Op.cit.

141. Lall, S., 2004, 'Reinventing Industrial Strategy: The Role of Government Policy in Building Industrial Competitiveness', Discussion Paper 28, United Nations Conference on Trade and Development, April.

142. Robinson, J.A., 2009, 'Industrial Policy and Development: A Political Economy Perspective', Paper prepared for the 2009 World Bank ABCDE Conference in Seoul, June 22-24.

143. Kiliçaslan, Y. and Taymaz, E., 2002, *The Structure of Structural Change and Growth,* Middle East Technical University: Department of Economics.

144. Steenkamp, E., Rossouw, R. and Viviers, W., 2014, *Analysis of Export and Employment Opportunities for South African Manufacturing Industries,* Avaiable at www.nuw.ac.za/af/trade/artikels.pdf

145. Kaldor, N., 1978, *Capitalism and Industrial Development: Some Lessons from Britain's Experience in Applied Economics,* London: Duckworth.

146. Op.cit.

147. Clark, N.L., 1994, *Manufacturing Apartheid State Corporations in South Africa,* Yale: Yale University Press.

148. Cornell, V., 2011, *South Africa Today: How Do We Characterise the Social Formation,* Papers from the 2011 ILRIG April Conference, April.

149. Chabane, N., Machaka J., Molaba N., Roberts S., and Taka M., 2003, *10 Year Review: Industrial Structure and Competition Policy,* University of the Witwatersrand: School of Economic and Business Sciences.

150. Bodibe O., 2007, 'Rethinking South Africa's Development Path: Economic Policy in the Era of Liberation', ANC Economic Transformation Policy Proposal, Vol. 20 no. 10, Centre of Policy Studies.

151. Edigheji, O., 2007, 'Rethinking South Africa's Development Path: Reflections on the ANC's Policy Conference Discussion Documents', *Special edition of Policy: Issues & Actors,* Vol. 20 no. 10, Centre for Policy Studies.

152. Ibid.

153. The Department of Trade and Industry (DTI), 2007, *National Industrial Policy Framework,* Pretoria: The Government of the Republic South Africa.

154. Ibid.

155. Ibid.

156. Ibid.

157. The Department of Trade and Industry (DTI), 2014, 'Special Economic Zone (SEZ)', Available at http://www.dti.gov.za/industrial_development/sez.jsp, Accessed on the 31 December 2014.

158. Ibid.

159. Tang, V., 2008, 'Zoning in on South Africa's Industrial Development Zones', TIPS Annual Forum, University of KwaZulu-Natal, School of Economics & Finance, October.

160. Davies, R., 2014, 'Address by the Minister of Trade and Industry, Dr Rob Davies to the National Council of Provinces (NCOP), on the Special Economic Zones Bill 2013 February', Available at https://www.thedti.gov.za/editspeeches.jsp?id=2997, Accessed on 30 December 2014.

161. Op.cit.

162. Netshitenzhe, J., 2013, *Why Inequality Matters: South African Trends and Interventions*, Mapungubwe Institute for Strategic Reflection (MISTRA), Johannesburg: Woodmead.

163. Davies R., 2006, 'Manufacturing Exports and Employment Growth', Employment Growth and Development Initiative, Human Sciences Research Council (HSRC), Available at: http://www.hsrc.ac.za

164. Public Financial Management Act (PFMA), 1999, Section 1 of the PFMA, Pretoria: National Treasury of South Africa.

165. The National Treasury of South Africa, 2006, 'Current Position Regarding Governance and State Owned Entities (SoE's) in South Africa', Pretoria: The Presidency.

166. Human Science Research Council, 2012, *Presidential Review Committee on State Owned Entities,* Pretoria: The Presidency.

167. Ibid.

168. Ibid.

169. The National Treasury of South Africa, 2006, 'Current Position Regarding Governance and State Owned Entities in South Africa', Pretoria: The Presidency.

170. Op.cit.

171. PricewaterhouseCoopers, 2011, *State Owned Enterprises: Governance Responsibility and Accountability*, PwC.

172. Alexkor, Undated, *Our History,* Available at: www.alexkor.co.za/our-history.htlm.

173. Eskom, Undated, Company Information, Available at: www.eskom.co.za/OurCompany/CompanyInformation/Page/Company-Information-1.aspx.

174. Department of Public Enterprises (DPE), Overview SAA, Available at: www.dpe.gov.za/soc/Page/SAA.aspz

175. Ibid.

176. SABC., Undated, *About SABC,* Available at: www.sabc.co.za/wps/portal/SABC/SABCMANDATE.

177. Armscor, Undated, Corporate Information, Available at: www.amoroc.co.za/about/CorpInfo.

178. Chaves, D., 2014, State of State: The State is Dead! Long Live the State! Avaliable at: www.tni.org/files/download/state-of-power/hyperlink.0.pdf

179. The South African Communist Party (SAPC), 2012, 'The South African Road to Socialism', 13th Congress Political Programme of the SAPC 2012-2017.

180. Ibid.

181. Morrell, P., 1998, Air Transport Liberisation in Europe: The Progress So Far, *Journal of Air Transportation WorldWide,* 13(1).

182. Rapoza, K., 2014, 'Why UAE and Qatar Have the «World's Best» Airline', Available at: www.forbes.com/site/kenrapoza/2014/04/01/WhyUAEandQatarHavetheWorld'sBestAirline

183. Ryerson, M. and Hanes, M., ud., 'Capturing the Impact of Fuel Price on Jet Aircrafts Operating Cost With Engineering and Econometrics Model, University of Calafornia Transportation Centre (UCTC) Research Paper No. 884.

184. Rudarakanchanan, N., 2014, 'Platinum Strike: What You Need to Know as South African Miners Drop Tool', *Internal Business Times,* Available at: www.ibtimes.com/platimunm-strike-what-you-need-to-know-souuth-african-miners-drop-tools-1546544.

185. Inggs, M., 2010, 'Mine Nationalisation Will be Disasterous for South Africa's Economy', *Mine Weekly,* Creamer Media's, Available at: www.miningweekly.com.article/mine-nationalisation-will-be-disasterous-for-south-african-economy-2010-09-01.pdf

186. Masito, M., 2007, *Afrikaner Economic Empowerment (1890-1990) and Lessons for Black Economic Empowerment,* University of Pretoria: The Gordon Institute of Business Science.

187. Ibid.

188. OECD, 2013, *Economic Survey of South Africa.*

189. Pottinger, B., 2008, *The Mbeki Legacy,* Cape Town: Zebra Press, p. 188.

190. Centre for Development and Enterprise, 2008, *Land Reform in South Africa: Getting Back on Track,* Johannesburg: Centre for Development and Enterprise.

191. Ibid.

192. Pepeteka, T., 2013, *Parliamentary Exhibition, June 2013: South Africa, Our land- the 1913 Land Act: One Hundred Years On,* Available at:www.parliament.gov.za/content/ Land%20Act%20-%20Paper%203%20- %20Kobus%20- %20Final.pdf.

193. Ibid.

194. Rugege, S., 2004, *Land Reform in South Africa: An Overview,* Available at: http:// ccs.ukzn.ac.za/files/landreforminSouthAfrica.pdf, p. 01.

195. Ramphele, M., 2008, *Laying Ghosts to Rest: Dilemmas in the Transformation of South Africa,*Cape Town: Tafeberg.

196. Op.cit. p. 02.

197. Ntsebenza, L., 2007, *Land Redistribution in South Africa: The Property Clause Revisited, Available at: www.yale.edu/macmillian/apartheid/apartheid_part1/Land _Reform.pdf,* p. 03.

198. Ibid. p. 03.

199. Partridge, A., 2014, *Institutions and Land Reform: Lessons from Land Redistribution Policy in Post-Apartheid South Africa,* Western Cape: University of Western Cape.

200. Department of Rural Development and Land Reform, 2011, *The Green Paper on Rural Development and Land Reform.* Available at: www.ruraldevelopment.gov.za/legislation-and-policies/categories/7-green-paper.

201. Binswanger-Mkhize, H., Bourguignon, C. and van der Brink, R., 2009, 'Introduction and Summary', in H. Binswanger-Mkhize, C. Bourguignon and R. van der Brink, ed., *Agricultural Land Redistribution: Towards Greater Consensus,* Washington DC, USA: The World Bank.

202. Partridge, A., 2014, *Institutions and Land Reform: Lessons from Land Redistribution Policy in Post-Apartheid South Africa, Western Cape:* University of Western Cape.

203. African National Congress (ANC), 1994,*The Reconstruction and Development Programme: A Policy Framework,* Johannesburg: ANC, pp. 9-10.

204. Department of Land Affairs, 1997, *The White Paper on South African Land Policy,* Pretoria: Department of Land Affairs.

205. Ibid.

206. Kahn, N., 2007, *Land and Agrarian Reform in South Africa,* Johannesburg: Centre for Policy Studies.

207. Department of Land Affairs, 1994, *Restitution of Land Rights Act 22 of 1994,* Pretoria: Department of Land Affairs.

208. Republic of South Africa,1996, *Constitution of the Republic of South Africa 106 of 1996,* Pretoria: Government Print.

209. Weideman, M., 2004, 'Who Shaped South Africa's Land Reform Policy?' *Politikon,* Vol 31(2),pp. 219-238.

210. Kloppers, H. J. and Pienaar, G. J., (nd), *The Historical Content of Land Reform in South Africa and Early Policy,* Available at:www.saflii.org/za/journals/PER/2014/20.html, pp. 678.

211. Department of Land Affairs, 1997, *The White Paper on South African Land Policy,* Pretoria: Department of Land Affairs.

212. Ibid.

213. Ibid., p. 678.

214. Op.cit.

215. United Nations, 1988, *Global Strategy for Shelter to the Year 2000,* Available at: http://www.un.org/documents/ga/res/43/a43r181.htm.

216. Centre for Development and Enterprise, 2008, *Land Reform in South Africa: Getting Back on Track,* Johannesburg: Centre of Development and Enterprise.

217. Op.cit.

218. Partridge, A., 2014, *Institutions and Land Reform: Lessons from Land Redistribution Policy in Post-Apartheid South Africa, Western Cape:* University of Western Cape.

219. Ibid.

220. Lahiff, E., 2007, 'Willing Buyer, Willing Seller: South Africa's Failed Experiment in the Market-led Agrarian Reform, *Third World Quarterly,* 28(8), pp. 1577-1597.

221. Op.cit.

222. Ibid.

223. Op.cit.

224. Op.cit.

225. Greenburg, S., 2004., *The Landless People's Movement and the Failures of the Post-Apartheid Land Reform,* University of Kwa-Zulu-Natal: School of Development Studies.

226. Op.cit.

227. Van der Merwe, D., 1989, *Land Tenure in South Africa: A Brief History and Some Reform Proposal.* Available at: www.saflii.org/za/journals/PER/2014/20.html

228. Niewoudt, W. and Vink, N., 1995, 'Financing of Land Purchases by Small-scale Farmers', *Development Southern Africa,* 12(4), pp. 509-517.

229. Op.cit.

230. Op.cit.

231. Ibid.

232. Jacobs, P., 2003, *Support for Agricultural Development*, Cape Town: University of Western Cape, Programme for Land and Agrarian Studies.

233. Op.cit.

234. Twala, C. and Selesho, J., 2013, *Rural and Agrarian Development Discourse in a Post-Apartheid South Africa: An Agro-Ecological Challenge.* Available at: www.krepublishers.com/.../JHE-41-1-009-13-2377-Twala-C-Tx[2].pmd.pdf.

235. Ibid.

236. Liversage, H., nd., *Smallholder Agriculture and Food Security in the 21st Century,* Available at: www.ifad.org/events/gc/32/roundtable/2.pdf, p. 32.

237. Gumede, V. 2014a, 'Land Reform in Post-Apartheid South Africa: Should South Africa Follow Zimbabwe's Footsteps?', *International Journal for African Renaissance Studies,* Vol. 9(1), pp. 50-68.

238. Moyo, S., 2013, 'The Land and Agrarian Question in Zimbabwe', in Buthelezi, S., ed., *The Land Belongs to Us: The Land and Agrarian Question in South Africa,* Alice: Fort Hare University Press.

239. Ibid.

240. Liversage, H., nd., Smallholder Agriculture and Food Security in the 21st Century. Available at: www.ifad.org/events/gc/32/roundtable/2.pdf, p. 32.

241. National Planning Commission, 2012, *The National Development Plan 2030*, Pretoria: The Presidency, Ministry of Planning, p. 219.

242. Ibid. 220.

243. Gumede, V. 2014a, 'Land Reform in Post-Apartheid South Africa: Should South Africa Follow Zimbabwe's Footsteps?', *International Journal for African Renaissance Studies,* Vol. 9(1), pp. 50-68.

244. Gumede, V., 2013b, 'Public Sector Reforms and Policy-making: A Case of Education in an Emerging Developmental South Africa', in A. Kanjee, M. Nkomo, and Y. Sayed, eds., *The Search for Quality Education in Post-apartheid South Africa,* Pretoria: HSRC Press.

245. Kraak, A., 2008, 'The Education-Economy Relationship in South Africa 2001-2005', in A. Kraak and K. Press, eds., *Human Resource Development Review 2008: Education, Employment and Skills in South Africa,* Cape Town: HSRC Press.

246. Hungwe, K., 1994, 'Educational Policy in African Colonial Context: The Case of Instructional Media in Southern Rhodesia (1930-1980)', *African Studies Monographs,* 15(1), p. 2.

247. Ibid. p. 3.

248. Ruddell, D., 1982, 'Class and Race: Neglected Determinants of Colonial «Adapted» Education Policies', *Comparative Education*, 18, p. 293.

249. Tabata, I.B., 1979, *Education of Barbarism: Bantu (Apartheid) Education in South Africa,* London: Unity Movement of South Africa, p. 3.

250. Ibid. p. 6.

251. Lapping, B.. 1987, *South African Apartheid Bantu Education Quotes.*Available at: http://www.africanhistory.about.com/od/apartheidQts1.htm

252. Tabata, I.B., 1979, *Education of Barbarism: Bantu (Apartheid) Education in South Africa,* London: Unity Movement of South Africa, p. 37.

253. Ibid.

254. Op. cit.

255. Ali- Dinar, A.B.,1994, *ANC Education Policy,* Available at: http://www.africa.upenn.edu/Govern_Political/ANC_Education.html.

256. Ibid.

257. Jansen, J. and Taylor, N., 2003, 'Educational Change in South Africa,1994-2003: Case Studies in Large Scale Education Reform', *Country Studies Education Reform and Management Publication Series,* Vol. 2(1), p. 3.

258. Ibid.

259. South African Presidency, 2014, *Twenty Year review South Africa,* Pretoria: Presidency, p. 56.

260. Ibid.

261. National Department of Education, 2001, *White Paper 6 on Special Needs in Education and Training,* Pretoria: National Department of Education.

262. Ibid. p. 135.

263. Modisaotsile, B.M., 2012, *The Failing Standard of Basic Education in South Africa,* Available at: www.ai.org.za.

264. Gumede, V., 2013a, 'Public Sector Reforms and Policy-making: A Case of Education in an Emerging Developmental South Africa', in A. Kanjee, M. Nkomo and Y. Sayed, eds., *The Search for Quality Education in Post-apartheid South Africa,* Pretoria: HSRC Press.

265. Ibid.

266. Ibid.

267. Ibid. P. 135.

268. Ibid. P. 135.

269. South African Presidency, 2014, *Twenty Year Review South Africa,* Pretoria: Presidency.

270. Brown, S., 2007, *Leadership and Legitimacy,* Pretoria: Institute of Justice and Reconciliation, p. 16.

271. South African Presidency, 2014, *Twenty Year Review South Africa,* Pretoria: Presidency.

272. National Department of Education, 1998, *Green Paper on Further Education and Training: Preparing for the 21 Century through Education, Training and Work,* Pretoria: Department of Education. p. 10.

273. Hoeckel, K., 2007, *Key Evidence on Vocational Education and Training from Previous OECD Work, EDU/EDPC/CERI(2007)6/ANN1,* OECD.

274. Akoojee, S., and McGrath, S., 2007, 'Public and Private Further Education and Training in South Africa: A Comparative Analysis of the Quantitative Evidence', *South African Journal of Education, 27*(2), pp. 209-222.

275. Booyens, J.C., 2009, 'The Value Attached to Teaching Qualifications by Educators and Other Stakeholders at a Further Education and Training College in Southern KwaZulu Natal', Unpublished dissertation, University of KwaZulu Natal, Durban.

276. Ibid.

277. Kgope. P. and Baatjes, I., 2014, 'White Paper on Post-School Education and Training: Some New Policy Directions', *Post School Education Journal*, Vol. 1. Issue 1.

278. Ibid.

279. National Planning Commission, 2012, *The National Development Plan 2030,* Pretoria: The Presidency, Ministry of Planning.

280. Ibid. P.200.

281. Op.cit. p.295.

282. Op.cit. p. 135.

283. Lumby, J., 2003, 'Transforming Health Centers: Managing the Change Process', in: Thurlow M., Bush, T. and Coleman, M. eds., *Leadership and Strategic Management in Iran Health Centres,* London: Commonwealth Secretariat, p. 161.

284. van der Berg, S., Taylor, S., Gustafsson, M., Spaull, N. and Armstrong, P., 2011, *Improving Education Quality in South Africa,* Report for the National Planning Commission, Stellenbosch University: Department of Economics, p. 4.

285. National Education Collaboration Trust, 2013, *Education Collaboration Framework.*Available at: http://www.naptosa.org.za/index.php/doc-manager/00-general/130-ecf-brochure/file, Accessed 23 November 2014.

286. Ibid.

287. Ibid. p. 131.

288. van der Berg, S., Taylor, S., Gustafsson, M., Spaull, N. and Armstrong,   P., 2011, *Improving Education Quality in South Africa,* Report for the National Planning Commission, Stellenbosch University: Department of Economics, p. 5.

289. National Education Collaboration Trust, 2013, *Education Collaboration Framework.*Available at: http://www.naptosa.org.za/index.php/doc-manager/00-general/130-ecf-brochure/file, Accessed November 2014.

290. Ngqela, N. and Lewis, A., 2012, Exploring Adolescent Learners' Experience of School Violence in a Township High School', *Child Abuse Research: A South African Journal,* 13(1), pp. 87-97.

291. Ibid.

292. Bloch, G., 2006, *Building Education Beyond Crisis,* Johannesburg: Development Bank of Southern Africa.

293. Kraak, A., ed., 2008, 'The Education-Economy Relationship in South Africa, 2001-2005', in A. Kraak and K. Press, eds., *Human Resource Development Review 2008: Education, Employment and Skills in South Africa,* Cape Town: HSRC Press.

294. Organisation of Economic Co-operation and Development, 2008, *Reviews of National Policies for Education: South Africa,* Available at: http://www.oecd.org/southafrica/reviewofnationalpoliciesforeducatio-southafrica.htm, Accessed 23 November 2014.

295. Policy Coordination and Advisory Services in the Presidency, 2008, *Towards a Fifteen Year Review, Synthesis Report on the Implementation of Government Programmes,* Pretoria: Government Communication and Information Systems, Available at: http://www.thepresidency.gov.za/main.asp?include+docs/15year/main.html, Accessed August 2014.

296. Department of Basic Education, 2012, *Education Statistics in South Africa 2010,* Pretoria: Department of Basic Education.

297. Organisation of Economic Co-operation and Development, 2008, *Reviews of National Policies for Education: South Africa,* Available at: http://www.oecd.org/southafrica/reviewofnationalpoliciesforeducatio-southafrica.htm, Accessed 23 November 2014.

298. Ministry of Monitoring and Evaluation, 2012, *Development Indicators 2011,* Pretoria: The Presidency.

299. Bloch, G., 2009, 'A Blueprint Learning', *Sunday Times,* 23 August 2013.

300. Moleke, P., 2006, *Finding Work: Employment Experience for South African Graduates,* Cape Town: HSRC Press.

301. Department of Higher Education and Training (DHET), 2012, *Green Paper for the Post School System,* Pretoria: DHET.

302. National Department of Education, 1997, *Education White Paper 3: A Programme for the Transformation of Higher Education,* Pretoria: Department of Education.

303. National Department of Education, 2001, *The National Plan on Higher Education,* Department of Education: Pretoria.

304. National Department of Education, 2012, *Green Paper for the School Education & Training,* Pretoria: Department of Education.

305. Breier, M. and Mabizela, M., 2008, 'Higher Education', in A. Kraak and K. Press, eds., *Human Resource Development Review 2008: Education, Employment and Skills in South Africa,* Cape Town: HSRC Press.

306. National Department of Education, 2012, *Green Paper for the School Education & Training,* Pretoria: Department of Education.

307. Breier, M. and Mabizela, M., 2008., 'Higher Education', in A. Kraak and K. Press, eds., *Human Resource Development Review 2008: Education, Employment and Skills in South Africa,* Cape Town: HSRC Press.

308. Ibid.

309. Op.cit.

310. Breier, M. and Mabizela, M., 2008., 'Higher Education', in A. Kraak and K. Press, eds., *Human Resource Development Review 2008: Education, Employment and Skills in South Africa,* Cape Town: HSRC Press.

311. Moleke, P., 2006, *Finding Work: Employment Experience for South African Graduates,* Cape Town: HSRC Press.

312. Barrera, M., 1979, *Race and Class in the Southwest: A Theory of Inequality,* London: University of Nortre Dame Press.

313. Verba, S., 2001, 'Thoughts about Political Equality: What Is It? Why Do We Want It?', Paper prepared for the Inequality Summer Institute, Harvard University, Harvard, p. 2.

314. Townsend, P., 1979, *Poverty in the United Kingdom,* Harmondsworth: Penguin.

315. Meth, C., 2006, 'Half-Measures: The ANC's Unemployment and Poverty Reduction Targets', in H. Bhorat and R. Kanbur, eds., *Poverty and Policy in Post-Apartheid South Africa,* HSRC Press: Pretoria.

316. Wilson, F., 2012, Historical Roots of Inequality in South Africa, *Economic History of Developing Regions,* 26(1), pp. 1-15.

317. Wilson, F., 2012, 'Historical Roots of Inequality in South Africa', *Economic History of Developing Regions,* 26(1), pp. 1-15.

318. Frye, I., Farred, G. and Nojekwa, L., 2011, 'Inequality in South Africa', in Jauch, H. and Muchena, D., eds., *Tearing Us Apart: Inequalities in Southern Africa,* Rosebank: OSISA.

319. Gumede, V., 2014b, 'Poverty and Poverty Lines in South Africa', in Kanbur, R. et al, eds., *Oxford Companion to the Economics of South Africa*, Oxford University Press, pp. 285-290.

320. Bhorat, H. and Van der Westhuizen, C., 2010, 'Poverty, Inequality and the Nature of Economic Growth in South Africa', in N. Misra-Dexter and J. February, *Testing Democracy: Which Way is South Africa Going?* Cape Town: IDASA.

321. Sen, A., 1999, *Development as Freedom,* New York: Anchor.

322. Gumede, V., 2015b, 'Inequality in Democratic South Africa', in X. Mangcu, ed., *The Colour of Our Future: Race and Identity in South Africa*, Johannesburg: Wits Press.

323. Gumede, V., 2008, 'Poverty and Second Economy Dynamics in South Africa: An Attempt to Measure the Extent of the Problem and Clarify Concepts', Development Policy Research Unit Working Paper 08/133, University of Cape Town, Cape Town.

324. Ibid.

325. Barrera, M., 1979, *Race and Class in the Southwest: A theory of inequality,* London: University of Nortre Dame Press.

326. Hirschman, C., 1980, 'Theories and Models of Ethnic Inequality', *Research in Race and Ethnic Relations, 2:1-20,* Available at: http://faculty.washington.edu/charles/pubs/ Theories_and_Models_of_Ethnic_Inequality.pdf, Accessed 22 February 2014.

327. Myrdal, G.,1944, *American Dilemma: The Negro Problem and Modern Democracy,* New Jersey: Transaction Publishers.

328. Ibid.

329. Van der Berg, S., 2010, *Current Poverty and inequality Distribution in the Context of South Africa's History,* University of Stellenbosch: Bureau of Economic Research.

330. Ibid.

331. Leibbrandt, M., Woolard, I. and McEwen, H., 2009, *Employment and Inequality Outcomes in South Africa: What Role for Labour Market and Social Policies?* Southern Africa Labour and Development Research Unit, University of Cape Town, Available: http:// www.oecd.org/els/emp/45282868.pdf, Accessed February 22, 2014.

332. Van der Berge, S., 2002, 'Education Poverty and Inequality In South Africa', Paper to the Conference of the Centre for the Study of African Economics on Economic Growth and Poverty in Africa, Cape Town: University of Stellenbosch.

333. Bhorat, H. and van der Westhuizen, C., 2012, 'Poverty and Inequality and the Nature of Economic Growth in South Africa', *Development Policy Research Unit (12)151,* Available at: http://www.clas.ufl.edu/user/marilynm/Theorizing_Black_ American_Syllabus_Files?Racial_Inequality.pdf, Accessed 22 February 2014.

334. Narayan, A. and Mahajan, S., 2002, *Inequality in Focus: The State of Opportunities in South Africa: Inequality among Children and in the Labor Market,* Available at: http:// www.worldbank.org/content/dam/Worldbank/document/ Poverty%20documents/Inequality-in-Focus-April2013.pdf, Accessed 18 December 2013.

335. Leibbrandt, M., Woolard, C., and Woolard, I., 2000, 'The Contributions of Income Components to South Africa's Income Inequality: A Decomposable Gini Analysis;, *Journal of African Economics,* 9(1), pp. 79-99.

336. Bhorat, H. and Hodge, J., 1999, 'Decomposing Shifts in Labour Demand in South Africa', *South African Journal of Economics*, 67 (3), pp. 348-380.

337. Frye, I., Farred, G. and Nojekwa, L.. 2011,'Inequality in South Africa', in Jauch, H. and Muchena, D., eds., *Tearing Us Apart: Inequalities in Southern Africa,* Rosebank: OSISA.

338. Seekings, J. and Nattrass, N., 2006, *Class, Race and Inequality in South Africa,* Connecticut: Yale University Press.

339. Bhorat, H. and van der Westhuizen, C., 2012, Poverty and Inequality and the Nature of Economic Growth in South Africa.*Development Policy Research Unit (12)151,* Available at:http://www.clas.ufl.edu/user/marilynm/ Theorizing_Black_American_Syllabus_Files?Racial_Inequality.pdf, Accessed February 2014.

340. Gumede, V., 2015b, 'Inequality in Democratic South Africa', in X. Mangcu, eds., *The Colour of Our Future: Race and Identity in South Africa*, Johannesburg: Wits Press.

341. Todes, A., Karam, A., Klug, N. and Malaza, N., 2009, 'Beyond Master Planning: New Approaches to Spatial Planning in Ekhuruleni South Africa', *Habitat International*, 34, pp. 414-420.

342. Ibid.

343. Thomas, N.H., 2003, Land Reform in Zimbabwe, *Third World Quarterly*, Vol. 24 (2), pp. 671-712.

344. Encyclopaedia Britannica, 'Group Act', Available at: www.britannica/EBchecked/topic/247103/Group-Areas-Act

345. Ibid.

346. The Presidency, 2006, *The National Spatial Development Perspective*, Pretoria: Government Press.

347. Ibid.

348. Ibid.

349. Ibid.

350. The Presidency, 2006, *The National Spatial Development Perspective*, Pretoria: Government Press.

351. South African Foreign Policy Initiative (SAFPI), 2012, Gautengs Contribution to South Africa, Africa GDP, BRICS Trade and Infrastructure, Available at: www.safpi.org/news/articles/2012/gauteng-contribution-south-africa-gdp-brincs-trade-and-infrustructure.

352. South African History Online, *Dutch East India Company (DEIC/VOC)*, Available at: http//www.sahistory.org.za/topic/dutch-east-india-company-deivoc

353. Gumede, V., 2014b, 'Land Reform in Post-Apartheid South Africa: Should South Africa follow Zimbabwe's Footsteps?', *International Journal for African Renaissance Studies*, 9(1), 2014, pp. 50-68.

354. Aartsma, H., 2008, *Early History of the Cape Colony, South Africa*, Available at: www.south-africa-tours-and-travels.com.

355. Mathebula, F.M., 2012, 'Imagining Governance in a Post-liberation Struggle Context: A Public Administration Perspective', Paper delivered at the 12th Annual Conference of South African Associates of Public Admistration and Management (SAAPAM) on the State of Governance in Africa at the Turn of the Century of the African National Congress: Reflective Perspective from Scholarship and Practice, Bloemfontein: University of Free State.

356. Apartheid Legislation in South Africa, Undated, Available at: http//www.scnc.ukzn.ac.za/doc/HIST?Apartheid%20Legislation%20in20%South%20Africa.htlm.

357. Gumede, V., 2008a, 'Public Policy Making in Post-Apartheid South Africa: A Preliminary Perspective. *Africanus: Journal of Development Studies*, 38(2), pp. 7-23.

358. Ramphele, M., 2008, *Laying Ghosts to Rest: Dilemmas of the Transformation in South Africa,* Cape Town: NB Publishers.

359. South African History Online, Undated, 'F. W. de Klerk Announces the Release of Nelson Mandela and Unbans Political Organisations', Available at: http// www.sahistoryonline.org.za/dated-event/fw-de'klerk-announces-release-nelson-mandela-and-unbans-political-organisations.

360. Ibid.

361. Ibid.

362. Republic of South Africa, 1996, 'Constitution of the Republic of South Africa, Act 108 of 1996', Cape Town: Parliament.

363. Ibid.

364. De Villiers, O., 2013, 'Francois Pienaar Relives 'Madiba Magic' of 1995', *The Mail & Guardian*, South Africa, Available At: http/mg.co.zs/articles/2013-07-04-francois-pinaar-relives-madiba-magic-of-1995.

365. Boreland, K., 2013, 'Madiba: Magic: Kryptonia for SA Sporting Opponents', *Daily Maverick*, Available at: http//www.dailymaverick.co.za/articles/2013-12-13/ madiba.magic-kryptonia-for-sa-sporting-opponents.

366. The Presidency, 'South Africa's National Anthem', Available at: www.thepresidency.gov.za/pebble.asp?relid=265.

367. Kane, J., 2001, *The Politics of Moral Capital,* Melbourne: Cambridge University Press, p 7.

368. Sison, A.J., 2003, 'The Moral Capital of leaders: Why Virtue Matters', *New Horizon Leadership Studies.*

369. Ibid.

370. Khunou, G., 2013, *What Middle Class? Dynamics Nature of Class Position,* Available at: http//www.resep.sun.ac.za/wp-content/uploads/2013/khunou-main-article-black-middle-class.pdf.

371. The South African Civil Society Information Service, 2013, 'Prof Sampie Terreblanche: White South African Will Have to Make Some Sacrifies', Available at: http// www.sacis.org.za/sites/article/1749.

372. Wale, K., 2014, *Reflecting on Reconciliation: Lessons from the Past, Prospects for the Future,* Cape Town: Institute of Justice and Reconciliation.

373. Ibid.

374. Gumede, V., 2013a, 'Socio-Economic Transformation in Post-Apartheid South Africa: Progress and Challenges', in Ngcaweni, B., ed., *The Future We Chose: Emerging Perspectives on the Centenary of the ANC,* Pretoria: AISA Press.

375. Bagchi, K.A., 2000, 'The Past and the Future of the Developmental State', *Journal of World Systems Research,* XI(2), pp. 398-442.

376. Mkadawire, T., 2001a, 'Thinking About Developmental States in Africa', *Cambridge Journal of Economics*, Vol 24, pp. 289-313.

377. Onis, Z., 1991, 'The Logic of the Developmental State'. *Journal of Comparative Studies*, Vol 24(1), pp. 109-126.

378. Johnson, C., 1982, *MITI and the Japanese Miracle*, Stanford: Standford University Press.

379. Ibid.

380. United Nations Economic and Social Council, 2013, *The Developmental State: What Options for Africa?*, Economic Commssion for Africa Governance and Public Administration Division, United Nations.

381. African National Congress, 2007, Strategy and Tactics: Building a National Democratic Society, Available online on http://www.anc.org.za/docs/pdf.

382. Castells, M., 1997, *The Rise of the Network Society, Volume* I, London: Blackwell.

383. Mkadawire, T., 2001a, 'Thinking About Developmental States in Africa', *Cambridge Journal of Economics*, Vol. 24, pp. 289-313.

384. Ibid.

385. Op.cit.

386. Ibid.

387. Ibid.

388. Edigheji, O., 2005, 'A Democratic Developmental State in Africa', A concept paper, Johannesburg: Centre for Development Studies.

389. Ibid.

390. Op.cit.

391. Terreblanche, S.J., 1999, *The Ideological Journal of South Africa: From RDP to GEAR Macro-Economic Plan in Religion in Public Life*, Available at: http//www.uct.ac.za/depts./ricsa/confer/me99/procs/pro_terr.thm,version11,29.2001.

392. Webster, E. and Adler, G., 1998, 'Towards a Class Comparison in South Africa "Double Transition": Bargained Liberalisation and the Consolidation of Democracy', Paper presented to the Seminar on Labour and Popular Struggle in the Global Economy, Columbia University, New York.

393. Visser, W., 2004, 'Shifting RDP to Gear: The ANC Government Dilemma in Providing an Equitable System of Social Security of the New South Africa', Paper presented at the 40th ITH Linzer Konferenz, 17 September 2004.

394. Ibid.

395. United Nations Economic and Social Council, 2013, 'The Developmental State: What Options for Africa?', Economic Commission for Africa Governance and Public Administration Division, United Nations.

396. Helper, D., Kruger, T. and Wial, H., 2012, *Why Does Manufacturing Matter? Which Manufacturing Matters?:* A Policy Framework, The Brooklyn Institute.

397. The Department of Trade and Industry, 2014, 'Industrial Policy Action Plan Economic Sector and Employment Cluster', *IPAP* 2013/14-2015/16

398. Department of Economic Development, 2011, *The New Growth Path: Framework*, Pretoria.

399. Natrass, N., 2011, 'The New Growth Path: Game Changing Vision or Cop-out?', *S Afr J Sci.* Vol. 107(3/4), Art. 638,8 pages. DOI: 10:4102/sajs.v107i3/4.638.

400. Department of Economic Development, 2011, *The New Growth Path: Framework,* Pretoria.

401. Zarenda, H., 2013, 'South Africa's National Development Plan a, nd its Implications for Regional Development', Trade Law Centre Working Paper No D13WP01/2013 June.

402. The National Planning Commission, 2012, *The National Development Plan: Vision 2030,* The Presidency of the Republic of South Africa.

403. CUTS International, 2014, 'Reinventing the Planning Commission: The Great Debate', Available at: http//www.cuts-international.org/pdf/reinventing_The_Planning_Commission_The_Great_Debate.pdf

404. Fritz, V. and Menocol, R., 2007, 'Developmental State in the New Millennium: Concepts and Challenges for the New Aid Agenda', *Development Policy Review,* Vol. 25(5), pp. 531-552.

405. Ibid.

406. Mkandawire, T., 2001b, 'Social Policy in a Development Context', Social Policy and Development Programme Paper number 7, United Nations Research Institute for Social Development, Geneva.

References

Aartsma, H., 2008, *Early History of the Cape Colony, South Africa*, Available online at www.south-africa-tours-and-travels.com, Accessed 19 December 2014.

Acemoglu, D., Gelb, S. and Robinson, J.A., 2007, *Black Economic Empowerment and Economic Performance in South Africa*, Johannesburg: The EDGE Institute.

Adamolekun, L., 2005, 'Re-orienting Public Management in Africa: Selected issues and Some Country Experiences', Economic Research Working Paper, African Development Bank: Tunis.

Adedeji, A., 1979, 'Statement to the Economic and Social Council of the United Nations', Second Regular Session, Geneva, July 12 1979.

Adelzadeh, A., 1999, 'From RDP to GEAR: The Gradual Embracing of Neo-Liberalism in Economic Policy', Occasional Paper No. 3, National Institute for Economic Policy (NIEP), Johannesburg.

Adesina, J., 2007, 'Social Policy and the Quest for Inclusive Growth: Research Findings from Sub-saharan Africa', Social Policy and Development Programme Paper No. 33, United Nations Research Institute for Social Development, Geneva.

Africa Commission, 2009, 'Global Financial Crisis Calls for Action', *Africa Commission Newsletter*, Issue 5, February 2009.

Africa Development Bank, 2009, 'Africa and the Global Economic Crisis: Strategies for Preserving the Foundations of Long-term Growth', Paper prepared for the 2009 Annual Meeting of the African Development Bank, May 13-14, 2009, Dakar: AfDB.

Africa Development Bank, 2010, *Assessing Progress in Africa Toward the Millennium Development Goals: MDG Report 2010*, Available online at http://www.afdb.org/fileadmin/uploads/afdb/Documents/Publications/MGDS202010 20Eng.pdf., Accessed 19 December 2014.

Africa Focus, 2009, *Africa: Global Economic Crisis, March 2009*, Available online at:.http://www.africafocus.org/docs09/gec0904b.php, Accessed 30 December 2014.

African Monitor, 2009, 'Dialogue on Africa's Response to the Global Financial Crisis', Available online at http://www.africanmonitor.org/Site index2.php?option=com_content&do_pdf=1&id=109, Accessed 22 December 2014.

African National Congress, 1992, 'Ready to Govern (R2G): ANC Policy Guidelines for a Democratic South Africa', Adopted at the National Conference, 28-31 May 1992, Available online at www.ancyl.org.za/docs/.../Politics%20Economy%20Manual%20for%20For%20Youth%20League.pdf., Accessed 16 December 2014.

African National Congress, 1994, *Reconstruction and Development Programme: A Policy Framework*, Johannesburg: Umanyano Publications.

African National Congress, 2007a, *Strategy and Tactics: Building a National Democratic Society,* Available online at: http://www.anc.org.za/docs/pdf., Accessed 22 December 2014.

African National Congress, 2007b, *Economic Transformation: African National Congress Policy Discussion Document*, Available online at: http://www.anc.org.za/docs/discus/2012/economic_transformations.pdf., Accessed 17 December 2014.

African National Congress, 2010, *Economic Transformation Discussion Document for the 2010 National General Council,* Available online at http://www.anc.org.za/docs/discus/2010/economicq.pdf., Accessed 23 December 2014.

African National Congress, 2012, *Economic Transformation, Land Policy Proposals,* Available online at http://www.anc.org.za/docs/discus/2012/landpolicyproposals.june2012g.pdf., Accessed 17 December 2014.

African National Congress, nd., 'The Freedom Charter', Available online at http://www.anc.org.za/show.php?id=72, Accessed 30 December 2014.

Aharonovitz, G.D., 2011, 'Why Cannot Poor Countries Utilise Existing Knowledge? Expansion of Firms and Human Capital Accumulation by Training', *Economic Enquiry*, Vol 49, No 1, pp. 108–121.

Ake, C., 2000, *Democracy and Development in Africa,* Maryland: Brookings Institution.

Akoojee, S. and McGrath, S., 2007, 'Public and Private Further Education and Training in South Africa: A Comparative Analysis of the Quantitative Evidence;, *South African Journal of Education*, Vol 27, No 2, pp. 209–222.

Alexandra, P., 2010, 'Rebellion of the Poor: South Africa's Service Delivery Protests – A Preliminary Analysis', *Review of African Political Economy*. Vol 37, No 123, pp. 25–40.

Alexkor, nd., *Our History,* Available online at www.alexkor.co.za/our-history.htlm, Accessed 13 December 2014.

Ali-Dinar, A.B., 1994, *ANC Education Policy*, Available online at http://www.africa.upenn.edu/Govern_Political/ANC_Education.html, 18 December 2014.

Altinay, H., 2011, *Global Civics: Responsibilities and Rights in an Interdependent World.* Washington DC: Brookings Institution Press.

Amin, S., 1972, 'Underdevelopment and Dependence in Black Africa: Historical Origin', *Journal of Peace Research*, Vol 9, No 2, pp. 105-120.

Amin, S., 1997, *Capitalism in the Age of Globalisation: The Management of Contemporary Society,* Cape Town, Zeb Books.

Amsden, A., 1989, *Asia's Next Giant: South Korea and Late Industrialisation,* New York: Oxford University Press.

Anuar, A.R., 2004, *Land Reform and Consolidation: A Comparison Between Malaysia and Some Selected European Countries,* Available online at http://www.instun.gov.za, Accessed 22 December 2014.

Ardington, C., Case, A. and Hosegood, V., (forthcoming), 'Labour Supply Responses to Large Social Transfers: Longitudinal Evidence from South Africa', To be published in the *American Economic Journal: Applied Economics*.

Armscor, 2010, *Corporate Information*, Available online at www.amoroc.co.za/about/CorpInfo, Accessed 14 December 2014.

Aryeetey, E., Devarajan, S., Kanbur, R. and Kasekende, L., 2012, *The Oxford Companion to the Economics of Africa*, New York: Oxford University Press.

Asante, M., 2007, *An Afrocentric Manifesto: Toward an African Renaissance*, Cambridge: Polity Press.

Bagchi, K.A., 2000, 'The Past and the Future of the Developmental State', *Journal of World Systems Research,* Vol XI, No 2, pp. 398-442.

Bahl, R. and Linn, J., 1994, 'Fiscal Decentralisation and Intergovernmental Transfers in Less Developed Countries in Publius', *The Journal of Federalism*, Vol 24, No 1, pp. 1-19.

Balchin, N., 2009, 'The Impact of the Global Financial Crisis in Africa', Available online at http://www.mthente.co.za/resources/reports-and-articles/mthente-in-the-news/The per cent20Impact per cent20of per cent20the per cent20Global per cent20Financial per cent20Crisis per cent20in per cent20Africa per cent20- per cent20Neil per cent20Balchin.pdf., Accessed 10 December 2014.

Bale, M. and Dale, T., 1998, 'Public Sector Reform in New Zealand and Its Relevance to Developing Countries', *The World Bank Research Observer*, Vol 13, No 1, pp. 103-121.

Barrera, M., 1979, *Race and Class in the Southwest: A Theory of Inequality,* London: University of Nortre Dame Press.

Barret, C., Carter, M. and Little, P., eds., 2006, 'Understanding and Reducing Persistent Poverty in Africa: Introduction to a Special Issue', *Journal of Development Studies*, Vol 42, No 2, pp. 167-177.

Baxter, R., 2008, 'The Global Economic Crisis and its impact on South Africa', Available online at http://www.reservebank.co.za/internet/Publication.nsf/LADV/21EFDE8DEE82935342257601003680B6/$File/Roger+Baxter.pdf., Accessed 15 December 2014.

Benjamin, P., 2005, *Labour Market Regulation: International and South African Perspective,* Cape Town: HSRC Press.

Bhorat, H. and Hodge, J., 1999, 'Decomposing Shifts in Labour Demand in South Africa', *South African Journal of Economics,* Vol 67, No 3, pp. 348-380. STOP

Bhorat, H. and van der Westhuizen, C., 2010, 'Poverty, Inequality and the Nature of Economic Growth in South Africa', in N. Misra-Dexter and J. February, eds., *Testing Democracy: Which Way is South Africa Going?*, Cape Town: IDASA.

Biko, S.B., 1996, *Steve Biko: I Write What I Like: A Selection of His Writings,* Randburg: Ravan Press.

Binswanger-Mkhize, H., Bourguignon, C. and van der Brink, R., 2009, 'Introduction and Summary', in H. Binswanger-Mkhize, C. Bourguignon and R. van der Brink, eds., *Agricultural Land Redistribution: Towards Greater Consensus,* Washington DC, USA: The World Bank.

Blas, J., 2009, 'Poor Still Hit By High Food Prices', *Financial Times,* 19 March 2009.

Bloch, G., 2006, *Building Education Beyond Crisis,* Johannesburg: Development Bank of Southern Africa.

Bloch, G., 2009, *The Toxic Mix,* Cape Town: Tafelberg.

Bodibe, O., 2007, 'Rethinking South Africa's Development Path: Economic Policy in the Era of Liberation – ANC Economic Transformation Policy Proposal', *Centre of Policy Studies*, Vol 20, No 10, pp. 75-80.

Bond, P., 2011, South African Splinters: From 'Elite Transition' to 'Small-as-Alliances', *Review of African Political Economy*, Vol 38, No 127, pp. 113–121.

Booyens, J.C., 2009, 'The Value Attached to Teaching Qualifications by Educators and Other Stakeholders at a Further Education and Training College in Southern KwaZuluNatal', Unpublished dissertation, University of KwaZulu Natal, Durban.

Boreland, K., 2013, 'Madiba: Magic: Kryptonia for SA Sporting Opponents', *Daily Maverick*, Available online at http//www..dailymaverick.co.za/articles/2013-12-13/madiba.magic-kryptonia-for-sa-sporting-opponents, Accessed 17 December 2014.

Bowman, Gilillan Attorney, 2012, 'Black Economic Empowerment Boucher', Available online at www.bowman.co.za/BEE/BEEBrochure-Ir.pdf., Accessed 22 December 2014.

Breier, M. and Mabizela, M., 2008, 'Higher Education', in A. Kraak, and K. Press, eds., *Human Resource Development Review 2008: Education, Employment and Skills in South Africa*, Cape Town: HSRC Press.

Brown, S., 2007, *Leadership and Legitimacy*, Pretoria: Institute of Justice and Reconciliation.

Buccus, I.,Hemson, D., Hicks, J. and Piper, L.,2007, 'Public Participation and Local

Governance', *Journal on Public Participation in Governance*, Available online at http://www.cpp.org.za/docs/reports/2007/lg-report0507.pdf., Accessed 22 December 2014.

Capehart, T. and Richardson, J., 2008, 'Food Price Inflation: Causes and Impacts',

Congressional Research Service: Report for Congress, Library of Congress, Available online at http://opencrs.com/document/RS22859, Accessed 22 December 2014.

Castells, M., 1997, *The Rise of the Network Society*, Volume I, London: Blackwell.Centre for Development and Enterprise,1999, 'Policy-making in New Democracy: South

Africa's Challenges for the 21st Century', Centre for Development and Enterprise, Johannesburg.

Centre for Development and Enterprise, 2008, 'Land Reform in South Africa: Getting Back on Track', Centre of Development and Enterprise, Johannesburg.

Chabane, N., Machaka J., Molaba N., Roberts, S. and Taka, M., 2003, '10 Year Review: Industrial Structure and Competition Policy', School of Economic and Business Sciences, University of the Witwatersrand.

Chambati, W., 2013, 'Changing Agrarian Labour Relations After Land Reform in Zimbabwe', in S. Moyo, and W. Chambati, eds., *Land and Agrarian Reform in Zimbabwe: Beyond White-Settle Capitalism*, Dakar: CODESRIA.

Chaves, D., 2014, 'State of State: The State is Dead! Long Live the State!', Available online at www.tni.org/files/download/state-of-power/hyperlink.0.pdf., Accessed 22 December 2014.

Cheadle, H., 2006, 'Regulated Flexibility and Small Business: Revisiting LRA &BCEA', University of Cape Town, Cape Town.

Chibber, V., 2002, 'Bureaucratic Rationality and the Developmental State', *American Journal of Sociology*, Vol 107, No 4, pp. 951-989.

Chikulo, B., 2003, 'Development Policy in South Africa: A Review', *PMN Bulletin,* Vol X, No 2, pp. 1-3.

Chipkin, I., 2007, *Do South Africans Exist? Nationalism, Democracy and the Identity of the People,* Johannesburg: Wits University Press.

Chisholm, L., 2003, 'The Politics of Curriculum Review and Revision in South Africa', Paper presented at the session on Culture, Context and Quality of Education, Oxford International Conference on Education and Development, 9–11 September.

Clark, N.L., 1994, *Manufacturing Apartheid State Corporations in South Africa,* Yale: Yale University Press.

Clarke, M., Godfrey, S., and Theron, J., 2002, *Workers' Protection: An Update on the Situation in South Africa,* Available online at http://www.oit.org/wcmsp5/groups/public/---ed_dialogue/---dialogue/documents/genericdocument/wcms_205380.pdf., Accessed 30 December 2014.

Cliffe, L., 2007, 'Policy Options for the Land Reform in South Africa: New Institutional Mechanisms?', Programme for Land and Agrarian Studies, University of the Western Cape.

Cloete, N. and Butler-Adam, J., 2012, 'Introduction', in H. Perold, N. Cloete and J. Papier, eds., *Sharping the Future of South Africa's Youth: Rethinking Post-school Education and Skills Training,* Centre for Higher Education Transformation, Cape Town.

Cohen, J. and Peterson, S.,1999, Administrative Decentralisation: Strategies for Developing Countries, West Hartford, CT: Kumarian Press.

Conceição, P. and Mendoza, R.U., 2009, *Is the Global Food Crisis Over?* Available online at http://www.voxeu.org/index.php?q=node/3459, Accessed 30 December 2014.

Constitution of the Republic of South Africa, 1996, Act 108 of 1996.

Constitutional Court of South Africa Judgement, CCT 100/09, 2010, Available online at http://www.saflii.org.za/za/cases/ZACC/2010, Accessed 23 December 2014.

Conyer, J.E., 2002, 'Racial Inequality: Emphasis on Explanations', *The Western Journal of Black Studies,* Vol 26, No 4, pp. 249-253.

Council on Higher Education, 2007, *Higher Education Monitor: A Case for Improving Teaching and Learning in South African Higher Education*, Council on Higher Education, Pretoria.

Cronin, J., 2008, 'The Future of the State: A Two-tier Cabinet is on the Cards', *Mail & Guardian*, 24-30 October 2008, p. 23.

Cross, E., 2009, 'The Cost of Zimbabwe's Continuing Farm Invasions', Cato Institute, African National Congress (ANC) 52nd National Conference Resolutions, 2007, Available online at http://www.anc.org.za, Accessed 13 February 2014.

Cullinan, K., 2006, 'Health Services in South Africa: A Basic Introduction', *Health-e News*, Service Department of Higher Education and Training.

Cummings, S. and Nørgaard, O., 2004, 'Conceptualising State Capacity: Comparing Kazakhstan and Kyrgyzstan', *Policy Studies*, Vol 52, No 4, pp. 685–708.

CUTS International, 2014, 'Reinventing the Planning Commission: The Great Debate', Available online at: http//www.cuts-international.org/pdf/reinventing_The_Planning_ Commission_ The_Great_Debate.pdf., Accessed 30 December 2014.

Daniel, J., Naidoo, P., Pillay, D. and Southall, R., 2010, *New South African Review 1 - 2010: Development or Decline?,* Johannesburg: Wits University Press.

Darralingam, S., 2009, 'Employment Creation Still Shoddy', in *SA Labour Market Report (QLF)*, Standard Bank.

Davies, R., 2006, 'Manufacturing Exports and Employment Growth', Employment Growth and Development Initiative, Human Sciences Research Council, Available online at http://www.hsrc.ac.za, Accessed 29 December 2014.

De Jager, N. and Meintjes C., 2013, 'Winners, Losers and the Playing Field in Southern Africa's 'Democratic Darlings': Botswana and South Africa Compared', *Politikon* Vol 40, No 2, pp. 233-253.

de Villiers, O., 2013, 'Francois Pienaar Relives 'Madiba Magic' of 1995', *Mail & Guardian,* South Africa, Available online at http/www.mg.co.zs/articles/2013-07-04-francois-pinaar-relives-madiba-magic-of-1995, Accessed 30 December 2014.

Department of Basic Education, 2012, *Education Statistics in South Africa 2010*, Pretoria: Government Printers.

Department of Economic Development, 2010, *The New Growth Path Framework,* Available online at http://www.economic.gov.za/communications/51-publications/151-the-new-growth-path-framework, Accessed 30 December 2014.

Department of Education, 1996a, 'Education White Paper 2: The Organisation, Governance and Funding of Schools, Notice 130, 14 February', *Government Gazette No. 16987*, Pretoria: Government Printers.

Department of Education, 1997a, 'Education White Paper 3: A Programme for Higher Education Transformation', *Government Gazette No. 18207,* Pretoria: Government Printers.

Department of Education, 1997b, 'Interim Policy for Early Childhood Development', Department of Education, Pretoria.

Department of Education, 1998a, 'Education White Paper 4: A Programme for the Transformation of Further Education and Training. Notice 2188, 25 September', *Government Gazette No. 19281*, Pretoria: Government Printers.

Department of Education, 2001a, 'Education White Paper 5 on Early Childhood Education: Meeting the Challenge of Early Childhood Development in South Africa', Pretoria: Government Printers.

Department of Education, 2001b, 'Education White Paper 6: Special Needs Education: Building an Inclusive Education and Training System', Pretoria: Government Printers.

Department of Education,2001c, *National Plan on Higher Education,* Pretoria: Government Printers.

Department of Education, 2001d, National Department of Education, Pretoria.

Department of Education, 2003, 'Plan of Action: Improved Access to Quality Basic Education for All', Department of Education, Pretoria.

Department of Health, 2003, *Essential Health Care for All South Africans: An Investigation into the Adequacy of Public Health Financing and the Equity of Provincial Health Resource Distribution,* Pretoria: Government Printers.

Department of Health, 2007, *A Policy on Quality in Health Care for South Africa,* Pretoria: Government Printers.

Department of Health, 2012a, 'South Africa Joins the World in Commemorating World Malaria Day on 25 April 2012', Available online at http://www.doh.gov.za/docs/misc/2012/malariaday2012.pdf., Accessed 30 December 2014.

Department of Health, 2012b, 'South Africa's National Strategic Plan for a Campaign on Accelerated Reduction of Maternal and Child Mortality in Africa', Department of Health, Pretoria.

Department of Health, 2013, *National Health Insurance: The First Eighteen Months,* Pretoria: Government Printers.

Department of Higher Education and Training, 2012, 'Green Paper for the Post-School System', Department of Higher Education and Training, Pretoria.

Department of Labour, 2001, *An Introduction to the Skills Development Strategy,* Pretoria: Government Printers.

Department of Land Affairs, 1997, 'The White Paper on South African Land Policy, Department of Land Affairs, Pretoria.

Department of Land Reform and Rural Development, 2012, *Land Reform Discussion Document*, Pretoria: Government Printers.

Department of Public Service and Administration, 1995, 'White Paper on the Transformation of the Public Service', Department of Public Service and Administration, Pretoria.

Department of Rural Development and Land Reform, 2011, *The Green Paper on Rural Development and Land Reform*, Available online at www.ruraldevelopment.gov.za/legislation-and-policies/categories/7-green-paper, Accessed 23 December 2014.

Department of Trade and Industry, 1995, 'White Paper on National Strategy for the Development and Promotion of Small Business in South Africa', Pretoria: Government Printers.

Department of Trade and Industry, 2003, 'Broad Based Economic Empowerment Bill', Pretoria: Government Print.

Department of Trade and Industry, 2005, 'Integrated Small-Enterprise- Development.

Department of Trade and Industry, 2007a, *National Industrial Policy Framework,* Pretoria: Government Press.

Department of Trade and Industry, 2007b, 'South Africa's Economic Transformation: A Strategy for Board- Based Economic Empowerment', Available online at https://www.environment.gov.za/sites/default/files/legislations/bbbee_act.pdf., Accessed 2 December 2014.

Department of Trade and Industry, 2010, *Industrial Policy Action Plan: 2013/14–2015/16,* Pretoria: Government Press.

Department of Trade and Industry, 2014, *Industrial Policy Action Plan Economic Sector and Employment Cluster: IPAP 2013/14-2015/16*, Pretoria: Government Printers.

Department of Trade and Industry, (Date?)'Special Economic Zone (SEZ)', Available online at http://www.dti.gov.za/industrial_development/sez.jsp, Accessed 31 December 2014.

Dikeni, L., 2012, *South African Development Perspectives in Question,* Johannesburg: Real African Publishers.

Dror, Y., 2006, 'Training for Policy Markers', in M. Moran, M. Rein, and R. Goodin, eds., Du Plessis, W.J., 2011, 'African Indigenous Land Rights in a Private Ownership Paradigm', PER, 2011, Vol. 14, No 7, p. 46.

Dye, T.R., 2002,*Understanding Public Policy*, New Jersey: Prentice Hall.

Edigheji, O., 2005, 'A Democratic Developmental State in Africa', A concept paper, Centre for Development Studies, Johannesburg.

Edigheji, O., 2007, 'The Emerging South African Democratic Developmental State and the People's Contract', Centre for Policy Studies, Johannesburg.

Edigheji, O., 2010, *Constructing a Democratic Developmental State in South Africa: Potentials and Challenges*, Cape Town: HSRC Press.

Evans, P., 1995, *Embedded Autonomy: States and Industrial Transformation,* Princeton: Princeton University Press.

Evans, P., 2007, 'In Search of the 21st Century Developmental State',University of California, Berkeley Campus, California.

Economic Commission for Africa, 2012, *Economic Report on Africa*, Addis Ababa: (PUBLISHER?)

El-Beltagy, K., 2009, 'Global Economic Crisis', Available on line at: http:// pathways.cu.edu.eg/news/news/uf/30/30293_4MPED-03-04.pdf., Accessed 02 December 2014.

Encyclopaedia Britannica, 'Group Act', Available online at www.britannica/EBchecked/ topic/247103/Group-Areas-Act, 15 December 2014.

Ertner, R.M., 2013, *Broad-Base Black Economic Empowerment, INTO SA eINFO: B-BBEE (2013),* Available   online   at   www.INTO_SA_eINFO_- Black_Economic_Empowermenr_South_Africa_2013_PDF., Accessed 2 December 2014.

Eskom, Undated, *Company Information,* Available online at: www.eskom.co.za/ OurCompany/CompanyInformation/Page/Company-Information-1.aspx, Accessed 02 December 2014.

Fanon, F., 1963, *The Wretched of the Earth*, New York: Grove Press.

Fedderke, J., 2014, 'South Africa's Growth Performance', in H. Bhorat, Q. Hirsch, R. Kanbur, H. Bhorat, A. Hirsch, and M. Ncube, eds., *Oxford Companion to the Economics of South Africa,* Oxford: Oxford University Press.

Federation of South African Women (1954-1963), 2013, 'The African Education Movement, Historical Paper Research Archive, Johannesburg.

Ferlie, E., Lynn, L. and Pollitt, C., 2007, *The Oxford Handbook of Public Management*, Oxford: Oxford University Press.

Ferlie, E., Pettigrew, A., Ashburner, L. and Fiztgereld, L., 1996, *The New Public Management in Action,* Oxford: Oxford University Press.

Fine, B. and Rustomjee, Z., 1996, *The Political Economy of South Africa: From Minerals-Energy Complex to Industrialisation,* Boulder, CO: Westview Press.

Finn, A., Leibbrandt, M. and Woodland, I., 2009, 'Income and Expenditure Inequality: Analysis of the NIDS Wave 1', Database Discussion Paper No. 5, Available online at http://www.nids.uct.ac.za/documents/discussion-papers/96-nids-discussion-paper-no05/file, Accessed 22 February 2013.

Finn, A. and Leibbrandt, M., 2013, 'Mobility and Inequality in the First Three Waves of NIDS', SALDRU Working Paper Number 120/ NIDS Discussion Paper 2013/2, SALDRU, University of Cape Town, Cape Town, Available online at http://www.nids.uct.ac.za/documents/discussion-papers/181-income-inequality-and-economic-mobility/file, Accessed 22 February 2013.

Fiske, E.B. and Ladd, H.F., 2005, *Educational Aspirations and Political Realities: Elusive Equity Education Reform in Post-apartheid South Africa,* Cape Town: HSRC Press.

Food and Agricultural Organisation, 2009, 'The Right to Food and the Financial and Economic Crisis', Submission to the United Nations Conference on World Financial and Economic Crisis, United Nations General Assembly, 24-26 June 2009, New York.

Food and Agricultural Organization, 2011, '2011 World Hunger and Poverty Facts and Statistics, State of World Food Insecurity Hunger Notes', Available online at http://www.worldhunger.org/articles/Learn/Number_of_hungry_people_in_the_world, Accessed 02 December 2014.

Freedom to Learn, 2013, 'A Look at South African Education', Available online at http://www.freedomtolearn.co.za/standards, Accessed 02 December 2014.

Fritz, V. and Menocol, R., 2007, 'Developmental State in the New Millennium: Concepts and Challenges for the New Aid Agenda', *Development Policy Review,* 2007, Vol 25, No 5, pp. 531-552.

Frye, I., Farred, G. and Nojekwa, L., 2011, 'Inequality in South Africa', in H. Jauch, and D. Muchena, eds., *Tearing Us Apart: Inequalities in Southern Africa,* Rosebank: OSISA.

Gelb, S., 2003, 'Inequality in South Africa', The EDGE Institute, Johannesburg.

Gelb, S., 2010, 'Macroeconomic Policy Development: From Crisis to Crisis', in B. Freund and H. Witt, eds., *Development Dilemmas in Post-Apartheid South Africa,* Scotsville: University of KwaZulu Natal Press.

Glaser, D., 2011, 'The New Black/African Racial Nationalism in SA: Towards a Liberal-egalitarian Critique', *Transformation,* Vol. 76, pp. 67-94.

Godfrey, S., 2003, 'Workers Protection: An Update on the Situation in South Africa: A Country Study, with M. Clarke and J. Theron', Report to the International Labour Organisation, Geneva, Available online at http://www.ilo.org/wcmsp5/groups/public/---ed_dialogue/--dialogue/documents/generic.document/wcms_205380.pdf., Accessed 02 December 2014.

Godfrey, S. and Theron, J., 1999, 'Labour Standards Versus Job Creation? An Investigation of the Likely Impact of the New Basic Conditions of Employment Act on Small Businesses', in *Development and Labour Monographs 1/99,* Institute of Development and Labour Law, University of Cape Town.

Godfrey S., Maree, J. and Theron J., 2006, 'Regulating the Labour Market: The Role of Bargaining Councils', *Industrial Law Journal*,Vol 27.

Government of the United States of America, 1997, *A Country Study: South Africa,* The Library of Congress, Federal Research Division, Washington, Available online at http://lcweb2.loc.gov/frd/cs/zatoc.html, Accessed 02 December 2014.

Green, D., 2009, *A Copper-Bottomed Crisis? The Impact of the Global Economic Meltdown on Zambia,* Oxford: Oxfam.

Greenburg, S., 2004, 'The Landless People's Movement and the Failures of the Post-Apartheid Land Reform', School of Development Studies, University of KwaZulu-Natal.

Greespan, A., 2013, *Financial Times*, October 25.

Griffith-Jones, S. and Ocampo, J., 2009, 'The Global Financial Crisis and Its Impact on Developing Countries', United Nations Development Working Paper, UNDP, New York.

Gumede, V., 2000, 'Import Demand Elasticities for South Africa: A Co-integration Approach', *Studies in Economics and Econometrics*, Vol. 2 No 1, pp. 21-38.

Gumede, V., 2003, 'Export Elasticities for South African Manufacturing – A Time-series Approach', *Studies in Economics and Econometrics*, Vol. 27(1), pp. 39-55.

Gumede, V., 2004, 'Export Propensities and Intensities of Small Manufacturing Enterprises in South Africa', *Small Business Economics: An International Journal,* Vol. 22(5), pp. 379-389.

Gumede, V., 2006, 'Small and Medium Manufacturing in South Africa: Constraints and Opportunities', in S. Roberts, ed., *Sustainable Manufacturing*, Cape Town: Juta Academic Press.

Gumede, V., 2007, 'Is Government Optimally Poised to Achieve Set Objectives and Targets in Time?', *Service Delivery Review Journal*, Vol. 5(3), pp. 48–51.

Gumede, V., 2008a, 'Public Policy Making in a Post-Apartheid South Africa – A Preliminary Perspective', *Africanus: Journal of Development Studies,* Vol. 38(2), pp. 7-23.

Gumede, V., 2008b, 'Social Protection in Latin America and Africa', Institute for Africa's Development', *Africa Notes,* Cornell University, Summer.

Gumede, V., 2008c, 'Poverty and Second Economy Dynamics in South Africa: An Attempt to Measure the Extent of the Problem and Clarify Concepts', Development Policy Research Unit Working Paper 08/133, University of Cape Town, Cape Town.

Gumede, V., 2010, 'Developmental States Remain a Pipedream in Africa', *The Thinker: Journal of Progressive Thought,* Vol. 19.

Gumede, V., 2011a, 'Policy Making in South Africa', in C. Landsberg, and A. Venter (4th ed.) *South African Government and Politics,* Pretoria: Van Schaik.

Gumede, V., 2011b, 'The Role of Public Policies and Policy Makers in Africa: Responding to Global Economic Crises', in D.R. Lee, and M. Ndulo, *The Food and Financial Crises in Sub-Saharan Africa: Origins, Impacts and Policy Implications,* CABI International.

Gumede, V., 2011c, 'Social and Economic Inclusion in Post-apartheid South Africa', *Transformation Audit,* Institute of Justice and Reconciliation, Cape Town.

Gumede, V., 2013a, 'Socio-Economic Transformation in Post-apartheid South Africa: Progress and Challenges', in Ngcaweni, B., ed., *The Future We Chose: Emerging Perspectives on the Centenary of the ANC*, AISA Press: Pretoria.

Gumede, V., 2013b, 'Public Sector Reforms and Policy-making: A Case of Education in an Emerging Developmental South Africa', in A. Kanjee, M. Nkomo and Y. Sayed, eds., *The Search for Quality Education in Post-apartheid South Africa*, Pretoria: HSRC Press.

Gumede, V., 2013c, 'African Economic Renaissance as a Paradigm for Africa's Socio-Economic Development', in K. Kondlo, *Perspectives in Thought Leadership for Africa's Renewal*, Pretoria: AISA Press.

Gumede, V., 2014a, 'Land Reform in Post-Apartheid South Africa: Should South Africa Follow Zimbabwe's Footsteps?', *International Journal for African Renaissance Studies*, Vol. 9(1), pp. 50-68.

Gumede, V., 2014b, 'Poverty and Poverty Lines in South Africa', in R. Kanbur, R. et al, eds., *Oxford Companion to the Economics of South Africa*, Oxford: Oxford University Press.

Gumede, V., 2014c, 'Millennium Development Goals: Towards a Post-2015 Development Agenda for South Africa', in J. Hofmeyer and A. Nyoka, A., eds., *Breaking the Mould: Prospects for Radical Economic Transformation, 2014 Transformation Audit*, Institute for Justice and Reconciliation, Cape Town.

Gumede, V., 2015a, 'Economic Policy in Post-apartheid South Africa', in N. De Jager, ed., *South African Politics*, Oxford: Oxford University Press.

Gumede, V., 2015b, 'Inequality in Democratic South Africa', in X. Mangcu, ed., *The Colour of Our Future: Race and Identity in South Africa*, Johannesburg: Wits University Press.

Habib, A., 2013, *South Africa's Suspended Revolution: Hopes & Prospects*, Johannesburg: Wits Press.

Hamilton, L., 2014, *Are South Africans Free?*, London: Bloomsbury.

Hall, R., 2003, 'A Comparative Analysis of Land Reform in South Africa and Zimbabwe', in M.C. Lee, and K. Colvard, *Unfinished Business: The land crisis in Southern Africa*, Pretoria: Africa Institute of South Africa.

Hall, R., 2007, 'The Impact of Land Restitution and Land Reform on Livelihoods', Programme for Land and Agrarian Studies, University of the Western Cape.

Halligan, J., 2007, 'Reintegrating Government in Third Generation Reforms of Australia and New Zealand', *Social Policy and Administration*, 22 (2), pp. 217-238.

Hamann, R., Khagram, S. and Rohan, S., 2008, 'South Africa's Charter Approach to Post-Apartheid Economic Transformation: Collaborative Governance on Hardball Bargaining', *Journal of South African Studies,* 23(1), pp. 21-37.

Hanival, S. and Maia, J., nd., *An Overview of the Performance of the South African Economy since 1994,* The Presidency: Government Press.

Hart, G., 2013, *Rethinking the South African Crisis: Nationalism, Populism and Hegemony*, Scottsville: UKZN Press.

Hassim, S., 2005, 'Gender, Welfare and the Developmental State in South Africa', Prepared for the United Nations Research Institute for Social Development (UNRISD) for the Project on Gender and Social Policy, Switzerland.

Hassim, S., 2010, *Social Justice, Care and Developmental Welfare in South Africa: A Capabilities Perspective in Development Dilemmas in Post-Apartheid South Africa*, KwaZulu Natal: University of KwaZulu Natal Press.

Hebinck, P. and Cousins, B. 2013, *In the Shadow of Policy: Everyday Practices in South African Land and Agrarian Reform,* Johannesburg: Wits Press.

Helper, D., Kruger, T. and Wial, H., 2012, 'Why Does Manufacturing Matter? Which Manufacturing Matters?: A Policy Framework', The Brooklyn Institute, February.

Hendricks, F., Ntsebeza, L. and Helliker, K., 2013, *The Promise of Land: Undoing a Century of Dispossession in South Africa,* Auckland Park: Jacana Media.

High Court of South Africa, Transvaal Provincial Division, 2014, 'Case No. 11678/06', Available online at http://www.lrc.org.za, Accessed 30 December 2014.

Hirsch, A., 2005, *Season of Hope; Economic Reform under Mandela and Mbeki, Scottsville:* University of Natal Press.

Hirsch, A., 2013, 'Aspirations to an Elusive Developmental State: The Obstacles to Deep Reform', in B. Ngcaweni, ed., *The Future We Chose: Emerging Perspectives on the Centenary of the ANC,* Pretoria: AISA Press.

Hirschman, C., 1980, 'Theories and Models of Ethnic Inequality', *Research in Race and Ethnic Relations,* 2, pp. 1-20, Available online at http://faculty.washington.edu/charles/pubs/Theories_and_Models_of_Ethnic_Inequality.pdf., Accessed 22 February 2014.

Hoeckel, K., 2007, 'Key Evidence on Vocational Education and Training from Previous OECD Work', *EDU/EDPC/CERI(2007)6/ANN1,* Paris: OECD.

Howlett, M. and Ramesh, M., 2003, *Studying Public Policy: Policy Cycles and Policy Subsystems,* Oxford: Oxford University Press.

Huddle, N., 2007, *Land in Zimbabwe,* pages 65-79, Available online at http://www.wiredspace.wits.ac.za, Accessed 30 December 2014.

Human Resources for Health South Africa, 2012, *HRH Strategy for the Health Sector,* Johannesburg: Wits Press.

Human Sciences Research Council, 2004, *Social Cohesion and Social Justice in South Africa: A Report Prepared for the Department of Arts and Culture,* Pretoria: HSRC.

Human Sciences Research Council, 2012, *Presidential Review Committee on State Owned Entities,* Pretoria: Human Sciences Research Council.

Hungwe, K., 1994, 'Educational Policy in African Colonial Context: The Case of Instructional Media in Southern Rhodesia (1930-1980)', *African Studies Monographs,* 15(1), pp. 1-36.

Hussain, M.N., Mlambo, K. and Oshikoya, T., 2009, 'Global Financial Crisis: An African Perspective', African Development Bank, Tunisia, Tunis, Available online at http://www.afdb.org/fileadmin/uploads/afdb/Documents/Publications/00157618-EN-ERP-42.PDF., Accessed 30 December 2014.

IJR, 2010, 'Transformation Audit', Institute of Justice and Reconciliation, Cape Town.

ILO, 1999, 'Decent Work: Report of the Director-General', International Labour Conference, 87th Session, Geneva.

ILO, 2003, 'Working Out of Poverty: Report of the Director-General', International Labour Conference, 91st Session, Geneva.

Inggs, M., 2010, 'Mine Nationalisation Will be Disastrous for South Africa's Economy', *Mine Weekly,* Creamer Media's, Available online at www.miningweekly.com.article/mine-nationalisation-will-be-desasterous-for-south-african-economy-2010-09-01.pdf., Accessed 29 December 2014.

International Monetary Fund, 2009, Impact of the Global Financial Crisis on Sub-Saharan Africa', Available online at http://www.imf.org/external/pubs/ft/books/2009/afrglobfin/ssaglobalfin.pdf., Accessed 30 December 2014.

International Monetary Fund, 2010, 'Sub-Saharan Africa Back to High Growth?: Regional Economic Outlook', *World Economic and Financial Surveys*, Washington DC: IMF.

Jacobs, P., 2003, 'Support for Agricultural Development', Programme for Land and Agrarian Studies, University of Western Cape, Cape Town..

Jagwanth, S., 2003, 'Democracy, Civil Society and the South African Constitution: Some Challenges', Management of Social Transformation, MOST Discussion Paper 65, UNESCO, Paris.

Jansen, J. and Taylor, N., 2003, 'Educational Change in South Africa 1994–2003: Case Studies in Large-scale Education Reform', *Country Studies: Education and Management Publication Series*.

Johnson, C., 1982, *MITI and the Japanese Miracle: The Growth of Industry Policy 1925-1975*, Stanford: Stanford University Press.

Johnson, C., 1999, 'The Development State: Odyssey of a Concept', in M. Woo-Cumings, ed., *The Developmental State*, Ithaca: Cornell University Press.

Kahn, N., 2007, *Land and Agrarian Reform in South Africa,* Johannesburg: Centre for Policy Studies.

Kaldor, N., 1978, *Capitalism and Industrial Development: Some lessons from Britain's Experience in Applied Economics,* London: Duckworth.

Kane, J., 2001, *The Politics of Moral Capital*, Melbourne: Cambridge University Press. Karamoko, J., and Jain, H., 2011, 'Community Protests in South Africa: Trends, Analysis and Explanations', Harvard Law School, Available online at http://www.mlgi.org.za/publications/publications-by-theme/local-government-insouthafrica/community-protests/Community_Protests_SA.pdf., Accessed 30 December 2014.

Khatiwada, S., 2009, 'Stimulus Packages to Counter Global Economic Crisis: A Review', Discussion paper, International Institute of Labour Studies, International Labour Organisation, Geneva.

Khunou, G., 2013, 'What Middle Class? Dynamics Nature of Class Position', Available online at http//www.resep.sun.ac.za/wp-content/uploads/2013/khunou-main-article-black-middle-class.pdf., Accessed 23 December 2014.

Klein, N., 2007, *The Shock Doctrine: The Rise of Disaster Capitalism,* Toronto: Alfred Knopf.

Kloppers, H.J. and Pienaar, G.J., nd., 'The Historical Content of Land Reform in South Africa and Early Policy', Available online at www.saflii.org/za/journals/PER/2014/20.html, Accessed 23 December 2014.

Kie-Song, M.R., 2009, 'The South African Expanded Public Works Programme (EPWP)', Conference on Employment Guarantee Policies 2004-2014, Pretoria, June.

Kiliçaslan, Y. and Taymaz, E., 2002, 'The Structure of Structural Change and Growth, Department of Economics, Middle East Technical University.

Koelbe, T., 2008, 'Market and the Economy', in N. Shepherd and S. Robins, eds., *New South African Keywords,* Johannesburg: Jacana.

Kovacevic, N., 2007, 'Righting Wrong: Affirmative Action in South Africa', *Harvard International Review*, Harvard.

Kraak, A., ed., 2008, 'The Education–economy Relationship in South Africa, 2001–2005', in A. Kraak and K. Press, eds., *Human Resource Development Review2008: Education, Employment and Skills in South Africa,* ape Town: HSRC Press.

Kruger, L.P., 2007, 'The Impact of Black Economic Empowerment (BEE) on South African Businesses: Focusing on Ten Dimensions of Business Performance', *Southern Africa Business Review*. Vol. 15(3), pp. 207-233.

Kunhle, S. and Hort, S., 2004, 'The Developmental Welfare State in Scandinavia: Lessons for the Developing World', Social Policy and Development Programme Paper Number 17, United Nations Research Institute for Social Development.

Kwon, H., 2005, 'Transforming the Developmental Welfare State in East Asia', Social Policy and Development Programme Paper Number 22, United Nations Research Institute for Social Development.

Lall, S., 2004, 'Reinventing Industrial Strategy: The Role of Government Policy in Building Industrial Competitiveness', Discussion Paper 28, United Nations Conference on Trade and Development, April.

Lahiff, E., 2007, 'Willing Buyer, Willing Seller: South Africa's Failed Experiment in the Market-led Agrarian Reform', *The Third World Quarterly,* Vol. 28(8), pp. 1577-1597.

Laishey, R., 1979, 'South Korea: Land Reform – Successes and Failures', *New Internationalist Magazine*.

Land Audit Complete: Minister, *SAPA and IOL News*, Available online at http://www.iol.co.za/news/politics/land-audit-complete-minister-1.1473275, Accessed 23 December 2014.

Land Reform in South Africa: Getting Back on Track, CDE Report No 16, 2008, Centre for Development Enterprise, Available online at http://www.cde.org.za/images/pdf., Accessed 23 December 2014.

Lapping, B., 1987a, *Apartheid: A History,* London: Grafton.

Lapping, B., 1987b, 'South African Apartheid Bantu Education Quotes', Available online at http://www.africanhistory.about.com/od/apartheidQts1.htm, Accessed 23 December 2014.

Larbi, G., 1999, 'The New Public Management Approach and Crisis States', UNRISD, Discussion Paper No. 112, pp. 1-50.

Lebert, T., nd., 'An Introduction to Land Reform in Zimbabwe', Available online at http://www.foodfirst.org, Accessed 23 December 2014.

Leftwich, A., 1995, 'Bringing Politics Back In: Towards a Model of a Developmental State', *Journal of Development Studies*. Vol. 31(3), pp. 400-427.

Leibbrandt, M., Woolard, C. and Woolard, I., 2000, 'The Contributions of Income Components to South Africa's Income Inequality: A Decomposable Gini Analysis', *Journal of African Economics,* Vol. 9(1), pp. 79-99.

Leibbrandt, M., Woolard, I. and Woolard, C., 2007, 'Poverty and Inequality Dynamics in South Africa: Post-apartheid Developments in Light of the Long-Run Legacy', South African Labour and Development Research Unit, University of Cape Town.

Leibbrandt, M., Woolard, I. and McEwen, H., 2009a, 'Employment and Inequality Outcomes in South Africa: What Role for Labour Market and Social Policies?', Southern Africa Labour and Development Research Unit, University of Cape Town, Available online at http://www.oecd.org/els/emp/45282868.pdf., Accessed 22 February 2015.

Leibbrandt, M., Woolard, I. and de Velliers, L., 2009b, 'Methodology', National Income Dynamics Technical Report, No. 1, *SALRDU,* Available online at http://www.nids.uct.ac.za/publications/citations/wave-1, Accessed 22 February 2015.

Leibbrandt, M., Woolard, I., Finn, A. and Argent, J., 2010,'Trends in South African Income Distribution and Poverty Since the Fall of Apartheid', OECD Social, Employment and Migration Working Paper No. 101, Available online at http://search.oecd.org/officialdocuments/displaydocumentpdf/?cote=DELSA/ELSA/WD/SEM(2010)1&doclanguage=e, Accessed 22 February 2015.

Levinston, M., 2010, 'GardenAfrica Works in South Africa, Swaziland, Namibia and Zimbabwe', Available online at http://www.cityfarmer.info/2010/05/16/gardenafricas-works-in-south-africa-swaziland-namibia-and-zimbabwe/, Accessed 22 February 2015.

Liversage, H., nd., *Smallholder Agriculture and Food Security in the 21st Century*, Available online at www.ifad.org/events/gc/32/roundtable/2.pdf., Accessed 23 December 2014.

Lissoni, A., Soske, J., Erlank, N., Nieftagodien, N. and Bashda, O., 2012, *One Hundred Years of the ANC: Debating Liberation Histories Today,* Johannesburg: Wits University Press.

Luiz, J., 2002, 'South African State Capacity and the Post-apartheid Economic Reconstruction', *International Journal of Social Economics,* Vol. 29(8), pp. 594-614.

Lumby, J., 2003, 'Transforming Health Centres: Managing the Change Process', in M. Thurlow, T. Bush and M. Coleman, eds., *Leadership and Strategic Management in Iran Health Centres*, London: Commonwealth Secretariat.

Macias, J. and Massa, I., 2009, 'The Global Financial Crisis and Sub-Saharan Africa: The Effects of Slowing Private Capital Inflows on Growth', ODI Working Paper Series, Overseas Development Institute, UK.

Mafeje, A., 2000, 'Africanity: A Combative Ontology', *CODESRIA Bulletin*, Nos. 1(4), pp. 66-71.

Mafeje, A., 2003, *The Agrarian Question, Access to Land, and Peasant Responses in sub-Saharan Africa*, UNRISD Programme Papers on Civil Society and Social Movements, Geneva.

Mamdani, M., 2013, *Define and Rule: Native as Political Identity*, Johannesburg: Wits University Press.

Masito, M., 2007, *Afrikaner Economic Empowerment (1890-1990) and Lessons for Black Economic Empowerment,* The Gordon Institute of Business Science, University of Pretoria.

Marais, H., 2010, *South Africa Pushed to the Limit: The Political Economy of Change.* Claremond: University of Cape Town Press.

Mathebula, F.M., 2012, 'Imagining Governance in a Post-liberation Struggle Context: A Public Administration Perspective', Paper delivered at the 12th Annual Conference of South African Associates of Public Administration and Management (SAAPAM) on the State of Governance in Africa at the Turn of the Century of the African National Congress: Reflective Perspective from Scholarship and Practice, University of Free State, Bloemfontein.

Mathekga, R., 2013, 'State Evolution and Sovereignty: The Case of South Africa', in M. Matondi, 2012, *Zimbabwe's Fast Track Land Reform.*, London: Zed Books.

Mayer, M., and Altman, M., 2006, *South Africa's Economic Trajectory: Implications for Skills Development*, Cape Town: HSRC Press.

Mbembe, A., 2012, 'Fifty Years of African Decolonisation', Chimurenga, 25 December 2010, Available online at http://www.chimurenga.co.za/page-147.html, Accessed 30 December 2014.

Mbeki, T., 1978, 'The Historic Injustice', Speech delivered at a seminar held in Ottawa, Canada, from February 19 to 22, 1978.

Mbeki, M., 2009, *Architects of Poverty: Why African Capitalism Needs Changing*, Johannesburg: Picador.

McGrath, S., 2004, 'The State of the South African Further Education and Training College Sector', in S. McGrath, A. Badroodien, A. Kraak, and L. Unwin, eds., *Shifting Understandings of Skills in South Africa,* Cape Town: HSRC Press.

McGrath, S. and Badroodien, A., 2006, 'International Influences on Evolution of Skills Development', *International Journal of EducationalDevelopment,* Vol. 29(5), pp. 483-494.

McKinsey Global Institute, *2010, Lions on the Move: The Progress and Potential of African Economies,* Johannesburg: McKinsey and Company.

Meegan, M., 2008, *Africa and the Global Financial Crisis: Disaster or Opportunity?* Available online at http://windyharbor.wordpress.com/2008/10/12/africa-and-the-global-financial-crisis-disaster-or-opportunity, Accessed 23 December 2014.

Mégie, A., 2004, 'Mise en ceuvre', in L. Boussaguet, S. Jocquot and P. Ravinet, *Diaïtionnaire des Poltiques Publiques,* Paris: Presses de le Foudation Nationale des Science Politiques.

Menocal, R.A., 2004, 'And If There Was No State? Critical Reflections on Bates, Polanyi and Evans on the Role of the State in Promoting Development', *Third World Quarterly.* Vol. 25(4), pp. 765-777.

Meth, C., 2006, 'Half-Measures: The ANC's Unemployment and Poverty Reduction Targets', in H. Bhorat and R. Kanbur, *Poverty and Policy in Post-apartheid South Africa,* Pretoria: HSRC Press.

Mhone, G., 2004, 'Organizational and Institutional Implications of a Developmental tate', Human Social Research Council paper, HSRC, Pretoria.

Ministry of Higher Education and Training, 2010, *Transformation, Social Cohesion and the Elimination of Discrimination in Public Higher Education Institutions,* Pretoria: Government Printers.

Ministry of Monitoring and Evaluation, 2012, *Development Indicators 2011,* Pretoria: The Presidency.

Mitchell, B., 2002, *Resource and Environment Management,* Harlow, England: Prentice Hall.

Mkadawire, T., 2001a, 'Thinking About Developmental States in Africa', *Cambridge Journal of Economics,* Vol. 24, pp. 289-313.

Mkandawire, T., 2001b, 'Social Policy in a Development Context', Social Policy and Development Programme Paper Number 7, United Nations Research Institute for Social Development, Geneva.

Mkandawire, T. and Soludo, C., 1999, *Our Continent Our Future: African Perspectives on Structural Adjustment*, Dakar: CODESRIA.

Mkokeli, S., 2011, Jobless Youth a 'Ticking Time Bomb' for SA, Vavi Warns', *Business Day*, June 7.

Mngxitama, A., n.d., 'Agrarian Reform and Social Movements: Problems and Prospects', *Surplus People Project*, Available online at http://www.spp.org.za/publications, Accessed 23 December 2014.

Mngxitama, A., 2000, 'South Africa: Land Reform Blocked', *Green Left Weekly Issue 406*, Available online at http://www.greenleft.org.au, Acessed 23 December 2014.

Modisaotsile, B.M., 2012, *The Failing Standard of Basic Education in South Africa*, Available online at www.ai.org.za, Accessed 23 December 2014.

Mohammed, S., 2010, 'The State of the South African Economy', in J. Daniel, P. Naidoo,

D. Pillay and R. Southall, eds., *New South African Review 1: 2010 – Development or Decline?*, Johannesburg: Wits University Press.

Moleke, P. , 2005, 'Inequalities in Higher Education and the Structure of the Labour Market', Human Science Research Council Paper Series, Employment and Economic Research Program, HSRC, Cape Town.

Moleke, P., 2006, *Finding Work: Employment Experiences for South African Graduates*, Cape Town: HSRC Press.

Morrell, P., 1998, 'Air Transport Liberalization in Europe: The Progress So Far', *Journal of Air Transportation WorldWide*, 13, No. 1, pp. 1-3.

Morse, K. and Struyk, J., 2006, *Policy Analysis for Effective Development*, Colorado: Lynne Reinner Publisher.

Moyo, S., 1998, *The Land Question and Land Reform in Southern Africa*, Available online at www.depot.gdnet.org/newkb/fulltext/moyo3.pdf., Accessed 23 December 2014.

Moyo, S., 2011, 'Three Decades of Agrarian Reform in Zimbabwe', *Journal of Peasant Studies*, Vol 38, No. 3, pp. 493-531.

Moyo, S., 2013a, 'Zimbabwe's Fast Track Land Reform; Implications for South Africa', in F. Hendricks, L. Ntsebeza and K. Helliker, eds., *The Promise of Land: Undiong a Century of Dispossession in South Africa*, Auckland Park: Jacana Media.

Moyo, S., 2013b, '*Land Reform in South Africa and Zimbabwe: Towards the Realisation of Socio-economic Rights?*', Available online at http://www.consultancyafrica.com/index.php?option=com_content&view=article&id=1323:land-reform-in-south-africa-and-zimbabwe.towards-the-realisation-of-socio-economic-rights&catid=91:rights-in-focus&Itemid=296, Accessed 26 December 2014.

Moyo, S., 2013c, 'The Land and Agrarian Question in Zimbabwe', in S. Buthelezi, ed., *The Land Belongs to the US: The Land and Agrarian Question in South Africa*, Alice: Fort Hare University Press.

Moyo, S. and Yeros, P., 2007, 'The Radicalised State: Zimbabwe's Interrupted Revolution', *Review of African Political Economy*, Vol. 111, pp. 103-121.

Moyo, S. and Murisa, T., 2008, 'Civil Society: Public Action Towards a Transformative Agenda?', in S. Moyo, K. Helliker, and T. Murisa, *Contested Terrain: Land Reform and Civil Society in Contemporary Zimbabwe*, Pietermaritzburg: S&S Publishing.

Murisa, T., 2013, 'Prospects for Small Holder Agriculture in Southern Africa in F. Hendricks, L. Ntsebeza and K. Helliker, eds., *The Promise of Land: Undiong a Century of Dispossession in South Africa,* Auckland Park: Jacana Media.

Mwakikagile, G., 1999, *Economic Development in Africa,* New York: Nova Science Publishers.

Myrdal, G., 1944, American Dilemma: The Negro Problem and Modern Democracy, New Jersey: Transaction Publishers.

Narayan, A. and Mahajan, S., 2002, 'Inequality in Focus: The State of Opportunities in South Africa – Inequality among Children and in the Labor Market', Available online at http://www.worldbank.org/content/dam/Worldbank/document/Poverty%20documents/Inequality-in-Focus-April2013.pdf., Accessed 23 December 2013.

National Planning Commission, 2012, *The National Development Plan 2030,* Ministry of Planning, The Presidency, Pretoria.

National Treasury, 2008, *Review of the Government Cluster System,* National Treasury, Technical Assistance Unit, Pretoria.

National Education Collaboration Trust, 2013, 'Education Collaboration Framework', Available online at http://www.naptosa.org.za/index.php/doc-manager/00-general/130-ecf-brochure/file, Accessed 14 December 2014.

Ndebele, N.S., 2012, 'Liberation Betrayed by Bloodshed', *City Press,* 26 August 2012.

Ndletyana, M. and Maimela, D., 2013, *Essays on the Evolution of the Post-Apartheid State: Legacies, Reforms and Prospects,* Johannesburg: Real African Publishers.

Ndlentyana, M., Makhalimele, P.O. and Mathekga, R., 2013, *Patronage Politics Divides Us: A Study of Poverty, Patronage and Inequality in South Africa,* Johannesburg: African Publishers.

Ndlovu-Gatsheni, S., 2013, *Coloniality of Power in Postcolonial Africa: Myths of Decolonisation,* Dakar: CODESRIA.

NEDLAC, 2009, *Framework for South Africa's Response to the Economic Crisis,* National Economic Development and Labour Advisory Committee, Johannesburg: NEDLAC.

Netshitenzhe, J., 2008, 'The Shift is Not Ideological', *in Mail & Guardian,* 31 October – 6 November 2008, p.23.

Netshitenzhe, J. 2012, 'A Continuing Search for Identity: Carrying the Burden of History', in A. Lissoni, J. Soske, N. Erlank, N. Nieftagodien and O. Bashda, eds., *One Hundred Years of the ANC: Debating Liberation Histories Today,* Johannesburg: Wits University Press.

Netshitenzhe, J., 2013a, *Why Inequality Matters: South African Trends and Interventions,* Mapungubwe Institute for Strategic Reflection (MISTRA), Pretoria.

Netshitenzhe, J., 2013b, 'A Pan-African Renaissance in the Next 50 Years', *The Thinker: Journal of Progressive Thought,* Vol. 51.

Ngongi, N., 2008, 'Policy Implications of High Food Prices for Africa, Alliance for a Green Revolution in Africa', Available online at http://www.ifpri.org/pubs/books/ar2007/ar07essay03.pdf., Accessed 23 December 2014.

Ngqela, N. and Lewis, A., 2012,'Exploring Adolescent Learners' Experience of School Violence in a Township High School', *Child Abuse Research: A South African Journal,* Vol. 13(1), pp. 87-97.

Niewoudt, W. and Vink, N., 1995, 'Financing of Land Purchases by Small- Scale Farmers', *Development Southern Africa,* Vol. 12(4), pp. 509-517.

Nørgaard's, O. and Cumming, S.N., 2004, 'Conceptualising State Capacity: Comparing Kazakhatan and Kyrgyzstan', *Political Studies.* Vol. 5(4), pp. 685-708.

Ntsebenza, L., 2007, *Land Redistribution in South Africa: The Property Clause Revisited,* Available online at www.yale.edu.com/macmillian/apartheid/apartheid_part1/Land_Reform.pdf., Accessed 30 December 2014.

OECD, 2013, *Economic Survey South Africa,* Johannesburg: OECD.

Okumu, W., 2002,*The African Renaissance: History, Significance and Strategy,* New Jersey: Africa World Press.

Oliver, M. and Shapiro, T., 1997, *Black Wealth-White Wealth: A New Perspective on Racial Inequality*, London and New York: Routledge.

Olver, C., Schaay, N., Sanders, D. and Kruger, V., 2011, *Overview of Health Sector Reforms in South Africa,* London: DFID Human Development Resource Centre.

Onis, Z., 1991, 'The Logic of the Developmental State', *Journal of Comparative Studies*, Vol. 24(1),pp. 109-126.

Organisation for Economic Co-operation and Development, 2008, 'Reviews of National Policies for Education: South Africa', Available online at http://www.oecd.org/southafrica/reviewsofnationalpoliciesforeducation-southafrica.htm, Accessed 23 December 2014.

Organisation for Economic Co-operation and Development, 2010, 'Development Aid Rose in 2009 and Most Donors Will Meet 2010 Aid Targets', Available online at http://www.oecd.org/document/11/0,3343,en_2649_34487_44981579_1_1_1_1,00.html, Accessed 23 December 2014.

Organisation for Economic Co-operation and Development, 2013, *OECD Economic Surveys: South Africa 2013,* Johannesburg, OECD Publishing.

Othman, P.F., 2001, 'Malaysia', in M.G. Chaudhry, ed., *Agrarian Reforms and Agricultural Productivity,* Asian Productivity Organisation, Available online at http://www.apotokyo.org/publications/files/agr-10-ar_ap.pdf., Accessed 23 December 2014.

Parliament of the Republic of South Africa, 2013, *Overview of Child Mortality in South Africa,* Research Unit, 4 March 2013.

Partridge, A., 2014, *Institutions and Land Reform: Lessons from Land Redistribution Policy in Post-Apartheid South Africa,* University of Western Cape, Western Cape.TOP

Pepeteka, T., 2013, Reversing *the Legacy of the 1913 Natives Land Act: Progress of Land Reform,* Parliament of the Republic of South Africa, Research Unit, Cape Town.

Persson, T. and Tabellini, G., 2000, *Political Economics: Explaining Economic Policy*, Cambridge: MIT Press.

Persson, T. and Tabellini, G., 2006, 'Electoral Systems and Economic Policy', in *The Oxford Handbook of Political Economy,* Oxford, New York: Oxford University Press.

Pheko, M., 1994, *The Land is Ours: The Political Legacy of Mangaliso Sobukwe*, New York: Pheko& Associates.

Pillay, U., 2011, 'Delivery Protests: National Problem Requires Local, Tailor-made Solutions', *Business Day*, 1 April.

Pillay, D., 2011, 'The Tripartite Alliance and Its Discontents: Contesting the National Democratic Revolution in the Zuma Era', in J. Daniel, P. Naidoo, D. Pillay and R. Southall, eds., *New South African Review 2: New Path, Old Compromises?* Johannesburg: Wits University Press.

Policy Coordination and Advisory Services in the Presidency, 2008a, *Towards a Fifteen Year Review, Synthesis Report on Implementation of Government Programmes,* Pretoria: Government Communications and Information Systems, Available online at http://www.thepresidency.gov.za/main.asp?include=docs/15year/main.html, Accessed 14 December 2014.

Pottinger, B., 2008, *The Mbeki Legacy,* Cape Town, Zebra Press.

Public Financial Management Act (PFMA), 1999, 'Section 1 of the PFMA', National Treasury, Pretoria.

PricewaterhouseCoopers (PwC), 2011, 'State Owned Enterprises: Governance Responsibility and Accountability', Available online at www.pwc.co.za, Accessed 29 December 2014.

Ramphele, M., 2008, Laying Ghosts to Rest: Dilemmas of the Transformation in South Africa, Cape Town: NB Publishers.

Rapoza, K., 2014, *Why UAE and Qatar Have the "World's Best" Airline?*, Available online at www.forbes.com/site/kenrapoza/2014/04/01/WhyUAEandQatarHavetheWorld'sBestAirline, Accessed 15 December 2014.

Rawls, J., 1999, *A Theory of Justice,* Cambridge MA: Harvard.

Republic of South Africa, 2012, 'National Strategic Plan on HIV, STIs and TB 2012-2016'.

Rudarakanchanan, N., 2014., 'Platinum Strike: What You Need to Know as South African Miners Drop Tool', *Internal Business Times*, Available online at www.ibtimes.com/platimunm-strike-what-you-need-to-know-souuth-african-miners-drop-tools-1546544, Accessed 23 December 2014.

Rugege, S., 2004, *Land Reform in South Africa: An Overview*, Available online at http://ccs.ukzn.ac.za/files/landreforminSouthAfrica.pdf., Accessed 2 December 2014.

Reuters, 2009, *Remittances to Kenya Rise in July from 2008,* Available online at http://www.africagoodnews.com/pan-africa/diaspora/882-remittances-to-kenya-rise-in-july-from-2008.html, 23 December 2014.

Robinson, J.A., 2009, 'Industrial Policy and Development: A Political Economy Perspective', Paper prepared for the 2009 World Bank ABCDE Conference in Seoul, June 22-24.

Robinson, M. and White, G., eds., 1998, *The Democratic Developmental State: Political and Institutional Design,* Oxford: Oxford University Press.

Rodney, W., 1973, *How Europe Underdeveloped Africa,* London: Bogle-L'Ouverture Publications and Dar-Es-Salaam: Tanzanian Publishing House.

Rothstein, C.M., 2004, 'Global Perspectives on Human Language: The South African Context. Overcoming Apartheid Policies Yesterday and Today: An Interview with a Former Bantu Education Student and Present-Day', Available online at http://www.stanford.edu/~jbaugh/saw/Chloe_Bantu_Education.html, Accessed 23 December 2014.

Ruddell, D., 1982, 'Class and Race: Neglected Determinants of Colonial Adapted Education Policies', in *Comparative Education*, Vol. 18, pp. 293-303.

Ryerson, M. and Hanes, M., nd.,'Capturing the Impact of Fuel Price on Jet Aircrafts Operating Cost with Engineering and Econometrics Model', University of Calafornia Transportation Centre (UCTC) Research Paper No. 884.

Sachs, J.D., 2005, *Investing in Development: A Practical Plan to Achieve the Millennium Development Goals*, UN Millennium Project, New York.

Sachs, J.D., McArthur, J., Schmidt-Traub, G., Kruk, M., Bahadur, C., Faye, M. and McCord, G., 2004, 'Ending Africa's Poverty Trap', *Brookings Chapters on Economic Activity*, (1), pp. 117–216.

Sadomba, W.Z. and Andrew, N., 2006, 'Challenging the Limits of the State's Market-based Land Resettlement Programme in Zimbabwe: The War Veterans as Catalyst of the Land Movement' in Stewart, P.D. S. ed., *Analysing Contemporary Debates and Issues,* Pretoria: University of South Africa.

Saul, J., 2012, 'Globalisation, Recolonisation and the Paradox of Liberation in Southern Africa', in A. Lissoni, J. Soske, N. Erlank, N. Nieftagodien and O. Bashda, eds., *One Hundred Years of the ANC: Debating Liberation Histories Today,* Johannesburg: Wits University Press.

Saul, J. and Bond, P., 2014, *South Africa: The Present as History, From Mrs Ples to Mandela and Marikana,* Aukland Park: Jacana.

Sayed, Y., Kanjee, A. and Nkomo, M., 2013, *The Search for Quality Education in Post-Apartheid South Africa,* Cape Town: HSRC Press.

Schacter, M., 2000, *Public Sector Reform in Developing Countries: Issues, Lessons and Future Directions,* Published by the Policy Branch of the Canadian International Development, Ottawa, Canada.

Schick, A., 1998, 'Why Most Developing Countries Should Not Try New Zealand Reforms', *The World Bank Research Observer,* Vol. 13(1), pp. 123-131.

Seekings, J. and Nattrass, N., 2006, *Class, Race and Inequality in South Africa,,*Connecticut: Yale University Press.

Sen, A., 1999, *Development as Freedom,* New York: Anchor.

Sen, A., 2009, *The Idea of Justice,* London: Allen Lane.

Shisana, O., 2011, *National Health Insurance: Green Paper,* Pretoria: HSRC.

Shivji, I., 2009, *Accumulation in an African Periphery: A Theoretical Framework,* Dar es Salaam: MkukinaNyota Publishers.

Shoko, T., 2004, *My Bones Shall Rise Again: War Veterans, Spirits and Land Reform in Zimbabwe,* Available online at http://www.ascleiden.nl/Pdf/workingpaper68.pdf., Accessed 26 December 2014.

Sison, A.J., 2003, 'The Moral Capital of Leaders: Why Virtue Matters', *New Horizon Leadership Studies Series,* Cheltenham: Edward Elgar.

Smith, J.M., 2011, *Connecting Young South Africans to Opportunity: Literature Review and Strategy,* CapeTown: DG Murray Trust, Available online at http://www.dgmt.co.za/files/2011/05/Literature-Review-Strategy.pdf., Accessed 10 December 2014.

Socio-economic Rights Institute, 2013, 'Access to Basic Services', Available online at http://www.seri-sa.org/index.php/2013-03-07-09-16-20/basic-services, Accessed 23 December 2014.

South Africa Overcoming Apartheid Building Democracy: BantuEducation, nd., vailable online at http://overcomingapartheid.msu.edu/sidebar.php?id=65-258-2&page=, Accessed 2 December 2014.

South African Broadcast Commission, 2014, *About SABC,* Available online at www.sabc.co.za/wps/portal/SABC/SABCMANDATE, Accessed 29 December 2014.

South African Foreign Policy Initiative (SAFPI), 2012, 'Gauteng's Contribution to South Africa, Africa GDP, BRICS Trade and Infrastructure', Available online at www.safpi.org/news/articles/2012/gauteng-contribution-south-africa-gdp-brincs-trade-and-infrustructure, Accessed 21 December 2014.

South African History Online, nd., 'Dutch East India Company', (DEIC/VOC), Available online at http//www.sahistory.org.za/topic/dutch-east-india-company-deivoc, Accessed 23 December 2014.

South African History Online, nd., 'F.W. de Klerk Announces the Release of Nelson Mandela and Unbans Political Organisations', Available online at http//www.sahistoryonline.org.za/dated-event/fw-de'klerk-announces-release-nelson-mandela-and-unbans-political-organisations, Accessed 27December 2014.

South African History Online, 2013, *Bantu Education Policy,* Available online at http://www.sahistory.org.za/topic/bantu-education-policy, Accessed 27 December 2014.

South African History Online, nd., 'Dutch East India Company', (DEIC/VOC), Available online at http//www.sahistory.org.za/topic/dutch-east-india-company-deivoc, Accessed 23 December 2014.

South African Institute of Race Relations, 2011, *Research and Policy Brief: Model C is the Model to Emulate,* Available at online at http://www.sairr.org.za/sairr-today-1/research-and-policy-brief-model-c-is-the-model-to-emulate-1-february-2011, Accessed 27 December 2014.

South African Institute of Race Relations, 2013, *Racial Transformation,* Johannesburg: SAIRR.

Southhall, R., 2010, 'South Africa 2010: From Short Term Success to Long Term Decline?', in J. Daniel, P. Naidoo, D. Pillay and R. Southall, eds., *New South African Review 1: 2010: Development or Decline?,* Johannesburg: Wits University Press.

Statistics South Africa, 2009, *Quarterly Labour Force Survey*, Pretoria: Statistics South Africa.

Statistics South Africa, 2012, *Census 2011,* Pretoria: Statistics South Africa.

Statistics South Africa, 2013, 'Mid-year Population Estimates', May 2013.

Statistics South Africa (various issues), *General Household Surveys,* Pretoria, South Africa.

Steenkamp, E., Rossouw, R. and Viviers, W., 2014, *Analysis of Export and Employment Opportunities for South African Manufacturing Industries,* Available online at www.nuw.ac.za/af/trade/artikels.pdf., 29 December 2014.

Stewart, J. and Walsh, K., 1992, 'Change in Management of Public Services', *Public Administration*, Vol. 70, No. 4, pp. 499-518.

Steyn, A., 2009, *Measuring Student Participation in the Higher Education Sector in South Africa,* Technical Report, University of Stellenbosch, Stellenbosch.

Stiglitz, J., 2002, *Globalization and Its Discontent,* New York: Norton.

Stiglitz, J., 2010, *Freefall, America, Free Markets and the Sinking of World Economy*, New York: WW Norton and Company.

Stiglitz, J., 2012, *The Price of Inequality: How Today's Divided Society Endangers Our Future*, New York: WW Norton and Company.

Stigliz, J., Sen, A. and Fitoussi, J.P., 2010, *Report by the Commission on the Measurement of Economic Performance and Social Progress,* Available online at http://www.stiglitz-sen-fitoussi.fr/documents/rapport_anglais.pdf., Accessed December 2014.

Stone, D., 2001, *Policy Paradox: The Art of Political Decision Making*, New York: Norton.

Swilling, M., Breda, J., Van Zyl, A. and Khan, F., 2006, *Economic Policy-making in a Developmental State: Review of the South African Government's Poverty and Development Approaches, 1994-2004,* Economic Policy and Poverty Alleviation Report Series, Research Report 3.

Stewart, J. and Walsh, K., 1992, 'Change in Management of Public Services', *Public Administration,* Vol. 70, No. 4, pp. 499-518. STOP

Tabata, I.B., 1979, *Education for Barbarism*, Available online at http://www.sahistory.org.za/archive/education-barbarism-ib-tabata-october-1979, Accessed 12 March 2015.

Taylor, M., nd., 'My Experience of the South African Rugby During Apartheid', Available online at http//www.rfu.com.images/museum/pdf/conference.john.taylor, Accessed 29 December 2014.

Terreblanche, S., 2002, *A History of Inequality in South Africa 1652-2002,* Scottsville: University of KwaZulu Natal Press and Sandton: KMM Review and Publishing Company.

Terreblanche, S., 2012, *Lost in Transformation: South Africa's Search for a New Future Since 1986,* Sandton: KMM Review Publishing Company.

The Department of Public Enterprises (DPE), 2013, *Overview Denel*, Available online at: www.dpe.gov.za/soc/Pages?Dene.aspx, Accessed 29 December 2014.

The Department of Public Works, 2010, *Annual Report: 2010/2011*, Pretoria: Global Campaign for Education, 2009, *The Global Campaign for Education Annual*

Report, Available online at http://www.campaignforeducation.org/docs/docs/resources/GCE%20Annual%20Report%20F.pdf, 23 December 2014.

The National Planning Commission, 2012, *The National Development Plan: Vision 2030*, Pretoria: The Presidency of the Republic of South Africa.

The National Treasury of South Africa, 2006, *Current Position Regarding Governance and State Owned Entities in South Africa,* National Treasury: Government Print.

The Presidency, 1996, *National Small Business Act of 1996. No 102 of 1996,* Pretoria: The Presidency.

The Presidency, 2006a, *Accelerated and Shared Growth Initiative for South Africa,* Pretoria: Government Press.

The Presidency, 2006b, *The National Spatial Development Perspective*, Pretoria: Government Press.

The Presidency, 2008, *Joint Initiative on Priority Skills Acquisition*, Pretoria: Government Press.

The Presidency, 2013, *South Africa's Economic Transformation: A Strategy for Broad- Based Black Economic Empowerment*, Available online at http://www.info.gov.za/view/DownloadFileAction?id=70187, Accessed 29 December 2014.

The Presidency, 2014a, *Twenty Year Review South Africa,* Pretoria, Government Print.

The Presidency, 2014b, 'South Africa's National Anthem', Available online at www.thepresidency.gov.za/pebble.asp?relid=265, Accessed 25 December 2014.

The South African Communist Party (SAPC), 2012, *The South African Road to Socialism,* 13th Congress Political Programme of the SAPC 2012-2017.

Think Africa Press, 2013, *South Africa Land Reform Debate and Natives Land Act, South Africa: Land Reform Debates Heat Up Again, 100 Years After the Natives Land Act,* Available online at http://thinkafricapress.com/south-africa/south-africa-land-reform-debate-natives-land-act, Accessed 24 December 2014.

Thomas, N.H., 2003, 'Land Reform in Zimbabwe', *Third World Quarterly,* Vol. 24, No. 2, pp. 671-712.

Thompson, L., 2000, *A History of South Africa,* Cape Town: Jonathan Ball Publisher.

Todes, A., Karam, A., Klug, N. and Malaza, N., 2009, 'Beyond Master Planning: New Approaches to Spacial Planning in Ekhuruleni, South Africa', *Habitat International,* Vol. 34, pp. 414-420.

Tomori, S., 1995, 'Evolving a New Development Paradigm for Africa', in B. Onimode and R. Synge, eds., *Issues in African Development: Essays in Honour of Adebayo Adedeji at 65,* Abuja: Heinemann Educational Books.

Townsend, P., 1979, *Poverty in the United Kingdom,* Harmondsworth: Penguin.

Triegaardt, J. and Patel, L., 2005, 'Social Security', in *Social Welfare and Social Development in South Africa,* Cape Town: Oxford University Press.

Turok, B., 2008, *Wealth Doesn't Trickle Down: The Case for a Developmental State in South Africa,* Cape Town: New Agenda.

Twala, C. and Selesho, J., 2013, 'Rural and Agrarian Development Discourse in a Post-Apartheid South Africa: An Agro-Ecological Challenge', Available online at www.krepublishers.com/.../JHE-41-1-009-13-2377-Twala-C-Tx[2].pmd.pdf., Accessed 23 December 2014.

UN Millennium Project, 2004a, *An Enhanced Strategy for Reducing Extreme Poverty by the Year 2015,* Interim Report, Task Force on Poverty and Economic Development, New York.

UN Millennium Project, 2004b, *Millennium Development Goals Needs Assessment: ackground Chapter to 'Ending Africa's Poverty Trap,* Working Chapter, New York, Available online at www.unmillenniumproject.org/html/background chapter.shtm, Accessed 23 December 2014.

UN Millennium Project, 2005a, *Combating AIDS in the Developing World,* New York: UN.

UN Millennium Project, 2005b, *Coming to Grips with Malaria in the New Millennium,* Report of the Task Force on HIV/AIDS, Malaria, TB, and Access to Medicines, Working Group on Malaria, New York.

UN Millennium Project, 2005c, Environment *and Human Well-Being: A Practical Strategy,* Report of the Task Force on Environmental Sustainability, New York.

UN Millennium Project, 2005d, *Halving Hunger: It Can Be Done,* Report of the Task Force on Hunger, New York.

UN Millennium Project, 2005e, *Health, Dignity and Development: What Will It Take?* Report of the Task Force on Water and Sanitation, New York.

UN Millennium Project, 2005f, *A Home in the City,* Report of the Task Force on Slum Dwellers, New York.

UN Millennium Project, 2005g, *Innovation: Applying Knowledge in Development.* Report of the Task Force on Science, Technology and Innovation, New York.

UN Millennium Project, 2005h, *Investing in Strategies to Reverse the Global Incidence of TB,* Report of the Task Force on HIV/AIDS, Malaria, TB, and Access to Medicines, Working Group on TB, New York.

Underhill Corporate Solution, 2011, *Literature Review on Small and Medium Enterprises' Access to Credit and Support in South Africa,* Available online at www.underhillsolutions.co.za, Accessed 02 December 2014.

United Nations, 1988, *Global Strategy for Shelter to the Year 2000,* Available online at http://www.un.org/documents/ga/res/43/a43r181.htm, 23 December 2014.

United Nations, 2010, *Africa Economic Outlook,* Available online at http://www.un.org/esa/dsd/resources/res_pdfs/publications/sdt_afri/AEO2010_part1_p76.pdf., Accessed 23 December 2014.

United Nations Development Programme, 2007, *Human Development Report,* New York: Palgrave Macmillan.

United Nations Development Programme, 2011, *Human Development Report,* New York: Palgrave Macmillan.

United Nations Development Programme, 2012, *Millennium Development Goals,* New York: Palgrave Macmillan.

United Nations Development Programme, 2013, *Human Development Report 2013,* New York: Palgrave Macmillan.

United Nations Economic Commission for Africa, 2008, *Overview of Economic and Social Conditions in Africa,* Meeting of the Committee of Experts of the 2nd Joint Annual Meetings of the African Union Conference of Ministers of Economy and Finance, Addis Ababa, Ethiopia.

United Nations Economic Commission for Africa, 2009, *Economic Report on Africa,* Available online at http://www.uneca.org/eca_resources/Publications/books/era2009/, Accessed 23 December 2014.

United Nations World Report, 2009, *World Report,* Available online at http//www.un.org/esa/policy/wess/wesp.html, Accessed 23 December 2014.

USAID, 2009, *USAID Responds to the Global Food Crisis,* Available online at http://www.usaid.gov/our_work/humanitarian_assistance/foodcrisis, Accessed 23 December 2014.

Vale, P. and Barret, G., 2009, 'The Curious Career of an African Modernizer: South Africa's Thabo Mbeki', *Contemporary Politics,* Vol. 15, No. 4, pp. 445-460.

van Aardt C.J., Ligthelm A.A. and van Tonder, J., 2011, A Broad Review of the New Growth Path Framework with Specific Emphasis on the Feasibility of Its Proposed Targets', Available online at www.unisa.ac.za/content/facilities/ems/docs/Press413.pdf., Accessed 24 December 2014.

van der Berge, S., 2002, ‚Education Poverty and Inequality in South Africa', Paper to the Conference of the Centre for the Study of African Economics on Economic Growth and Poverty in Africa, University of Stellenbosch, Cape Town.

van der Berg, S., 2010, *Current Poverty and Inequality Distribution in the Context of South Africa's History,* Bureau of Economic Research, University of Stellenbosch.

van der Berg, S., Taylor, S., Gustafsson, M., Spaull, N. and Armstrong, P., 2011, *Improving Education Quality in South Africa,* Report for the National Planning Commission, Department of Economics, Stellenbosch University.

van der Merwe, D., 1989, 'Land Tenure in South Africa: A Brief History and Some Reform Proposals', Available online at www.saflii.org/za/journals/PER/2014/20.html., Accessed 23 December 2014.

Velde, D.W., 2008, *The Global Financial Crisis and Developing Countries,* Overseas Development Institute, Available online at http://www.odi.org.uk/resources/download/2462.pdf., Accessed 23 December 2014.

Vettorri, 2005, *The South African Legislative Framework Regarding Collective Bargaining,* University of Pretoria, Pretoria.

Visser, W., 2004, 'Shifting RDP to Gear: The ANC Government Dilemma in Providing an Equitable System of Social Security of the New South Africa', Paper presented at the 40th ITH Linzer Konferenz, 17 September 2004.

Wai Yip So, B., 2007, *Does China Follow the Path of Taiwan's Developmental State Model? The Rise of Hsinchu Science Park and Zhongguancun Science Park,* Department of Public Policy and Management, I-Shou University, Taiwan.

WaThiong'o, N., 1986, *Decolonising the Mind: The Politics of Language in African Literature,* Oxford, James Currey.

Webster, E. and Adler, G., 1998, 'Towards a Class Comparison in South Africa Double Transition: Bargained Liberalisation and the Consolidation of Democracy', Paper presented to the Seminar on Labour and Popular Struggle in the Global Economy, Columbia University, New York.

Weick, K.E., 1979, *The Social Psychology of Organising Reading,* New York: McGraw-Hill Humanities.

Weideman, M., 2004a, 'Why Land Reform', Unpublished doctoral dissertation, Witwatersrand University, Available online at http://wiredspace.wits.ac.za, Accessed 11 December 2014.

Weideman, M., 2004b, 'Who Shaped South Africa's Land Reform Policy?', *Politikon,* Vol. 31, No. 2, pp. 219-238.

Wenzel, P., 2007, 'Public-sector Transformation in South Africa: Getting the Basics Right', *Progress in Development Studies,* Vol. 7, No. 1, pp. 47-64.

White Paper on South Africa Land Policy, 1997, Department of Land Affairs.

Wilkinson, R. and Pickett, K., 2010, *The Spirit Level: Why Greater Equality Makes Societies Stronger,* New York: Bloomsburry Press.

Wilson, F., 2012, 'Historical Roots of Inequality in South Africa', *Economic History of Developing Regions,* Vol. 26, No. 1, pp. 1-15.

World Bank, 1997, *World Development Report,* Washington DC: World Bank.

World Bank, 2005a, 'Concept Note: Rethinking Social Policy', World Bank Conference inArusha Tanzania (12-15 December 2005), Available online at worldbank.org/website/external/topics, Accessed 22 December 2015.

World Bank, 2005b, *World Development Indicators*, Washington DC: World Bank.

World Bank, 2009, 'Swimming Against the Tide: How Developing Countries Are Coping with the Crisis', Background paper prepared for the G20 Finance Ministers and Central Bank Governors Meeting, Horsham, UK, 13-14 March.

World Bank, 2006, 'Global Economic Prospects', Available online at http://www-wds.worldbank.org/external/default/WDSContentServer/IW3P/IB/2005/11/14/000112742_20051114174928/Rendered/PDF/343200GEP02006.pdf.

World Bank, 2010, *Global Monitoring Report: Achieving the MDGs in the Aftermath ofthe Global Economic Crisis*, Washington DC: World Bank.

World Bank, 2011, *Global Economic Prospects Report 2011: Navigating String Currents*, Washington: World Bank, Available online at http://siteresources.worldbank.org/INTGEP/Resources/335315-1294842452675/GEPJanuary2011FullReport.pdf.

World Bank, 2014a, *South Africa Economic Update Fiscal Policy and Redistribution in an Unequal Society*, Washington, DC: World Bank.

World Bank, 2014b, *South Africa Economic Update Focus on Export Competitiveness*, Washington, DC: World Bank.

World Bank, 2014c, *South Africa Economic Update: Fiscal Policy and Redistribution inan Unequal Society*, Washington, DC: World Bank.

World Economic Forum, 2014, *Information Technology Report*, Available online at www.slideshare.net/worldeconomicforum/world-economic-forum-network, Accessed 23 December 2014.

World Food Programme and the World Bank Group, 2009, *Rethinking School Feeding: Social Safety Nets, Child Development and the Education Sector*, Available online at http://www.un.org/en/ga/second/64/socialprotection.pdf., Accessed 23 December 2014.

Zamchiya, P., 2011, 'A Synopsis of Land and Agrarian Change in Chipinge District, Zimbabwe', *Journal of Peasant Studies*, Vol 38, No 5, pp. 1093-1122.

Zarenda, H., 2013, 'South Africa's National Development Plan and its Implications for Regional Development', Trade Law Centre Working Paper No D13WP01/2013 June.

Zenex Foundation, nd., 'Shifts in Education Policy: 1994-2012', Available online at http://www.zenexfoundation.org.za/zenex-news-archive/item/117-shifts-in-education-policy-1994-2012, Accessed 24 December 2014.

Zimbabwe Institute, nd., *Zimbabwe Land Policy Study,* Available online at http://www.kubatana.net/docs/landr/zim_institute_land_policy_0508.pdf., Accessed 22 December 2014.

Index

A

ABET (Adult Basic Education and Training), 101, 110
Accelerated economic growth, 57
accelerating economic growth, 41
Accessed, 157–59, 161–63, 170, 172–73, 179–88, 190–205
Accessed 27December, 200
acknowledgement, 26, 107
ACSA (Airport Company South Africa), 84
activities, value-adding, 71
actors, 24, 26, 92, 162
Adapted Education Policies, 168
administration, 19, 21–22, 70, 185, 189, 201
  post-apartheid South African, 6
Adult Basic Education and Training (ABET), 101, 110
adults, 97–101
Advisory Services, 29–30, 170, 198
Africa, 3, 64, 68, 70, 129–30, 156, 168, 173–77, 179–81, 185–86, 188, 191, 193–94, 196, 202–4
Africa and southern Africa's development, 16
Africa Development Bank, 179
Africa Economic Outlook, 203
Africa Governance, 176–77
Africa Institute of South Africa, 189
African and international markets, 60
African Colonial Context, 167, 190
African communities, 11–12, 14–15, 98–99, 116
African countries, 3, 6, 103
  post-independent, 144
African Development, 202
African Development Bank, 179, 190
African Economic Renaissance, 189

African Economics, 173, 192
African Economics on Economic Growth and Poverty in Africa, 173, 204
African Education Movement, 186
African Indigenous Land Rights, 186
African inhabitants of South Africa, 126
African people, 16, 88–89
African Political Economy, 180, 182, 195
African population group, 122–23
African provinces and neighbouring countries, 129
African Renaissance Studies, 167, 174, 189
Africans, 5–6, 12, 15, 33–34, 55, 62, 64, 87–89, 95, 98–101, 121–22, 125–26, 141, 144, 190
  enrolment of, 111–12
African Union Conference of Ministers of Economy, 203
Africa's Poverty Trap, 199
Africa's Socio-Economic Development, 189
Africa VII, 156–57
Afrikaner Economic Empowerment, 164, 193
Afrikaner nationalism, 143
age groupe, 37
age groups, 50–51, 108–9
agenda, 4, 8, 10, 91–92, 146, 189, 195
agenda setting, 25–26
Agrarian Development Discourse, 167, 202
Agrarian Question, 167, 193, 195
agrarian reform programmes, 93
agrarian reforms, 87, 89, 93–95, 165–66, 182, 190–92, 195, 197
Agrarian Studies, 167, 183, 189, 191
Agricultural Land Redistribution, 165, 181

www.ingramcontent.com/pod-product-compliance
Lightning Source LLC
Chambersburg PA
CBHW060034030426
42334CB00019B/2316